The Globalization Turbulence

The Globalization Turbulence

Emerging Tensions in Indian Society

Edited by
Prashant Kumar Trivedi

Council for Social Development, New Delhi

RAWAT PUBLICATIONS
Jaipur • New Delhi • Bangalore • Hyderabad • Guwahati

ISBN 978-81-316-0451-9

Published by
Prem Rawat for **Rawat Publications**
Satyam Apts, Sector 3, Jawahar Nagar, Jaipur 302 004 (India)
Phone: 0141 265 1748 / 7006 Fax: 0141 265 1748
E-mail: info@rawatbooks.com
Website: www.rawatbooks.com

New Delhi Office
4858/24, Ansari Road, Daryaganj, New Delhi 110 002
Phone: 011 2326 3290

Also at *Bangalore, Hyderabad* and *Guwahati*

Typeset by Rawat Computers, Jaipur
Printed at Chaman Enterprises, New Delhi

Contents

Foreword

Globalization as a process of social, economic, political and cultural transformation encompassing the whole world has always remained a debated concept. But during the past two decades the debate has narrowed down to two issues: the centrality of communication and information revolution and global capital as the driving force. Everyone agrees that the developments in communication technology have integrated the world through greater connectivity. However, one very obvious question that arises here is whether the communication revolution itself or the global capital is the driving force is the issue of debate. In the initial years of the 1990s many commentators put forth the common sense idea, rather naively, that the communication revolution was the driving force being itself a class-neutral, objective, value-free process. After about two decades of experiencing turbulence in many spheres of society and economy more and more analysts now accept the view that there is a political economy of the process of globalization whose driving force was capitalism and whose ideology was neo-liberalism. The process involved not only privatization of public enterprises, liberalization of controls over entrepreneurs and opening of the country's economy to foreign capital, but also a whole set of cultural, educational and communication policies which affected every sphere of society. The essays in this volume, contributed by some of India's best-known social scientists, eminently capture that turbulence in Indian society in the wake of globalization.

Two themes are pronounced through the volume. One is the trend of rising inequalities in each sphere of society, class, caste, gender, region, ethnicity, religion and in several combinations of them. What is striking is the argument that inequality is not just a consequence of globalization, but its very pattern of growth is based on generation of inequalities. Aggravation of class differences both in income and basic opportunities such as health, education and employment is borne out by many studies. However, it is also true that there has been a steady expansion of the middle class which is the economic base of globalization both as a market and as the ideological flag bearer. Thus globalization and liberalization have sharply divided society into two-class blocks – the entrepreneur and middle class on the one hand and the large masses of working people on the other. The papers on caste make it clear that Dalits have been great sufferers as globalization assumes that the actors have some asset to operate the new opportunities and most Dalits are without assets. Same with women who have experienced new inequalities and deprivations with informalization of labour and as a consequence of dismantling of public support systems as well as some other steps taken in the name of mainstreaming of gender.

Besides the increasing inequalities, it is the cultural consequences of globalization which have caused enormous anxieties in society. A culture of consumerism has been promoted by global agencies and the media that has created unsustainable demands on natural resources. Local creativity has been subsumed by the tidal waves of homogenized world culture that allow only marginal or superficial role to the indigenous forms. That may sometimes produce what one author calls 'glocal' culture. But whether the local retains its authority is an open question. As is argued by an author the movement for people's empowerment may have been sidelined in the process

In fact, this volume belongs to a new stage of discourse on globalization when the world has experienced a major economic crisis that put into question many tenets of neo-liberalism and once again put the state back in centre stage of social and economic policy. There is a new phase of history when some developing countries have emerged as players on world stage – BASIC is the newly popular acronym for this phenomenon (Brazil, South Africa, India and China) or BRICS if one adds Russia to it. Above all this a historical moment when we see the emerging era of self-determination of people. This is an era when deprived groups are asserting their human rights – classes, castes, races, ethnicities, religious minorities, regions, nationalities and women seeking fulfilment of their legitimate aspirations and new solidarities especially intersectional solidarities – within countries, continents and globally are in the formation. The new moment is evident in many positive and negative manifestations – not only in the upsurge of social movements and political mobilizations in elections and mass movements but also in the outbreaks of various kinds of violence including terrorism, farmers suicides and other acts of protest. There are some welcome responses from the state in the form of guaranteeing employment, education, health facilities and the like. But until dominant forces at every level acknowledge the character of the new moment the confrontation will continue to be intense. Essays in this volume highlighting the trends of inequities and cultural alienation growing out of the neo-liberal policies make a valuable contribution to the understanding of the social turbulence of our time.

Manoranjan Mohanty
Council for Social Development, New Delhi

Acknowledgements

I am grateful to Prof. Muchkund Dubey, President, Council for Social Development (CSD), New Delhi for taking keen interest in the publication of this volume. Dr T. Haque, Director, CSD, has always encourged me for my publications, this is an opportune moment to thank him. I feel it important to put on record that Ravi Kumar was the one who not only helped me conceptualize the theme but also consistently pushed me to publish this volume. Besides, Dr Kurian was another person who not only facilitated me to complete this project but also as the director of CSD gave me full freedom and support for my other assignments as well.

Contributors to this volume deserve special thanks as despite the fact that most of them are well-known scholars, they generously accepted my invitation to contribute chapters to this volume. This clearly shows their willingness to encourage younger people. Prof. Mohanty whom I regard more as my teacher than a senior colleague readily agreed to write foreword to this volume for which I owe a debt of gratitude to him. Finally, My spouse Abha, daughter Veera, mother Vibha Trivedi and father S.D. Trivedi have been the real support and strength for me.

List of Contributors

Maitrayee Chaudhuri is Professor at the Centre for the Study of Social Systems, Jawaharlal Nehru University, New Delhi.

Satish Deshpande is Professor of Sociology at Delhi School of Economics, Delhi University, New Delhi.

Ravi Kumar is Associate Professor, Department of Sociology, South Asian University, New Delhi.

Neetha N. is Senior Fellow at the Centre for Women's Development Studies (CWDS), New Delhi.

T.K. Oommen is Professor Emeritus at the Centre for the Study of Social Systems, Jawaharlal Nehru University, New Delhi.

Utsa Patnaik, was Professor at the Centre for Economic Studies and Planning, Jawaharlal Nehru University, New Delhi.

P. Radhakrishnan was Professor of Sociology at Madras Institute of Development Studies, Chennai.

Rowena Teresa Robinson is Professor at Centre for the Study of Social Systems, Jawaharlal Nehru University, New Delhi.

Rohini Sahni is Associate Professor at Department of Economics, University of Pune, Pune.

V. Kalyan Shankar is Research Scholar at Department of Economics, University of Pune, Pune.

Prashant Kumar Trivedi is Associate Fellow, Council for Social Development, New Delhi.

Surya Prakash Upadhyay is Research Scholar of Sociology at the Department of Humanities and Social Sciences, Indian Institute of Technology Bombay, Mumbai.

Introduction

Indian Society in the Era of Neo-liberal Reforms

PRASHANT KUMAR TRIVEDI

This volume is a collection of papers presented at the 'National Seminar on Structural Transformation and Development in Post-liberalization India' organized jointly by the India International Centre and the Council for Social Development (CSD) at New Delhi in January 2008. The volume critically examines the way neo-liberal globalization has affected different facets of Indian society including caste, class, gender, religion and social movements. It also seeks to assess the impact of these economic policies on the lives of oppressed sections of our society. This is an opportune moment to do so as this set of policies completes almost two decades in India taking off in 1991.

Globalization

A contested concept like globalization, many feel, has been hijacked by market fundamentalists to further their neo-liberal agenda after the demise of socialist bloc at international level during the 1980s. It has got different connotations in different contexts and one way of understanding it is with reference to neo-liberal ideology that believes in free market as panacea of all problems relating to underdevelopment. It rests on the premise that by bringing all human actions into the domain of the market and by maximizing the reach and frequency of market transactions, social good could be maximized.[1] It seeks to limit state intervention in economy believing that free market itself leads to efficient outcomes and promotes 'free society'. This doctrine pronounces that removal of trade barriers and closer integration of national economies is the only way to get rid of the problems of underdevelopment. For this it prescribes lifting of barriers on the cross-border movement of goods, services and capital. But many accuse advanced capitalist countries of hypocrisy as they have pushed poorer countries to eliminate trade barriers but kept their own.[2]

Not everybody would subscribe to the idea of conceptualizing globalization only with reference to neo-liberalism or capitalism. Rohini Hensman[3] insists on defining it independent of imperialism, capitalism and neo-liberalism. For her, the reasonable definition of globalization would be "free movement of products, money, ideas and people around the globe". She considers national boundaries as the only major obstacle to such movement and that is why globalization is seen as "weakening or eventual elimination of those boundaries". Hensman makes a strong plea for unity of workers around the globe against capital for many reasons. First, free movement of products, money, people and ideas appears to be a romantic idea in today's world market dominated by transnational corporations of hitherto unheard sizes. In fact, many economists indicate that any kind of movement – be it of products or of ideas – is not autonomous of dynamics of capitalism. Second, she seems to be conceptualizing 'national boundaries' as something that can be understood without referring to capitalist markets. Third, there cannot be any disagreement with her on the question of an international working class movement but as Mary John[4] argues, "has it not become much easier in the era of global outsourcing – to pit workers against each other".

Globalization in India

In India, 1991 is considered to be a turning point in the context of neo-liberal policies but the rudiments of new policy were put in place in the early 1980s against the backdrop of India's $5 billion loan agreement with International Monetary Fund (IMF) to cushion balance of payments deficit arising from 1979–80 oil shock and higher costs for growing imports under various liberalization measures. The process was furthered with various steps taken by the governments during the 1980s including the launching of 'New

Industrial Policy'. These macro-economic reforms came with full force in the early years of 1990s. These set of policies included drastic cut back in the number of industries reserved for public sector, removal of licensing to start new enterprises for private sector in almost all the industries, devaluation of rupee, removal of quantitative restrictions on imports, heavy reduction in the tariffs for imports and several exemptions given to foreign firms to operate in India.[5] These policies emphasize on reducing fiscal deficit and advocate tax cuts across the board. As a result, the obvious outcome, of course, is that the prospects of expanding public expenditure got constrained. Moreover, it is typically public investment and welfare expenditure that bear the brunt of the adjustment.[6]

The neo-liberal policies changed the whole scenario of economic growth in India. Agriculture was replaced from its earlier position. Majumdar[7] observed that in the current euphoria about liberalization and globalization of the Indian economy, the agricultural sector has taken a back seat. This again widened the gap between agriculture-dependent and non-agriculture-dependent population. Among agriculturalists too, the impact has not been even. A section of rich farmers took advantage of these policies but vast majority of peasants suffered a setback in terms of growing input costs and volatile market conditions. In this context, Utsa Patnaik raises a very pertinent question that why neo-liberal reforms be necessarily accompanied by agricultural depression, food insecurity, poverty and acute distress in particular region. In her chapter 'On Deepening Poverty of Masses including Deprived Social Groups in Rural and Urban India under Economic Reforms', while commenting on the above question, she takes a position that neo-liberal reforms bring these sufferings with them by advocating expenditure deflationary policies that directly impact population in unorganized sector, especially the peasantry. As a consequence, rising unemployment accompanies falling incomes. In addition, the peasantry is exposed to global markets that lead to change in land use patterns away from food grains to cash crops. Volatile global markets often ruin small producers. Patnaik's direct estimate of persons below the poverty line in rural India is much higher than official estimates.

In the same way, income disparities in the urban areas went up drastically. With growing concentration of resources and opportunities, urban areas expanded at a higher pace. India may boast of growing number of billionaires in post-reforms period but simultaneous increase in the poverty incidence reflects widening caste-class divide. Analysing the data from two quinquennial surveys of NSSO conducted in 1999–2000 and 2004–05 respectively, Satish Deshpande underlines worsening urban inequalities during reform period. Although there may be a slight improvement in the rural situation, particularly at the lower levels of MPCE distribution but according to his analysis presented in his chapter 'Recent Trends in Caste Inequalities: Comparison of NSSO Consumption Expenditure Data of 2000 and 2005', rural STs and urban SCs are worse off groups in contemporary Indian society.

Sociology of Globalization

A great amount of research has gone into understanding the post-liberalization India. These researches range from efforts to understand the changes in economy to that of cultural and social transformations. Many studies make efforts to locate the interconnections between the changes in economy and the diverse structural aspects that characterize the society. The society as well as economy has been in turmoil since the initiation of liberalization process. For instance, a boom in certain kinds of employment has been observed, though accompanied by the process of informalization of labour force. The pattern of employment and labour market has undergone some significant changes. The expansion of the middle class and the penetration of market also effected transformations in the cultural sphere.

The hegemony of market and subservience of cultural forms to it has been a notable phenomenon in these times. Political scientists have been arguing that when two cultures come into each other's contact, their negotiation appears to be informed by political and economic arrangements accompanying them. This could result in *hierarchy of cultures*. In this situation the globalization of culture seems to assign different spaces to different cultures in 'global culture'.

This kind of power relations between cultures could be seen in India too. The marginalization of folk music, for instance, if it cannot attract customers and simultaneous booming business of Hollywood movies, often dubbed in Indian languages, is one such example. However, for consumption of larger audience, indigenized versions of these cultural products such as 'Indi-pop' are also available. "Globalization in combination with mechanization is wielding a devastating influence on the traditional arts and crafts of India at present. The case of the traditional artisan community of Kerala, otherwise called visvakarmas, becomes a sordid tale of pauperization and dispossession in this context".[8] These changes should not come as a surprise to us as we live in policy regime that seeks to bring in maximum possible human actions into the realm of market and we know that music, dance and other art forms flourish or even survive only if they satisfy the needs of the market.

Although one cannot claim cultural exchange to be either new or direct fallout of globalization only but there is no doubt that the process gained momentum during this period and simultaneity of these two phenomena calls for further engagement with it. Besides, today, one is neither willing to live in a tight container nor allergic to 'western' and 'foreign' culture. In fact, what we tend to brand as 'western' is more of a culture promoted by multi-national corporations (MNCs) that seeks to reduce human beings with consumers and takes good of market as good of society. Avijit Pathak[9] further elaborates this point saying that "it seeks to nurture a consciousness that is oriented to pleasure: pleasure in unlimited consumption of goods – material as well as symbolic. Indeed, globalization as it exists is impossible to imagine without this consumptionist/pleasure-seeking/mass culture ...". It seems that cultural symbols are used for furthering commercial interests of MNCs and for this purpose they do not mind or in fact prefer selective appropriation of 'native' cultural symbols and 'local' traditions. It is in this context that we can understand the strengthening of 'dowry system'. One more thing that haunts us is why most of the time these MNCs choose to rely on retrograde traditions like dowry, why not they pick up something else? The answer to this question lies in analysis of nature of growth in this period done by Amit Bhaduri.[10] He notes that it is not just the case that inequality is growing but it is a pattern of growth that requires increasingly growing inequalities. It is thus not surprising to see that in this period already existing inequalities based on caste, class, gender, region etc., have not just continued but aggravated further.

It is this interplay of consumer goods, globalization and culture that has been brilliantly explored by Rohini Sahni and V. Kalyan Shankar in their chapter on 'Usurping Differences, Reproducing Homogeneity: Cultural Changes in the Midst of Global Markets'. The authors argue that the way we engage with popular culture is increasingly getting defined through the conduits of material culture and this change has an international dimension to it, wherein both the forms of culture are drawing their influences from global trends. They take up an interesting example of famous TV programme 'Indian Idol' to demonstrate their point.

Besides, one should also investigate another very interesting phenomenon that Avijit Pathak describes as an effort to keep culture and economy relatively autonomous. "It is like believing that even if there is reason to celebrate economic globalization, it is possible to retain autonomy and specificity of our culture. Culture need not lose its historicity and its core values in the name of being globalized". He cites NRI phenomenon and its affinity with cultural symbols or its search for 'roots' to ably demonstrate this kind of cultural nationalism. One very obvious question that arises here is why upper caste/class Indian loves to have both Indian culture and economic globalization together, is there anything common between these two? One wild guess could be that both privilege these people. Although this is not a convincing argument but this phenomenon needs to be investigated further. Just opposite to Hindu right-wing position of supporting economic globalization and opposing cultural globalization, one strand[11] of Dalit–Bahujan politics appears supporting cultural globalization as it negates 'brahminic myth of purity and pollution' and opposes economic globalization because it enriches rich and makes poor poorer. One thing seems common in these apparently contradictory stands is that both try to keep economy and culture relatively independent of each other.

When popular culture is undergoing such a transformation, we do not expect other aspects of social life to remain unaffected by this strong wind of change, even though it is supposedly conservative part of life such as religion. Studies have indicated that media explosion has refashioned religious experience like never before. For one reason this is more so. Electronic media, being a defining feature of this era and visual impact carried by it with its capacity of carrying information in no time regardless of distance, has equipped it with hitherto unheard power. This in fact has redefined media itself. This media boom has given rise to a phenomenon of 'tele-gurus'. The overwhelming presence of these 'gurus' is so visible in public realm that we cannot avoid a serious and informed debate on the subject anymore. This volume has included two chapters both covering different dimensions of religion as experienced in public realm with changing times. In their paper, Surya Prakash Upadhyay and Rowena Robinson indicate a very interesting phenomenon, i.e., coincidence of profusion and streamlining. They see a movement towards a greater degree of abstraction and an implicit, and sometimes explicit, trend towards the formal, more highly philosophical ideas of the great tradition.

P. Radhakrishnan too suggests that while globalization has strengthened Brahminic Hinduism and its institutionalized sites and structures, it has weakened the religious symbols, sites, shrines, and practices of the lower strata or what may be called 'folk religion'. Radhakrishnan unearths 'unhealthy nexus between faith and politics'. He refers to Adam's Bridge – Ramar Sethu controversy and incidence of communal flare up in Baroda in 2006 when in the process of widening public roads some of the 'religious road blocks' were removed. Radhakrishnan's analysis makes significant contribution to our understanding of interface between faith, politics and development in India but we need to be careful about the context in which these incidences take place. Post-2002 Gujarat with Narendra Modi as chief minister backed by RSS–VHP combine is not comparable with context in which Ramar Sethu controversy took place. Besides, one is inclined to suggest that minority communalism and majority communalism should be studied in their contexts.

When the cultural significance of the collective enforced through different cultural traits has been on decline, in the field of social movements and social mobilization as well, there have been enormous changes. The declining active participation of people in general elections, especially among urban middle class, to the absence of organized macro forms of dissent and resistance are only some examples. With growing antipathy for politics among urban middle classes in this period, we witness proliferation of what Shekhar Gupta[12] calls 'candidates of cocktail party' those who want lateral entry in the system. Media critiques like P. Sainath[13] regularly warn us that NGO activism backed by mainstream electronic and print media has contributed to push ideological bankruptcy to a new height. Referring to campaigns launched by several NGOs during the last parliamentary elections, Sainath notes that "at points, the campaigns even raised this sense in young people – of voting to feel good about yourself. Not for any political reason. Some of the groups asked voters to focus on the individual candidates. Not his or her political platform. So it's okay if your 'clean' candidate has a genocidal political agenda. This cannot help much with a young generation already depoliticized and exposed daily to the media scorn of politics and all that goes with it".

One cannot claim that this process of *depoliticization of politics* is autonomous of neo-liberal agenda. Perhaps, this is necessary precondition for its smooth taking off. Somewhat on similar lines, Ravi Kumar in his chapter 'Violence, Aspirations and Migration in Post-liberalization Rural India: Conflict and Change in a Strife-Torn Village' argues that weakening of radical left forces and their delegitimization by the state has become necessary for the neo-liberal capital to expand without hindrance because the notions of a harmonious, non-conflictual order (within an essentially inegalitarian and hierarchically structured society) become important for stability of a system as it provides an unhindered expansionist possibility of its interests. Ravi Kumar's discussion on the character of state reminds us on discourse 'hard state' vs 'soft state' and withdrawal of state in the era of globalization. Manoranjan Mohanty[14] argues that that as part of neo-liberal agenda, state is supposed to retreat from economic and social welfare arena, "hand over economic functions to private capital, allow much arena of autonomous socio-economic activities to NGOs, both national and international, but acquire more power to suppress all forces that challenge this new political economy".

This chapter gives us a very clear idea that changes have occurred in the rural India too, completely debunking the possibility of any debate regarding its isolation, as penetration of capital, migration, new aspirations and the information revolution alter their social, cultural and economic fabrics. These changes compel us to look at the transformations that have occurred with the interaction of the larger economic transformations within the social, economic and cultural structures. It is the appropriate time, after nearly two decades of the beginning of the process of liberalization to analyse and understand the nature of changes that have taken place.

Caste, Class, Gender and the Complex Matrix of Liberalized Economy

Many social scientists have reflected upon the changing caste, class and gender relations in the period of globalization. Referring to the changing context, Avijit Pathak comments that "modernity has acquired a new meaning in global era. And culture-specific identities, far from withering away, are redefining their roles". In the same way, Andre Beteille[15] notes that rapid change is taking place in the balance between agricultural and industrial economies but "fluidity of class divisions in changing society does not mean that economic inequalities or conflict arising from them are disappearing, or even declining". While, on the one hand, he underlines increasing inequalities but on the other hand he observes substantial growth in the size of middle class and its changing social composition. He notes that it has not only grown in size but also become socially more diverse. Beteille also comments that in India, liberalization and privatization have given boost to both downward and upward mobility of somehow equal quantum. It is interesting to note that in the same article he "inequalities exist and may sometimes be on the increase" and then comments that "upward mobility subverts polarization thesis". This juxtaposition of two observations poses certain question for the social scientists.

The emergence of urban middle class, particularly new middle class, believed to be product of economic liberalization, has drawn attention of social scientists studying post-liberalization Indian society. Well-known sociologist T.K. Oommen, in his chapter 'Structural Transformation and Developmental Politics in Post-Liberalization India' notes that even 'global Indians' seem to be inextricably intertwined in primordial identities. He calls them 'glocal'. These observations lead him to underline intertwining between caste and class in influencing the behaviour of individuals and collectivities. Referring to the case of Karnataka State Farmers Association (KRRS), Oommen points out that while opposing globalization at macro level, farmer organization's own functioning at local level is moulded by class domination, caste hierarchy and patriarchy. This takes us to another observation that traditional identities are having a new lease of life in secular spaces.

Persistence of primordial identities in this period does not mean that nothing has changed. Caste too has not remained unaffected by strong wave of economic changes. The idea of caste as the defining character of social structure has also been witness to debates since the economy opened up. M.N. Panini[16] hopes that "economic globalization in the long run is likely to weaken the hold of caste over economy" but his apprehension is that "if the policy of liberalization and with it possibility of rapid economic development is thwarted, it will mainly be because of the backlash produced by the caste system". Many reports and data from NSS reveal not only growing inter-caste inequalities but also widening intra-caste inequalities. It leads us to a situation where class composition of caste groups and caste composition of classes are changing but even then an overview of Indian society reflects correlation between caste and capitalist class structures. Exploring data provided by NSS 55th round, Satish Deshpande[17] notes that the difference between caste groups are too strong and too stable to be artifacts. Ghanshyam Shah[18] also supports the idea of overlapping between caste and class even in contemporary society. Social scientists argue that it happens so because liberalization and privatization have not only carried forward handicaps based on caste but also weakened support system provided by welfare state that remained an important contributing factor for bringing out changes in caste-class congruence.

While at the one level the changes are brought about within the discourses of marginalization such as the Dalit discourse with one strand of this discourse arguing for the need to produce the bourgeoisie within Dalits and therefore sees no harm with the neo-liberal onslaught but only demands certain concessions to facilitate the growth of this section. At a political level and in terms of mobilization, there have been new developments such as the forging hitherto inconceivable alliances between the so-called *savarna* castes and the Dalit political formations. But for majority of Dalits, liberalization is another betrayal by upper castes, the first being nationalist agenda, as leaders like Ambedkar and Phule perceived Indian nationalism as upper caste agenda. Globalization operates only with those people who already have something to operate with but Dalits, mostly being wage labour, have nothing to operate with. So Dalits see this system working against them. This is a system of class domination. My own chapter 'When Neo-liberal Agenda Negotiates Dalit Agenda: The Case of BSP in Uttar Pradesh' further adds that in the scheme of liberalization, private sector has been given a major share and Dalits are loosing job opportunities reserved in government sectors. For Dalits, liberalization is another way of reinventing inequalities. While discussing 'redistribution' 'recognition' dilemma in the context of BSP, I have submitted for further discussion that this Dalit party is taking more interest in distributing resources in favour of small well-off section among Dalits, instead of large masses of poor Dalits.

The nature of discourses treating women as their subject has also witnessed a great change. On the one hand, while notions of 'empowerment' and 'development' have been redefined, on the other hand the negative impact on women's lives in light of informalization of economy or co-existence of traditional forms of normative patriarchal structures, along with the new demands imposed by the economy for enhanced economic participation of women, have generated new complexities in the lives of women. Maitrayee Chaudhuri identifies very interesting phenomenon of 'certain mainstreaming of gender' in development programmes, corporate and media but with redefinition of notions such as freedom, choice, justice, equity, autonomy etc., differently than articulation presented by women's movement. Besides, 'NGOization' of both women's studies and women's movement is also evident in increasing efforts to 'gender sensitise' and 'gender train'. In her chapter 'Gender Discourse and Its Many Avatars: How Critical? How Mainstream?', Chaudhuri underlines neo-liberal vision at work in affirmation of the individuated, entrepreneurial middle class women in public discourse, especially in mainstream media and major shift in development vision vis-à-vis poor women.

The discourses on development empowerment and participation put forth by World Bank have come under severe criticism in this context. These international agencies have come under fire from feminists for their advocacy for what Mary John[19] would term 'people's capitalism' kind of development paradigm. "The central argument of this perspective is that providing economic and social security to poor women in the informal sector is the proper pragmatic response to a world where both the public and private sectors – in short, almost the entire formal sector which has been the backbone of India's mixed economy – are facing erosion."[20] For detailed discussion on the subject, one may like to revisit debates on micro-credit programmes.

Last two and a half decade of globalization have popularized phrases like 'feminization of poverty'[21] and this language of discourse itself reveals changing status of women in this era. But not everybody would[22] subscribe to these ideas. "From the standpoint of women workers, especially those in the Third World, the anti-globalization makes no sense. If successful, it would simply deprive them of a large proportion of their employment opportunities as well as the possibility of improving employment conditions through global solidarity and coordination." Gail Omvedt[23] too finds it problematic to oppose globalization because "it is impossible and even undesirable to withdraw from the global economy and social system". Further explaining her point she comments that "to ask Dalits, women and others to simply 'fight globalization' at the cost of taking up real democratic demands, at the cost of a real analysis and understanding of how to deal with situation they find themselves in, is a recipe of disaster".

The comments made by well-known scholars like Gail Omvedt and Rohini Hensmen are indeed controversial and for further clarity on the subject Neetha N. provides macro-level data analysis in her chapter 'Changing Dimensions of Women's Work and Gender Inequality in Post-reforms Period'. Exploring the data from NSS and Census of India, Neetha finds that growing social and economic crisis is locking vast sections of women workers into a downward spiral resulting in a deepening of gender-based inequalities. She opines that increased participation of women in employment should be seen as their desperate search for livelihood options than actual labour market expansion for at least two reasons. One, women workers are not in a position to exercise their choice regarding the kind of their employment in the context of increasing burden to support their family on them. Two, asymmetrical power relations and sexual division of labour leave women doubly disadvantaged as household work and reproductive responsibilities still seen as women's work outside the sphere of production. In Neetha's analysis, what is clearly evident is inextricable link between gender and class or in fact caste too as it is not too difficult to assume that vast majority of women workers in unorganized sector belongs to lower rungs of caste hierarchy.

This book raises certain questions pertaining to structural transformation during the last two decades. This engagement with the kind of changes experienced post-1991 Indian society in terms of gendered representation, transformations in caste and class structures, in conjunction with the political economy of development, will open up new avenues for understanding contemporary Indian society. This understanding will also help us explain the direction of development, its intent and the need for changing its course, if any.

Notes

1. David Harvey, 2005. *A Brief History of Neoliberalism*, Oxford University Press, Oxford, p. 3.
2. Joseph Stiglitz, 2002. *Globalisation and its Discontents*, Allen Lane, The Penguin Press, London, pp. ix–xiv & p. 7.
3. Rohini Hensman, 2004. "Globalisation, Women and Work: What Are We Talking About?", *Economic and Political Weekly*, 39(10), pp. 1030–34.
4. Mary John, 2009. "Reframing Globalisation: Perspectives from the Women's Movement", *Economic and Political Weekly*, 44(10), pp. 46–49.
5. Francine Frankel, 2005. *Political Economy of India, 1947–2003: The Gradual Revolution*, Oxford University Press, New Delhi, pp. 585–91.
6. Praveen Jha, 2005. "Withering Commitments and Weakening Progress: State and Education in the Era of Neoliberal Reforms", *Economic and Political Weekly*, August 13.
7. N.A. Majumdar, 1999. "Investment in Agriculture and the Globalisation Syndrome", *Economic and Political Weekly*, April 3.
8. George Varghese K., "Globalisation Traumas and New Social Imaginary: Visvakarma Community of Kerala", *Economic and Political Weekly*, 38(45), pp. 4794–802.
9. Avijit Pathak, 2006. *Modernity, Globalisation and Identity: Towards a Reflexive Quest*, Aakar Books, New Delhi.
10. Amit Bhaduri, 2008. Presentation in a panel discussion on "Developmental Politics in Post-Liberalization India: The Emerging Scenario", in 'National Seminar on Structural Transformation and Development in Post-Liberalisation India' organized jointly by the India International Centre and the Council for Social Development in New Delhi in January 2008.
11. Kancha Ilaiah, 2003. "Cultural Globalisation", *The Hindu*, February 22, p. 10.
12. Shekhar Gupta, 2009. "The Glorious Certainties", *Indian Express*, April 18.
13. P. Sainath, 2009. "Celeb Crusades and the Death of Politics", *The Hindu*, May 4.
14. Manoranjan Mohanty, "Kilvenmani, Karamchedu to Khairlanji: Why Atrocities on Dalits Persist?"
15. Andre Beteille, 2007. "Classes and Communities", *Economic and Political Weekly*, March 17, pp. 945–52.

16. M.N. Panini, 1996. "The Political Economy of Caste", in M.N. Srinivas (ed.), *Caste: Its Twentieth Century Avatar*, Penguin Books, New Delhi, pp. 28–68.
17. Satish Deshpande, 2003. "Caste Inequalities in India Today" in *Contemporary India: A Sociological View*, Penguin Books, New Delhi, pp. 98–124.
18. Ghanshyam Shah, Harsh Mander, Sukhadeo Thorat, Satish Deshpande and Amita Baviskar, 2006. *Untouchability in Rural India*, Sage Publications, New Delhi, pp. 19–61.
19. Mary John, 2009. Op. cit.
20. Renana Jhabvala and R.K.A. Subrahmanya (eds.), 2000. *The Unorganised Sector: Work Security and Social Protection*, Sage Publications, New Delhi.
21. Johanna Brenner, 2006. "The Feminization of Poverty, Comparable Worth and Feminist Political Discourse", in *Women and the Politics of Class*, Aakar Books, New Delhi, pp. 101–17.
22. Rohini Hensman, 2004. Op. cit.
23. Gail Omvedt, 2005. "Capitalism and Globalisation, Dalits and Adivasis", *Economic and Political Weekly*, November 19, pp. 4881–85.

Part I
Social Structure

1

Structural Differentiation and Developmental Politics in Post-liberalization India

T.K. OOMMEN

Post-liberalization India is not even two decades old. To attribute structural transformation and its impact on developmental politics in India *via* economic liberalization is indeed too hasty. Broadly speaking, there are but two sources of social transformation: revolution, understood as sudden, forceful and violent upturns of governments, and structural differentiation, that is, a gradually evolved division of labour between different institutional clusters in society – a prerequisite for modernization. While revolutionary upheaval occurs suddenly, it takes a long period to mature. At any rate, social transformation, which follows revolution, is invariably a long *duree* process. And, structural differentiation is indeed slow, piecemeal and gradual. Structural adjustment programme (SAP) or economic liberalization is the most recent example of structural differentiation in human history – a process which started in ancient India through bifurcation of the distinct spheres of the king and the priest, much before the division of labour between the church and the state came about in the West.

I need to make a methodological comment here. If two phenomena occur simultaneously or even in quick succession the general tendency is to link them causally, which is not logically sound because their simultaneous or successive occurrence could be independent of each other. At any rate, if the analyst wants to link them causally s/he has to resort to one of the following methodological devices. One, identify two units (village, district, state, nation), one in which the phenomenon (in the present case, economic liberalization) is absent and the other into which it is introduced and then make a comparative analysis. If some additional/extra changes are observed in the unit where the new factor is introduced, it is reasonable to attribute the changes to the new phenomenon. Such an approach, usually referred to as synchronic, which compares two spaces is untenable in the present context because economic liberalization treats India as one indivisible space. The other, that is, diachronic approach, which analyses the units through time is also not feasible because the time-chunk which elapsed after the introduction of economic liberalization is too short to bring about social transformation. Even if one ignores this constraint, s/he confronts the problem of near total absence of systematic data for two time points, say 1980 a decade before the introduction of liberalization and 2000 a decade after it.

This brings me to another introductory comment I want to make which is prompted by the thematic focus of this volume – class, caste and gender. Class analysis is not very strong in Indian social science not only because of the contentious nature of the concept of class between the different schools of thought but also because those analyses are invariably related to industrialized societies and India remains predominantly agrarian to this day. Agrarian classes are more elaborate and often interlaced with additional elements such as feudal and/or caste oppression, which makes class analysis more complicated, if not vexatious. In the case of caste, the tension between the 'ought' and the 'is' persists vehemently; the Indian state has wished away the reality of caste system from Indian society and consigned it to tradition (see Deshpande, 2003: 98–124). The Indian census does not even identify the population based on castes, save the two social clusters of Scheduled Castes (SCs) and Scheduled Tribes (STs). And, this is done to enable the state to extend special entitlements to them.

One more introductory observation related to the interdisciplinary nature of this volume is called for. Much of the 'class analysis' in India is but number crunching, undertaken by economists, invoking the massive data collected by official agencies. These analyses invariably ignore the interpenetration between class, caste and gender. Analyses of caste, the patented sphere of sociologists and social anthropologists, were impervious not only to the material conditions of caste groups in general but also to the institutionalized oppression to which the lower castes were subjected to by those above them.[1] The trend to view women's issues through the gender lense surfaced only recently with the emergence of women's studies as a separate discipline, which itself is partly a product of women's movement. To analyse the impact of liberalization on these three social categories, conventionally studied by three disciplines – economics, sociology and gender studies – and to link it with developmental politics is to bring in a fourth discipline, viz., political science. Given this stupendous agenda of the seminar I can only scratch it here and there.

One may assert without the fear of being contradicted that India has not witnessed a revolution[2] in the sense in which I have referred to it earlier. The anti-colonial movement did bring about a change in government but the transfer of power was far from sudden or bloody. Sporadic violent attempts to overthrow the government in independent India such as the Naxalbari revolt were limited in their scope, confined as they were, to specific pockets and remain abortive. Therefore, the major source of social transformation in independent India is structural differentiation, the culmination of which may be witnessed in the introduction of SAP in 1991. Keeping this in mind I propose to provide a short history of this structural differentiation in independent India[3] in Section I. Section II will focus on the impact of structural differentiation, particularly economic liberalization, on class, caste and gender. Section III will concentrate on the link between the emerging social transformation and developmental politics.

I

Broadly speaking, there were two competing models of society when India attained political freedom. One model was that of the capitalist democracies of the West. These democracies had evolved gradually on the principle of separation between the state, market and civil society. The underlying assumptions of this separation were the following: First, the state is an agency of coercion and is motivated by power. Therefore, the process of acquiring and exercising power should be well-defined and checked through legal mechanisms. Second, economic activity is motivated by material incentives and is to be regulated by the market mechanism in terms of free exchange. Third, civil society is the space for free voluntary activity for the citizens, between the state and the market, the zone in which a variety of political actions could be initiated to moderate the potential authoritarianism of the state and the likely rapacity of the market. In the West, state, market and civil society emerged successively and each of these spheres acquired a certain level of autonomy.

In contrast to the separation principle of capitalist democracies, the socialist societies functioned on the institutional principle of fusion of the state, market and civil society (see Kaminiski, 1992). Here, the party–state monopolized all powers and regulated the market and the civil society. From the command economy of the socialist state the market disappeared and civil society was absorbed by the state. The conjoint activities of the one-party system and its numerous front organizations came to be christened as people's democracy!

In the beginning capitalist democracies were only concerned with creating congenial conditions for citizens to pursue their preferred pattern of life, protecting them from external aggression and providing them with internal security. But, the emergence of socialist states which attended to the economic welfare of their citizens posed major challenges to the capitalist democracies. Understandably, 20th century capitalist states tended to become welfare states. Thus, what were considered to be the private worries of individual citizens became public issues to be handled by the state (Mills, 1959). Most of the colonial states became politically independent by the mid-20th century and took over the agendas of the socialist and the welfare states in different combinations. Inevitably, post-colonial societies became substantially state-centric and India was no exception.

Independent India opted for what came to be referred to as the 'third way', that is, combining multi-party democracy, one of the distinctive features of capitalist states, with planned economy, the hallmark of the socialist states. This was indeed a challenging experiment in that efforts were made to fuse the best of both in the two models. However, it was the planned economy and the associated state centrism which assumed saliency in the first quarter century of India's independence. The state intended to promote economic development with an accent on distributive justice and also initiated a number of measures to introduce and institutionalize people's participation in the context of planned development (see GoI, 1951: 2; 1956: 3; 1985: 24–25 and 68).

The state in India wanted to retain its centrality not only in initiating planned economic development but also in promoting and sustaining the civil society. Although one-party dominance persisted for most of the time in independent India, it did not become a party-state or usurp the space of civil society. However, by the 1970s one witnessed a proliferation of organizations which started interrogating the state. While some of these organizations are not explicitly anti-state, quite a few are. Further, some are neither anti-state nor pro-state, but objected to the unanticipated consequences of state-initiated development leading to the ravaging of the ecology and the environment. The prominent new collective actors are women, Dalits, adivasis, religious minorities, rural poor, urban slum dwellers, environmentalists, and so on. They heralded a new beginning and manifested a new stirring – the emerging vibrant civil society.

It is far from my intention to suggest that civil society crystallized in India only recently. Quite the contrary, India had a long tradition of anti-establishment mobilizations (see Oommen, 2001: 219–35). In fact, the 'national' state and civil society reinforced each other in independent India (although the former was far too strong as compared with the latter), and some agencies in civil society became inimical to the state only during the emergency (1975–77) and since then.

Free India's state was committed not only to usher in and sustain political democracy but also to foster economic development. Understandably, a large number of giant high-tech ventures have been sponsored and financed by the state; these were even sacralized. Jawaharlal Nehru's allusion to them as the 'temples' of modern India is an example of this. But gradually the ill-effects of big projects surfaced. Not only did most of them cause environmental degradation, some of them also led to the uprooting of millions of natives from their habitats. This gave birth to a large number of political actions by environmentalists who are invariably unattached to any political party and are anti-state. In this context, the state was accused of 'destructive development', that is, reckless development which ignores the human dimension. Some have dubbed this accusation as 'ecological fundamentalism' and argue that environmentalists ignore the ground reality of poverty and underdevelopment in India. According to them, these problems could be successfully tackled only through substantial application of science and technology, which are likely to bring about some negative consequences for the environment. But, the trade-off is worth it according to the 'developmentalists'. The point is, in a democratic society a wide variety of articulations crystallize which in itself is a testimony to the existence of a vibrant civil society.

While civil society tried to assert its autonomy, in independent India right from the beginning the story of the market is almost the reverse. The Bombay Plan of 1944 conceived by a few Indian industrialists wanted state intervention in planning, financing and managing industrial development (Stern, 1993: 210). Thus, even before independence, economic nationalism pursued by the big bourgeoisie in India prompted state intervention. However, two points may be noted here. One is that the all-India bourgeoisie was seeking protection from its foreign colonial counterpart through the state as the presence of the latter would continue even after the political withdrawal of the colonial power. The other point is that the small bourgeoisie of different linguistic regions (nations) also wanted protection from the state against the all-India big bourgeoisie. This is an important dimension of conflicts between 'little nationalism' and 'great nationalism' in India (Guha, 1979: 455–78).

The national state, which succeeded the colonial state, invariably started with adequate legitimacy as an agent of economic intervention and development. Understandably, the Indian state had initiated a series of measures to achieve this objective. The two earliest measures were the instituting of the Planning Commission in March 1950 and the passing of the Industries (Development and Regulation) Act of 1950. The first was an instrument to initiate the process of long-term economic development and the second was intended to curb monopolistic tendencies and to avoid waste emanating from undesirable competition between private industrial houses (Panini, 1995: 35).

The Industrial Policy Resolution of 1956 sectoralized Indian industries into public and private, reserving investments in basic and heavy industries for the public sector, which eventually came to occupy the 'commanding heights' in the economy. But, the real problem was that the public sector in India was perceived more as a social service agency than as an economic venture competing with other agencies and generating at least modest profits. On the other hand, the Companies Act was amended in 1956 to reduce the control of family members over industrial corporations. This was followed by the abolition of the Managing Agency System and the nationalization of commercial banks in 1969. Following close on its heels was the passing of the Monopolies and Restrictive Trade Practices Act of 1970 which prescribed that big business houses needed to obtain permission from the government to expand their enterprises. Further, the share of foreign investment in Indian companies was restricted to 49 per cent of the equity capital. Finally, stringent rules for repatriation of profits and on foreign exchange transactions were introduced through the Foreign Exchange Regulation Act of 1973. Truly, India's was licence-permit raj.

The rural economy was moulded by the state basically through land reforms and the 'green revolution'. Land reforms sought to abolish absentee landlordism and intermediaries between the landowner and the actual tiller of the land, the idea being to make those who worked on the land its real owners. The hope was to bring about: "A land reform which breaks the power of large farmers and the rural elite, will ... provide a framework within which public goods and services can be directed to the target groups with minimum leakage" (Chenery et al., 1974: 135). But due to serious implementation lags and gigantic leakages the objectives could not be achieved. Although the 'green revolution' provided for the subsidization of agricultural inputs and ensured the marketing of agricultural produce at an agreed and often agreeable prices, it mainly benefited the rural rich.

The state thus was a decisive actor in the affairs of the Indian economy from 1947 till 1990. The announced aim of this involvement was to bring about economic development and distributive justice. But neither of these goals have been achieved. According the Economic Survey of 1994–95 (GoI, 1995), the rate of return from the public sector enterprises remains a measly 3 per cent. The restrictions imposed on the private companies did not produce the intended results as licensing favoured the big business houses (GoI, 1969). In spite of the emphasis on distributive justice, not only did the disparity between the rich and the poor increase, but even the absolute proportion of the population below the poverty line increased. These developments prompted the liberalization of the economy, thereby conceding autonomy to the market. That is, while the civil society wrested its autonomy from the state, autonomy was invested on the market by the state.

The implications of the progressive reduction in state centrism and autonomization of civil society and market are to be noted. First, the state is increasingly compelled to share its sovereignty not only with other spheres within the domestic polity but is also constrained to undergo an erosion of its sovereignty vis-à-vis the Bretton Woods institutions. This is evident from the success with which the World Trade Organization (WTO) and such other agencies can impose their conditionalities on the Indian state (Oommen, 1993: 1–38). Second, while the market in India has achieved a certain degree of autonomy vis-à-vis the state, the global market substantially erodes the Indian market's autonomy – witness the manner in which even the retail trade is taken over by multinationals. Third, civil society has to fight its battle at two fronts, the state and the market – both formidable adversaries. This structural differentiation is likely to mould developmental politics in India, which I will discuss later in Section III.

II

Economic liberalization, like any other phenomenon, produces both winners and losers; if the winners are many and the losers are a few, its acceptability and legitimacy will increase. Keeping this in mind we need to examine the quality of social transformation brought about through economic liberalization. There is enough reports in the media which indicate that the number of Indian billionaires is increasing and they are shining in the post-liberalization era; the most visible beneficiary being Mukesh Ambani whose wealth is increasing "by roughly 40 lakh every single minute" (see *Times of India*, 8th October 2007). On the other hand, India's ranking in Human Development Index (HDI), undertaken by United Nations Development Programme (UNDP), hovers between 120 and 130, the rank being 128 in 2007, among the 170 countries subjected to this exercise since 1990 by UNDP.

Thus, there is a huge stable sinking bottom of India's citizenry and a minuscule few shining at the top. Further, analysts have pointed out that the Indian states vary substantially in their economic performance in post-reforms period (see Ahluwalia, 2000: 1637–48) and the average per capita income of northern states fell below that of southern states by the end of the 1990s (see Mathew, 2004: 564–79). The reason for the increasing regional disparities is partly attributed to increased share of the private sector, since early 1980s and got accelerated after the introduction of liberalization in 1991 (see Kurian, 2000: 538–50). Finally, not only that poverty did not decline in post-reforms period as compared with the pre-reforms period but inequality increased significantly in the post-reforms period as compared with the previous decades (see Dev and Ravi, 2007: 509–21). But, the focus of this seminar being the impact of economic liberalization on three social categories – class, caste and gender – I will confine my analysis to them.[4]

Ignoring the conceptual contentions about class I shall limit my analysis to two class categories – working class and middle class – in the urban context while discussing the impact of liberalization.[5] While the working class seems to be by and large losers, the prosperous middle class, particularly the new middle class (NMC), is believed to be a product of economic liberalization. In rural India, those with substantial land holdings are the only gainers, while both the middle peasantry as well as the agrarian poor (that is, marginal farmers and agricultural labourers) is losers. In fact, "... globalization has led to shock and crisis and contributed to increased loss of livelihoods, deprivation, insecurity, debt and death in the lives of many, specially in agriculture" (Mehta and Ghosh, 2004–05: 115).

According to the 1991 census data, which was collected before liberalization was launched, the size of labour force was 317 million of which 8.5 per cent (i.e., 27 million) was in the formal sector (Davala, 1995: 5). Women constituted one-third of the informal sector and one-seventh of those in the formal sector. There were 75 million agricultural labourers and 110 million small and marginal farmers who supplemented their income by working as labour (Dutt, 1996: 5), that is, 185 million were in the rural informal sector. The NSSO sample survey in 1999–2000 (55th round) revealed that out of a total workforce of 397 million, only 28 million were in the formal sector. The Census of India, 2001 report the size of labour force as 400 million. Of this, only 28 million (7.5%) was in the formal sector. The urban informal sector comprised around 100 million. The 2004–05 Economic Survey, (GoI, 2005: 230) reports that the employment as on 31st March in the formal sector was 27 million. All these indicate that informalization of labour increased after economic liberalization.

It is more pertinent to note here that the wages of those employed in the formal sector are substantially higher as compared to those employed in the informal sector; one estimate is that the wages in the formal sector are four to five times higher than that in the informal sector (see CMIE, 1989). More importantly, the workers in the informal sector are under inferior employment conditions; they have no legal proof of having employed, often subjected to subcontracting, denied the right to unionize, face constant threat of being dismissed, irregular working hours and less number of annual employment days. Based on the hearings the National Commission of Women had with women workers from primary, secondary and tertiary sectors drawn from different parts of the country, it has been concluded that liberalization has led to the deterioration of women workers (see Sudershan, 2004).

Additionally problems such as lack of parity in wages with men workers, non-availability of separate latrines, crèches for children, not to speak of sexual harassment from male co-workers and superiors exist in the case of women workers. Thus, one can conclude without doubt that because economic liberalization spawns informalization it leads to a general decline in the welfare of workers.

The government is not impervious to this unhappy trend. Thus, the Second National Labour Commission appointed by the previous government submitted its report in 2002 and proposed a legislation provisioning social security for all workers, including those in the informal sector. The present government set up the National Commission on Enterprises in the Unorganized Sector, which proposed a number of measures to provide social security to the workers in the informal sector. Yet another laudable initiative of the present government is the National Rural Employment Guarantee Act (NREGA) providing a minimum of 100 days of employment for those living in rural India. While the legislations proposed by the two commissions are yet to be passed, it is too early to evaluate the impact of NREGA.

Some have argued that the introduction of technology in rural India in the field of agriculture is not leading to polarization but 'income diffusion' between small and big farmers (see for an example, Sharma and Poleman, 1994). Similarly, some others emphasize the role of local markets in making technological inputs easily accessible in rural areas (see Shah, 1993; Shah and Ballabh, 1997: A183-A190). While accessibility is a necessary condition, it is not a sufficient one in that affordability is crucial particularly for the small and marginal farmers. Therefore, it is rightly argued that in so far as the unequal distribution of land and other resources persist, adoption of technology and access to market will not decrease the dependence of small farmers on those who wield economic, social and political power in rural India but will persist and exacerbate (see Wilson, 2002: 1229–38). Thus, there is no evidence to suggest that liberalization has improved the economic conditions of peasantry and agricultural workers.

Although economic liberalization advocates the retreat of the state from the sphere of social welfare, there are two areas, which are considered to be the responsibility of state – primary education and primary health. But liberalization creates an ethos of privatization, which encapsulates even these areas. Proliferation of low quality private primary schools, which use English as the medium of instruction and charge exorbitant fees, has become common even in rural India (see Jha, 2005: 3677–84). This is disastrous for creating a sound education system, a prerequisite for building the much heralded knowledge society. Equally dismal is the consequence of privatization of primary health, another vital prerequisite to develop the much required human resource for economic liberalization (see Saxena, 2006: 133–76).

At any rate privatization of education and health hits very hard, particularly the poor who cannot afford to pay the high fees/charges. To complicate matters, even the food insecurity has increased during the post-liberalization period (see Degaonkar, 2006: 391–401). The privatization spree has not even spared water making it unaffordable to the poor (see Iyer, 2003: 239–66). A predictable consequence of the conjunction of these factors is the tendency to terminate life in desperation. The widely reported phenomenon of farmer's suicide is a manifestation of this. According to K. Nagaraj, an agrarian crisis has gripped India's countryside caused by commercialization of agriculture, scarcity of water, withdrawal of state investments in agriculture, increase in the cost of cultivation and crash of prices in the post-liberalization period (see *The Hindu*, November 13, 2007, p. II). It is significant to recall here that it is not the rural poor who are committing suicides but small and medium farmers who fall into the debt trap from states, which have performed relatively well according to the official estimates (see Mehta and Ghosh, 2004–05).

The role of middle class in Indian society varied across time. The middle class was in the forefront of the anti-colonial struggle and the most important professional category was the lawyers. After independence, those in the top echelon of administration and professionals such as doctors, engineers, university teachers and the like assumed crucial significance in the project of 'nation-building'. Those professionals who left the country in search of greener pastures were viewed as an 'anti-national' and 'unpatriotic' bunch, because 'brain drain' decelerated the process of nation-building. With economic liberalization, all these changed: not only that graduates of Indian Institutes of Technology (IITs), Indian Institutes of Management (IIMs) and those trained in Information Technology (IT) are added to doctors and engineers, their spatial mobility across the world is facilitated and they got incorporated into the 'global brain pool'.

Traditionally, the upper castes, constituted by the three twice-born *varnas*, viz., Brahmins, Kshatriyas and Vaishyas, had a near monopoly in administration and professions, with the Brahmins dominating. But, the policy of reservation provided to SCs and STs and some of the policy measures extended to the Other Backward Classes (OBCs) gradually started eroding the monopoly of those castes entrenched in administration and professions. The upper castes, particularly the Brahmins, who were the most affected, quickly shifted to the new market economy of the 1990s unleashed by liberalization. Equipped as they were with appropriate social, cultural and economic capital, drawn from tradition and acquired during the mixed economy phase of modernization, the Brahmins were well placed to become transnationals when liberalization was introduced. Perhaps it is no accident that Indian upper castes acquired substantial presence in the Silicon Valley, the IT hub of the United States of America and subsequently to replicate it in India. Thus, Bangalore, the 'silicon valley of India', has visible presence of South Indian Brahmins (see Bairy, 2006: 177–219).

It is fascinating to note here how the high-tech profession of IT gets inextricably intertwined with Brahmins. In an article published in September 2000 in *Vipra Nudi*, a caste periodical, one reads:

> The computer field, which recognizes only merit and is rid of caste, community etc., today is overflowing with brilliance. It is indeed the greatest achievement of the 21st century that the Brahmin community, which was being stamped out in the name of reservation, is occupying 60 per cent of this field .... Even before the angry eyes of the government and politicians fall on it, it is generating billions worth foreign exchange and according an important place for the country in the eyes of the world. (quoted in Bairy, 2006: 207–8)

And, one Mr Sadashivaiah provides the rationalization for the Brahmin dominance to Bairy on 1 March 2000, in the course of fieldwork:

> In the Silicon Valley there is no reservation. If you have merit, you will survive; otherwise you don't .... Here (in India) you might de-recognise us on the basis of our caste, but we will always remain indispensable because of our brains ... you cannot for ever rule the society with a crown, but it is possible with knowledge. And who else but the Brahmin is the knowledge center? Who else but the Brahmins have pursued knowledge for its own sake? (see Bairy, 2006: 2009)

The inferences that one can make based on these articulations are basically three. One, even the super specialty middle class global Indian of our times seems to be inextricably intertwined in primordial identities – caste, religion, language, region, tribe – indeed s/he is at best glocal. Although some concessions and compromises are shown in beliefs and rituals, marriage and dietary practices, traditional identities are having a new lease of life in secular spaces. This brings me to the second point. The much-touted 'cultural capital' is available only to the upper castes and it can be, and often it is, an undying source of social arrogance leading to hegemonic tendencies. Thirdly, class and caste can be dissociated as tools constructed for analysis, but in everyday life they are inextricably intertwined influencing the behaviour of individuals and collectivities. However, this is not to deny the enormous contextual compartmentalization in human behaviour which makes it possible to hold forth or back one or another dimension.[6]

I have indicated above the potential of the urban middle class drawn from upper castes celebrating liberalization. In contrast, the rural middle class, drawn partly from upper castes and partly from the OBCs, perceives economic liberalization as a great threat. During the Green Revolution era, this group greatly benefited from the state patronage in the form of subsidized inputs for agricultural production and assured prices for agricultural products. But this pattern of state–farmer relationship is an anachronism in the regime of economic liberalization. Understandably, the state has withdrawn or gradually withdrawing them. Expectedly, a large number of farmers' movements anchored to particular linguistic regions/provincial states emerged all over India with the explicit agenda of opposing liberalization. Some of them, such as the one led by Sharad Joshi in Maharashtra, displayed considerable ambivalence in its attitude to liberalization, while some other such as those in Uttar Pradesh, led by Mahendra Tikait, were not very vocal in expressing their opposition to liberalization. But, the farmers' movement, which virulently opposed economic liberalization and achieved world visibility, is the Karnataka State Farmers' Association (KRRS) led by Nanjudaswamy, an academic by profession. The KRRS is an interesting case to analyse the interpenetration between class, caste and gender.

KRRS has been an integral part of the People's Global Action (PGA), an anti-liberalization network which co-ordinates activities across the world. Most of the 400 farmers who participated in the PGA Inter-Continental Caravan across Europe in 1999 were its members. And, Nanjudaswamy declared in the *KRRS Newsletter* (No. 1) in 1999:

> We the participants in the Inter-Continental Caravan for Solidarity and Resistance ... have come here to build bridges between people who want to reclaim their future, to disobey the institutions that run the current, self-destructive system of global economic, political and military governance, and to take power in their hands in order to construct a different world. A world where local people are in control of their local economy, where centralized economic and political power disappear. (quoted in Pattenden, 2005: 1978)

While KRRS eminently succeeded in building horizontal solidarity with anti-liberalization protestors across the world, at the local level its affairs are dominated by men drawn from the local dominant groups (see Assadi, 1997; Nadkarni, 1987); class domination, caste hierarchy and patriarchy mould the local level functioning of KRRS. While egalitarianism is preached at the global level inequality and oppression are practised at the local level by KRRS, its glocality is bristled with utter contradictions. The organization was mainly focusing on benefits to be wrested from the state for rich and middle farmers, it ignored issues such as agricultural wages, interest rates on private loans, distribution of ration cards based on income levels, caste exploitation and gender oppression (Assadi, 1997; Nadkarni, 1987). However, it may also be noted that a section of low caste, particularly men, are becoming more vocal and started asserting their social rights. But even their behaviour at home smacks of patriarchal values. That is, vertical class, caste and gender relations persist at the micro level, in spite of the success of KRRS at the macro level – global, national, provincial – as an opponent of liberalization (see Pattenden, 2005: 1975–85).

There is some evidence of the deteriorating condition of women, which is expressed through the notions such as feminization of poverty and the presence of women in greater proportion, as compared with men, in the informal sector of the economy. But some writers argue that liberalization provides an opportunity to women to get some employment with all the precarious conditions associated with it. Further, these employment also provides them with an opportunity to resist the oppression they face within the household where the values of patriarchy persists (see for example, Hensman, 2004: 1030–34). Similarly, in the case of Dalits and Adivasis, the leading tendency is to suggest that they should resist liberalization because the rolling back of the state from welfare measures would adversely affect them. But, there are authors who argue that liberalization has become an irreversible process and therefore the subalterns should also tap the benefits they are likely to accrue from it (see for an example, Omvedt, 2005: 4881–85). The benefits are: one, economic not only through employment but also demanding better prices for their products; and two, get aligned to global networks and highlight the human rights violations they face.

These pragmatic suggestions cannot be ignored. But, in the case of the subaltern classes, particularly the Adivasis, there is an acute additional problem. While the high-tech projects result in considerable displacement affecting several castes and classes, the proportion of displacees is disproportionately high in the case of Adivasis. The estimates regarding displacement vary vastly. According to one such estimate, some 35 to 55 million people have been displaced in independent India. Of these, displacement due to large projects according to the government, between 1951 and

1985, is sixteen and a half million. But critics estimate that the figure for 1951–1990 is little over twenty one million (see Sen, 1995: 243). According to the latest reported statistics, in 2007, displacees in India count 1.4 million and of these 79 per cent are Adivasis (see *Hindustan Times*, December 20, 2007). The fact that the Adivasis constitute only 8 per cent of India's population makes the problem of displacement evidently acute in their case.

Indeed, it is true that limited displacements are unavoidable in the course of development and the process began soon after India started its journey of planned economic development. But, during the post-liberalization period, not only that the process of displacement got accelerated but it also started affecting those areas where dams are not constructed or mining is not done. The forcible launching of the special economic zones (SEZs) in spite of acute resistance by the oustees, is the most telling example of the onslaught administered through the liberalization regime (see Oommen, 2006: 267–80).

The analysis, which so far provided evidence of the impact of economic liberalization on class, caste and gender, mainly confined to the micro levels and to the increasing informalization of the economy. Let me now turn to an analysis of the persisting broad correlation between class and caste in India, liberalization notwithstanding.

As the data relating to castes and communities are not collected in the censuses of independent India, save the two constitutionally recognized deprived groups of SCs and STs. But the National Sample Survey Organization (NSSO) started providing these data since 1999 based on which the correlation between income categories and castes and communities has been worked out.[7] The data relating to 1999–2000 and 2004–05 are presented in Tables 1a and 1b.

It is clear, from the tables that the percentage of those below the poverty line increased for STs, SCs, UC-Muslims, UC-Hindus and UC-Sikhs in rural India although in differing proportions; as clusters of castes and communities they are losers as liberalization proceeds. In contrast, those below the poverty line decreased in the cases of OBCs, UC-Christians and UC-Others; the decrease being phenomenal in the case of the last category. It is also important to note that the top 5 per cent MPCE had increased for all categories in rural India except the STs, UC-Hindus and UC-Sikhs. Reasons for this may be entirely different. In the case of STs the substantial displacement they suffered due to high-tech projects in rural India could be a plausible explanation. In the cases of UC-Hindus and UC-Sikhs the decrease in their shares of rural population may be the reason. In the case of UC-Christians and UC-Others those in the top 5 per cent of MPCE group has increased substantially.[8]

Table 1a

Comparative Distribution of Monthly Per Capita Consumption Expenditure (MPCE) by Caste-Community Groups, Rural India, 1999–2000 and 2004–05

Caste and Community Groups	*Below Poverty Line 1999–2000= Rs 327 2004–05=Rs 356.30*		*Approx. Top 5% of MPCE 1999–2000=Rs 1,000 2004–05=Rs 1,200*		*Estimated Shares of Rural Population*	
	1999–2000	*2004–05*	*1999–2000*	*2004–05*	*1999–2000*	*2004–05*
ALL-ST	45.8	47.6	1.4	1.2	10.5	10.6
ALL-SC	35.9	36.8	1.7	2.1	20.5	20.9
UC-Mus	26.8	27.3	2.0	3.2	7.5	6.7
ALL-OBC	27.0	26.7	3.3	4.1	37.6	42.8
UC-Hin	11.7	12.7	8.6	8.5	22.0	17.5
UC-Chr	9.6	6.6	18.9	29.2	0.7	0.6
UC-Skh	0.0	0.4	31.7	29.1	1.0	0.8
UC-Oth	16.0	2.7	17.9	29.8	0.2	0.1
All Groups	27.0	28.3	4.3	4.5	100.0	100.0

ST = Scheduled Tribes,
UC = Upper Castes,
OBC = Other Backward Classes,
Chr = Christians,
SC = Scheduled Castes,
MUS = Muslims,
Hin = Hindus,
Skh = Sikhs,
Oth = Others.

Source: Computed from NSSO 61st Round data. Cells show percentage share of each caste-community group in the relevant MPCE size-class; last column shows share of each group in total rural population. Poverty Line is as per official estimate of Planning Commission Expert Group. Columns may not add up due to rounding.

Table 1b

Comparative Distribution of Monthly Per Capita Consumption Expenditure (MPCE) by Caste-Community Groups, Urban India, 1999–2000 and 2004–05

Caste and Community Groups	*Below Poverty Line 1999–2000= Rs 454 2004–05=Rs 538.60*		*Approx. Top 5% of MPCE 1999–2000=Rs 2,000 2004–05=Rs 2,500*		*Estimated Shares of Urban Population*	
	1999–2000	*2004–05*	*1999–2000*	*2004–05*	*1999–2000*	*2004–05*
ALL-ST	35.6	33.9	1.8	1.7	3.4	2.9
ALL-SC	38.3	39.8	0.8	1.6	14.4	15.7
UC-Mus	34.2	38.7	1.6	2.5	11.4	10.0
ALL-OBC	29.5	30.9	2.0	2.3	30.4	35.6
UC-Hin	9.9	10.5	8.2	9.6	36.9	32.9
UC-Chr	5.4	6.9	17.0	16.5	1.3	1.0
UC-Skh	4.9	1.6	15.1	15.7	1.1	1.1
UC-Oth	2.7	3.3	14.4	22.9	1.1	0.9
All Groups	23.4	25.6	4.5	5.1	100.0	100.0

Source: Computed from NSSO 61st Round data. Cells show percentage shares of each caste-community group in the relevant MPCE size-class; last column shows share of each group in total urban population. Poverty line is as per official estimate of Planning Commission Expert Group. Columns may not add up due to rounding.

The situation in urban India is substantially different (see Table 1b) in that poverty reduction occurred only in the cases of STs and UC-Sikhs: in the case of the former moderately and in the case of the latter, substantially. As for all others urban poverty has increased the worst hit being UC-Muslims followed by UC-Others. The loosers in urban India in terms of their presence in the top five per cent MPCE group are only STs and UC-Christians. Over all, the principal gainers both in rural and urban India are UC-Others. In the case of UC-Muslims, while incidence of poverty increased both in rural and urban India, so did their presence in the top 5 per cent MPCE group, which points to the emerging economic polarization among them.[9]

Three general points emerge from the NSSO data presented in Tables 1a and 1b. They are: (1) the impact of liberalization varies across castes and communities and their internal disparities get exacerbated. To arrest the increasing class polarization those who benefit less should be explicitly targeted. (2) The traditionally privileged upper castes benefit more, irrespective of their religious backgrounds, as compared with STs, SCs and OBCs, again irrespective of their religious affiliations. Thus caste (and not religion) seems to be the relevant variable in determining gainers and loosers in the context of liberalization. (3) The share of STs decreased in the top 5 per cent MPCE groups both in rural and urban India. This is in contrast to SCs who have improved their representation in the top 5 per cent MPCE group both in rural and urban India. This reveals the fact that constitutionally mandated provisions in themselves are not sufficient for upward mobility of the traditionally underprivileged groups.

III

Armed with this understanding of the impact of economic liberalization on class, caste and to a lesser extent on gender, I propose to look at the nature of developmental politics in contemporary India.[10] I suggest that three factors in combination condition the nature of developmental politics in post-liberalization India. One, the conceptions different political formations hold about the future of India. Two, their attitude towards economic liberalization. Three, the place the political formations accord to civil society organizations (CSOs)/non-governmental organizations (NGOs).

Elsewhere I have designated four competing conceptions, which prevalent in contemporary India (see Oommen, 2004: 745–55, reproduced in Oommen, 2005: 208–22) as cultural monism, cultural pluralism, cultural federalism and cultural subalternism. Implicit in these conceptions are the differing ideas the political formations have about the nature of Indian polity they want to evolve. The cultural monists conceive India as a cultural monolith with one dominant mainstream as articulated through the slogan: one nation, one culture, one people. Anchoring itself firmly to India's Aryan Hindu past, the cultural monists want to exorcise all the 'undesirable' accretions, particularly those of Muslims and Christians, subordinate indigeneous non-Aryan Adivasis and Dravidians and 'integrate' Indian protestant religions, such as Jainism, Buddhism and Sikhism into the Hindu mainstream.

In tune with this value orientation the cultural monists should have rejected economic liberalization and opted for a 'swadeshi' regime in economics. But political compulsions, both national and global, prompted them to endorse economic liberalization. However, all who attest cultural monism do not unanimously accept this. Witness, for example, the position articulated by the Swadeshi Jagran Manch (SJM) on liberalization, widely believed to be the economic think tank of Rashtriya Swayamsevak Sangh (RSS), the fountain-spring of the idea of cultural monism. However, for pragmatic reasons, the cultural monists combine economic globalization and 'cultural nationalism'. Generally speaking, political parties float their front organizations of workers, peasants, youth, students, women, teachers and the like, usually referred to as 'mass organizations' (see Mohanty, 2004: 388–406). But, in the case of Bharatiya Janata Party (BJP), this relationship is reversed; BJP is the political instrument of RSS, which claims to be only a cultural organization. Thus, several CSOs/NGOs inspired by the RSS ideology co-ordinate and reinforce their activities with the BJP. Needless to say, there are moments of contentions and conflicts within this ideological fraternity. In spite of this, the cultural monists constitute a distinct collective actor in the context of developmental politics in post-liberalization India. This strand of politics combines cultural nationalism, economic globalism and subservience of the party to ideological hegemony of Hindutva.

In contrast, the cultural pluralists conceive India as a product of gradual and continuous accretion of cultural elements drawn from ancient medieval and modern or Aryan, Dravidian, Mughal and European elements each of which made a significant contribution to the 'composite culture' of India. They strive to establish 'unity in diversity' and the principal political party, which identifies with this value orientation is the Indian National Congress (INC). Cultural pluralists attest secularism, understood as according equal respect to all religions, as a cardinal principle.

The Congress opted for planned economic development of India, but after four decades of experimenting with it adopted liberalization in 1991 due to pragmatic economic reasons as I have noted in Section I. While the Congress party is not averse to concede freedom to CSOs, it cannot be said that the party always stood by this principle, as exemplified by the declaration of internal emergency during 1975–77, a salient feature of which was suppression of CSOs. While, the Congress too have several front organizations, the relationship between the party and these organizations is not clearly defined; it is neither subservient as in RSS–BJP relationship nor the party has a dominant role as in the case of left parties. The relationship between the Congress party and its front organizations is characterized by reciprocity and autonomy. Thus, the combination of cultural pluralism, economic liberalization and interdependent relationship with CSOs provide a distinct flavour to the developmental politics pursued by the Congress party.

What I designate as cultural federalism is an objective pursued by parties with four distinct bases: nationality (for example, some of the Tamil, Telugu and northeast parties), caste (for example, some of the parties in Bihar and Uttar Pradesh), religion (for example, some of the parties in Punjab, Jammu & Kashmir) and class (for example, left parties). In spite of these differing social bases, two factors are common to them. One, they have a firm anchorage in at least one provincial state where they were/are in power, and two, they are against a strong centre – be it manned by the Congress or the BJP. Their alliance with or opposition against these two parties, with all-India spread, is largely based on pragmatic considerations, except in the case of left parties, who oppose 'communal' BJP and selectively support 'secular' Congress.

The cultural federalists vary in their orientation to economic liberalization. Except the left parties, none seem to have taken a clear position; the remaining parties seem to be ambivalent to liberalization. Even the Communist Party (Marxist) of India, (CPM), the only left party which has enough presence in three states to capture power, its opposition to capitalism and endorsement of socialism in principle notwithstanding, in practice the CPM governments vary as illustrated by the difference between West Bengal and Kerala.

The relationships between these parties and CSOs/NGOs too vary vastly. All the left parties have well-formed 'mass organizations', which are dependent on the parties for their ideology and organizational framework; indeed they are subservient to the parties. This pattern is quite different from that of RSS–BJP relationship as noted above. The attitude of the left parties to 'autonomous' CSOs/NGOs would vacillate between friendship and hostility depending upon the position these organizations take in particular contexts and/or on specific issues. As for the remaining political parties included under the rubric of cultural federalism there is no distinct pattern. For example, Asom Gana Parishad (AGP) is a party, which emerged out of the student movement, which created the organization, All Assam Students' Union (AASU), and AGP's dependence on AASU is well known. This pattern applies to some other 'nationalist' parties of northeast also. On the other hand, there are no other strong mass organizations of the type associated with the parties of northeast. In the case of parties anchored to religious and caste identities there are no strong mass organizations, although autonomous religious and caste associations often exert pressure on them.

The cultural subalternists are disenchanted with all the above three conceptions of India. According to them, cultural monists are pursuing the goal of reinforcing the hegemony of the traditionally privileged caste Hindus, the Manuvadis, to recall an evocative phrase from the lexicon of the most visible political formation of cultural subalternists, the Bahujan Samaj Party (BSP). While the cultural subalternists perceive both pluralists and leftists as 'moderates', some of the dominant castes drawn from the OBCs – Jats, Yadavas, Kurmis – are perceived as the worst oppressors of Dalits in contemporary rural India. In the perception of subalternists the traditional elites along with the emerging OBC elites grabbed the fruits of planned economic development. Economic liberalization continue to provide new opportunities to them and the Dalits continues to be deprived. This is the rationale behind the demand to extend the policy of reservation to the fast expanding private sector and the Bhopal Declaration, which demanded the participation of Dalits in the goods and services to be produced and sold in the wake of liberalization (see Omvedt, 2005: 4881–85). The cultural subalternists do not oppose liberalization as such but want to have a fair deal in the distribution of its benefits. For this to be realized they felt that the Dalit–Bahujans constituted by Adivasis, Dalits, the Most Backward Classes (MBCs) and those religious minorities drawn from the above groups should acquire political power and rule the country.[11]

It is fascinating to note here that BSP gradually emerged out of CSOs, started and nurtured by its founder Kanshi Ram. In turn, a large number of NGOs of Dalit women, college/university teachers, workers, students and the like have emerged and operate both at the all-India and at the regional/local levels. But, the relationship between these organizations and BSP is not clear or even visible; indeed it is tenuous and occasionally hostile. While some of the organizations support the party implicitly, a section of the Dalit bourgeoisie and intellectuals are critical of BSP's tendency to change quickly its policies and strategies. It may be noted that unlike the regionally anchored groups – tribes, castes and nationalities – the Dalits are spatially dispersed all over India. For the success of its developmental politics BSP champions the Dalit cause on an all-India basis.

Three factors – the visions of political parties regarding India's future, their disposition to economic liberalization, and the level of autonomy conceded to CSOs – conjointly mould the developmental politics of post-liberalization India. Whether or not a political formation support or oppose specific policies is dictated by the political-payoffs it hopes to harvest in electoral terms. It is this crass political pragmatism, which gives birth to the frequently denounced but eagerly sought after vote bank politics. All parties indulge in this brand of politics; the only difference is that the 'banks' they bank with differ – religious communities, caste clusters, regional-linguistic groups and even gender. The class factor which cuts through all these categories, admittedly in differing proportions, gets relegated to the background. Consequently, instead of pursuing distributive justice based on the principle – greater the deprivation larger the benefits of development – the perverse practice of 'betting for the strong' in terms of electoral harvest assumes salience, not only across castes and communities but also within them. This results in cumulative exclusion of the weak and cumulative domination by the strong. This is the basic feature of developmental politics in post-liberalization India.

Notes

1. For example, the phenomenon of untouchability is scarcely studied. See Desai (1976) for an early exception. Recently, a team of social scientists and activists undertook a study of untouchability in rural India (see Shah et al., 2006), but such studies are indeed rare.
2. It may be noted here that the term 'revolution' is invoked in a variety of contexts such as industrial revolution and information revolution. The Indian brands are 'non-violent', 'total', 'green' and 'white' revolutions. But I am referring to the term in its strict classical sense alluding to violent political revolutions.
3. This section draws from an earlier publication of mine (Oommen, 1996: 191–202), reproduced in Oommen (2004: 107–27).
4. In fact, two other social categories – Scheduled Tribes and religious minorities – too should have been included in the scope of this seminar and I will refer to them as and when necessary and possible.
5. The fact that those at the top of the class pyramid are substantial gainers is widely endorsed. At any rate, they are not losers.
6. Latterly, there has been some discussion in sociology and social anthropology regarding the death of 'caste as a system' from contemporary India, although there is no consensus (see Srinivas, 2003: 455–59; Beteille, 2007: 945–52; Shah, 2007: 109–16). I am inclined to suggest that one should not hasten to write an 'obituary' on caste even as a 'system' because the institution has shown prodigious potentiality to re-invent itself constantly as Indian experience for more than 3,000 years show.
7. I thank profusely Prof. Satish Deshpande of Delhi University for providing these tables.
8. The increase/decrease of those below the poverty line calls for analysis and explanations which cannot be provided here. I may hazard two hunches: One, the change in the shares of rural population for the castes/communities and two, in the case of UC – other which includes Jains who seem to have gained substantially from liberalization because of their traditional occupations – trade, commerce etc., – which got a great boost under the liberalization regime. This hunch seems to be applicable in understanding the substantial increase in the top 5 per cent of MPCE for UC – Christians also in rural India.
9. The specificities of the Muslim case are elaborately reported and explained in GoI (2006).

10. Developmental politics in contemporary India is moulded by two other factors – the corporations (Indian and foreign) in pushing policies which accelerate economic liberalization, and some of the NGOs pursuing non-party politics in arresting it. But since their conception about the future of India is not articulated I leave them out of this analysis.
11. The recent shift in the strategy of BSP to change its constituency from Dalit–Bahujans to one that encapsulates all (sarvajan) is an interesting one. Whether it indicates a mere shift in strategy to achieve electoral success or a real change in value-orientation is too early to say.

References

Ahluwalia, M.S. 2000. "Economic Performance of States in Post-Reforms Period", *Economic and Political Weekly*, May 6, pp. 1637–47.

Assadi, M. 1997. *Peasant Movement in Karnataka 1980–94*, Delhi: Shipra.

Bairy, T.S. 2006. "Unpacking Globalisation: Historicising the Globalising Brahmin", in S. Somayaji and G. Somayaji (eds.), *Sociology of Globalization: Perspectives from India*, Jaipur: Rawat Publications, pp. 177–219.

Beteille, A. 2007. "Classes and Communities", *Economic and Political Weekly*, March 17, pp. 945–52.

Chenery, H., S. Ahluwalia, C.L.G. Bell, J.H. Duloy and R. Joly. 1974. *Redistribution with Growth*, New Delhi: Oxford University Press.

Davala, S. (ed.). 1995. *Unprotected Labour in India*, Delhi: Friedrich Ebert Stiftung.

Degaonkar, C. 2006. "Globalization, Food Security and the Poor in India", in S. Somayaji and G. Somayaji (eds.), op. cit., pp. 391–401.

Desai, I.P. 1976. *Untouchability in Rural Gujarat*, Bombay: Popular Prakashan.

Deshpande, S. 2003. *Contemporary India: A Sociological View*, New Delhi: Penguin.

Dev, M.S. and C. Ravi. 2007. "Poverty and Inequality: All India and States, 1983–2005", *Economic and Political Weekly*, February 10, pp. 509–21.

Dutt, R. (ed.). 1996. *Organizing the Unorganized Workers*, Delhi: Vikas Publishing House.

Government of India. 1951. First Five-Year Plan: A Draft Outline, New Delhi: Planning Commission.

——. 1956. Second Five-Year Plan: A Draft Outline, New Delhi: Planning Commission.

——. 1969. Report of the Industrial Licensing Policy Enquiry Committee, New Delhi: Ministry of Industrial Development.

——. 1985. Seventh Five-Year Plan: 1985–89, Vol. I, New Delhi: Planning Commission.

——. 1995. Economic Survey of 1994–95, New Delhi: Ministry of Finance.

——. 2005. Economic Survey for the Year 2004–05, New Delhi: Ministry of Finance.

——. 2006. Social, Economic and Educational Status of Muslim Community of India, Prime Minister's High Level Committee, Cabinet Secretariat, New Delhi.

Guha, A. 1979. "Great Nationalism, Little Nationalism and the Problems of Integration: A Tentative View", *Economic and Political Weekly*, 14 (7 & 8), pp. 455–58.

Hensman, R. 2004. "Globalization, Women and Work: What are We Talking About?", *Economic and Political Weekly*, March 6, pp. 1030–34.

Iyer, R. 2003. "Water Privatization and People's Organizations", in P.G. Jogdand and S.M. Michael (eds.), *Globalizations and Social Movement: Struggle for Humane Society*, Jaipur: Rawat Publications, pp. 239–66.

Jha, P. 2005. "Withering Commitments and Weakening Progress: State and Education in the Era of Neoliberal Reforms", *Economic and Political Weekly*, August 13, pp. 3677–84.

Kaminiski, B. 1992. *The Collapse of Socialism*, Princeton, NJ: Princeton University Press.

Kurian, N.J. 2000. "Widening Regional Disparities in India: Some Indicators", *Economic and Political Weekly*, February 12, pp. 538–50.

Mathew, Joseph. 2004. "Performance of the Northern States: A Comparative Analysis", *Economic and Political Weekly*, February 7, pp. 564–79.

Mehta, A.K. and S. Ghosh. 2004–05. "Globalization, Loss of Livelihoods and Entry into Poverty", *Alternate Economic Survey India*, pp. 115–26.

Mills, C.W. 1959. *The Sociological Imagination*, New York: Oxford University Press.

Nadkarni, M. 1987. *Farmer's Movements in India*, Delhi: Allied.

Omvedt, G. 2005. "Capitalism and Globalization, Dalits and Adivasis", *Economic and Political Weekly*, November 19, pp. 4881–85.

Oommen, M.A. 1993. The Political Economy of Globalization, ISS Discussion Paper II, New Delhi: Institute of Social Science.

Oommen, T.K. 1990. *State and Society in India*, New Delhi: Sage Publications.

——. 1996. "State, Civil Society and Market in India: The Context of Mobilization", *Mobilization: An International Journal*, 1(2), pp. 1991–2002 (reproduced in Oommen, T.K. 2004. *Nation, Civil Society and Social Movements*, New Delhi: Sage Publications, pp. 107–27).

——. 2001. "Civil Society: Religion, Caste and Language in India", *Sociological Bulletin*, 50(2), pp. 219–35 (reproduced in Oommen, T.K. 2004. Ibid., pp. 128–43).

——. 2004. "Futures India: Society, Nation-State and Civilisation", *Futures*, Vol. 36, pp. 745–55 (reproduced in Oommen, T.K. 2005. *Crisis and Contention in Indian Society*, New Delhi: Sage Publications, pp. 208–22).

——. 2006. "Coping with Development Pathologies: Resistance to Displacement", *Sociological Bulletin*, 55(2), pp. 267–80.

Panini, M.N. 1995. "The Social Logic of Liberalization", *Sociological Bulletin*, 44(1), pp. 33–62.

Pattenden, J. 2005. "Trickle-Down Solidarity, Globalization and Dynamics of Social Transformation in a South Indian Village", *Economic and Political Weekly*, May 7, pp. 1975–85.

Saxena, K.B. 2006. "The Shrinking Sovereign Space: Globalization and Health Policy", in S. Somayaji and G. Somayaji (eds.), op. cit., pp. 133–76.

Sen, Jai. 1995. "National Rehabilitation Policy: A Critique", *Economic and Political Weekly*, February 4, pp. 241–44.

Shah, A.M. 2007. "Caste in the 21st Century: From System to Elements", *Economic and Political Weekly*, November 3, pp. 109–16.

Shah, G., H. Mander, S. Thorat, S. Deshpande and A. Baviskar. 2006. *Untouchability in Rural India*, Delhi: Sage Publications.

Shah, T. 1993. *Ground Water Markets and Irrigation Development: Political Economy and Practical Policy*, New Delhi: Oxford University Press.

Shah, T and V. Ballabh. 1997. "Water Markets in North Bihar: Six Village Studies in Muzaffarpur District", *Economic and Political Weekly*, December 27, A183-A190.

Sharma, R. and T.T. Poleman. 1994. *The New Economics of India's Green Revolution: Income and Employment Diffusion in Uttar Pradesh*, New Delhi: Vikas Publishing House.

Srinivas, M.N. 2003. "An Obituary on Caste as a System", *Economic and Political Weekly*, February 1, pp. 455–59.

Stern, R.W. 1993. *Changing India: Bourgeois Revolution in the Subcontinent*, Cambridge: Cambridge University Press.

Sudershan, R.M. 2004. Globalization and its Impact on Women: Findings from Hearings Conducted by National Commission for Women, paper presented at the Conference on Impact of Globalization on Women, National Commission for Women, September 17, New Delhi.

Wilson, K. 2002. "Small Cultivators in Bihar and 'New' Technology: Choice or Compulsion?", *Economic and Political Weekly*, March 30, pp. 1229–38.

2

Recent Trends in Caste Inequalities

Comparison of NSSO Consumption Expenditure Data of 2000 and 2005

SATISH DESHPANDE

This paper has the limited objective of making a comparative caste-disaggregated analysis of monthly per capita consumption expenditure data from the last two quinquennial (big sample) surveys of the NSSO conducted in 1999–2000 and 2004–05 respectively. Only two time points separated by five years are not sufficient to establish long-term trends; moreover, consumption expenditure data – as different from measures of income and wealth – tends to understate economic inequalities. However, the 55th and 61st rounds are the first two of the new generation of surveys that allow for a reasonably comprehensive caste profiling of Indian society. As such, they are worth analysing for preliminary indications of trends in inter-caste inequality, for an overall sense of the ways in which caste continues to be a salient aspect of economic status, and for the emerging patterns of social mobility (or immobility) in contemporary society.

Three kinds of comparisons are made here: average consumption expenditure levels across castes; comparison of the different internal segments of the consumption expenditure distribution of each caste; and comparison of the relative 'caste gap' separating the so-called 'upper' castes from the other caste and tribe groups. It is found that, after adjusting for inflation, average consumption levels have increased slightly for all castes in the rural sector, whereas they have stayed the same or declined slightly in the urban sector, specially for the Scheduled Castes (SCs) and the Other Backward Classes (OBCs). The Upper Castes (UCs) are the only ones to have registered an unequivocal increase in average consumption by all measures in both sectors, while urban Scheduled Tribes (STs) seem to have witnessed a minor spurt in consumption levels. Coming to a disaggregated analysis of segments of the class spectrum (taking the 5th, 25th, 50th, 75th and 95th percentiles of consumption expenditure), it is found that for all castes and in both sectors, gains in consumption levels are most at the top quarter of the distribution, though there are anomalies and exceptions. It is noteworthy that the bottom quarter of all castes in the urban sector registers a small decline in consumption levels – in urban India, the poorest sections seem to have become slightly worse off in the first five years of this century. In terms of the 'caste gap' – or the gap between respective percentiles of consumption expenditure for the UCs compared to the three other caste groups – it generally increases as we go up the distribution. In other words, the gap in consumption expenditure between UCs and other castes increases as we go from the 5th to the 95th percentile. In the rural sector, there has been no significant change in the caste gaps between 2000 and 2005, but in the urban sector the gaps seem to have increased slightly, except for the STs who display a peculiar pattern of caste inequality relative to the UCs.

These are preliminary findings, to be confirmed or refuted, once data from the next big sample survey become available. Nevertheless, they establish beyond doubt the strong correlation between caste and economic status in contemporary India, and thus the urgent need for caste sensitive analyses of economic inequality.

Data Issues

It is only relatively recently that social scientists have begun to pay attention to the social patterning of economic inequality. Traditionally, research interest in poverty and inequality related issues has been channeled strictly along class lines with some heed paid to regional distribution. Caste in particular was for a long time a 'politically incorrect' variable for the analysis of inequality. This attitude was also reflected in the official statistics, which made it impossible to distinguish any castes other than the SCs and STs. Barring partial exceptions, cross-tabulations of religion and caste were also not available.

The political mobilization around caste and the renewed salience of religious identities have changed this decisively over the last decade. The Mandal reforms extended interest in caste beyond the scheduled categories, and also highlighted the fact that the so-called 'upper castes' have been – statistically speaking – the most elusive social group in modern India. More recently, the Sachar Committee made a pioneering attempt to produce a detailed socio-economic profile of the Muslim community. Even, the World Bank now devotes considerable effort to analysing the social composition of the poor. All these initiatives have depended heavily on data from the National Sample Survey Organization (NSSO).

The key innovation was effected in the NSSO's 55th round survey conducted in 1999–2000. Beginning with this round, the NSSO began to report data separately for the OBCs. Given that it had also begun to provide unit-level data to users, it became possible, for the first time in independent India, to construct a fairly comprehensive cross-classification of religious and caste groups. Since OBC data was now available, the residual category of 'Others' – those not belonging to the ST, SC or OBC categories – could legitimately be treated as being roughly equivalent tc the 'upper castes'.[1] Moreover, cross-tabulation with religion data allowed for the identification and analysis of caste-based differences within religious groups and religion-based differences within caste groups. Although not taken up in this paper, intra-caste and intra-religion differences allow us to take advantage of macro indicators of economic status when examining the claims of different interest groups.

As with all large data sets, specially those based on sample surveys, the NSSO data are not without their own problems. One issue that is often raised is that in the NSSO surveys, both caste and religion data are self-reported and are not subjected to any further checking or verification by investigators, as is done in the census. While it needs monitoring, this is not as yet an insurmountable obstacle. On the whole, estimates of ST and SC population shares as per the NSSO have been slightly higher but have remained within acceptable distance of the census shares extrapolated for the survey years.[2] A second problem is that disaggregated analyses are often ruled out due to inadequate sample size in the relevant sub-categories. Thus, what is a perfectly acceptable sample size for rural or urban India as a whole quickly shrinks to statistically unacceptable levels as disaggregation across caste, religion or region is introduced. This is a well-known issue with sample surveys, and has to be met with judicious strategies of analysis. A much more serious issue that has come to light with the 61st round survey of 2004–05 is that of the significant increase in the sample proportion, and hence the estimated population share, of the OBC category compared to the 55th round survey of 1999–2000.

Table 1

Weighted Sample Sizes in the 55th and 61st Round Surveys of the NSSO 1999–2000 and 2004–05, by Caste, by Sector

Caste Groups	*RURAL INDIA*				*URBAN INDIA*			
	Weighted SS	*Estimated % of Popn*		*Weighted SS*	*Weighted SS*	*Estimated % of Popn*		*Weighted SS*
	55R	*55R*	*61R*	*61R*	*55R*	*55R*	*61R*	*61R*
ST	47,113	10.5	10.3	46,051	5,121	3.4	3.0	4,665
SC	91,732	20.4	21.3	95,709	21,656	14.4	15.0	23,053
OBC	168,525	**37.5**	**42.9**	192,702	45,839	30.4	36.0	55,288
UC	141,061	**31.4**	**25.5**	114,450	78,003	51.7	45.9	70,500
Missing	708	0.2	0.1	373	256	0.2	0.0	41
Total	449,140	100.0	100.0	449,286	150,876	100.0	100.0	153,547

Note: Weights used are the multipliers supplied with NSSO unit level data on disk; sample sizes show number of persons rounded to nearest integer. 'Missing' refers to records with no data in the caste field. All caste groups include members of all religions. UC = 'Upper' Caste, i.e., those not belonging to ST, SC or OBC.

Table 1 shows the weighted sample sizes, by caste and by sector, for the two relevant surveys of the NSSO, namely, the quinquennial 55th and 61st rounds conducted in 1999–2000 and 2004–05 respectively. It has to be emphasized that the complex sampling design followed by the NSSO does not take into account of any social identities, specially caste or religion. The design does consider size of settlements (villages or urban blocks), and it also tries to oversample affluent households, which would otherwise be very scarce in a national sample. But, there is no attempt to create strata based on caste or religion, and their incidence in the sample is supposed to be a by-product of the representativeness achieved through rigorous sampling techniques.

As can be seen from Table 1, the estimated share of the rural and urban population belonging to the STs and SCs does not vary greatly across the two rounds. The significant changes are for the OBC and for the residual UC group (figures in bold type), and these changes seem to be mutually compensatory. It would seem that between the 55th and 61st rounds, the rural OBC population share increased by roughly five-and-a-half percentage points (from 37.5% to 42.9%), while the UC population share declined by almost six percentage points (from 31.4% to 25.5%). In the urban sector, both the magnitude and the direction of change in population shares for these two caste groups is almost the same as that in the rural sector. The urban OBC share has risen by 5.4 per cent (from 30.4% to 36.0%) while the UC share has declined by 5.8 per cent (from 51.7% to 45.9%). Since the OBC category is a relatively new one with many regional variations, it is possible that the increase over five years reflects better awareness and administrative clarity about the category, so that people who were not sure of their status before are now able to return themselves as OBCs. However, we will have to wait until the next quinquennial round of the NSSO before the matter can be settled. If the population share of the OBCs continues to be unstable in three consecutive big sample rounds, then, there is surely cause for worry. If this share settles down around the levels shown in the 61st round – which, by the way, remain quite plausible – then this issue can be laid to rest.

Yet another issue unrelated to the caste question is that of the 'contamination' caused by the canvassing of two different reference periods in the 55th round survey of 1999–2000. As is now well-known, the simultaneous use (on adjoining pages of the survey instrument) of the traditional thirty-day reference period as well as a newly introduced seven-day reference period for most items of everyday consumption raised the strong possibility that respondents and investigators would have tended to use a single reference period and simply convert it to the other by either dividing or multiplying by four to move from month to week or vice versa. Since the seven-day reference period tended to produce consistently higher estimates of consumption, and earlier surveys had used the month as the reference period, there was bound to be some 'contamination' of data. Although many attempts were subsequently made to minimize the impact of such contamination, the authoritative view, as expressed by the Planning Commission, is that the 'mixed recall period' (MRP) consumption estimates of the 61st round are the ones that are roughly (but not exactly) comparable to the 55th round estimates.[3] The MRP involves use of 365-day recall (or reference) period for five infrequently purchased non-food items, namely, clothing, footwear, durable goods, education and medical expenses, and 30-day recall period for all other items. Accordingly, this paper relies exclusively on the MRP estimates of consumption for the 61st round. However, this caveat regarding comparisons between the 55th and 61st rounds should also be kept in mind – even with the use of the MRP, the 55th round data remain aberrant and are not strictly comparable with the 61st round. This is another reason why comparative exercises must await the next big sample survey before they can draw any firm conclusions.

One final reminder: this paper discusses economic inequality, but it does so based on consumption expenditure data. In the Indian context, consumption expenditure data has been preferred to income data because of the greater accuracy and reliability of such estimates, and also because of the special usefulness of such data in analysis of extreme poverty. However, it has long been recognized that consumption expenditure data tends to significantly understate inequality because it does not take into account savings, investments and stocks of wealth. Given that the share of these non-consumption components of income tends to increase with income levels, it is obvious that looking at consumption expenditure alone will heavily underestimate real differences in economic status. In keeping with general (Indian) practice, and given the absence of reliable macro data on incomes, consumption data provides a fairly good sense of economic inequality in a poor country like India.

Comparison of Average Levels of Consumption Expenditure

The first set of comparisons considered are those of average levels of consumption expenditure. Two dimensions are taken up: first, comparisons across caste groups and second, comparisons across the 55th and 61st rounds, or 1999–2000 and 2004–05 respectively. As already indicated, the MRP estimates of consumption expenditure are used for the 61st round. The consumption expenditure data from the 55th round is adjusted to 61st round price levels by using the Labour Bureau price indices as per the Planning Commission Expert Group practice. The price indices in question are, for the rural sector, the Consumer Price Index for Agricultural Labourers (CPIAL) with base year 1986–87=100, and the Consumer Price Index for Industrial Workers (CPIIW) with base year 1982=100. Since both the NSSO surveys considered here were conducted from July to June, the midpoint of this period, or January, is taken as the reference point, and the respective price indices for January 2000 and January 2005 are used to derive the price deflator to be used on the 55th round consumption expenditure estimates.[4]

Table 2

Median Monthly Per Capita Consumption Expenditure by Caste, by Sector (MPCE in constant 2004–05 Rupees)

Caste Groups	*RURAL INDIA*			*URBAN INDIA*		
	1999–2000	*2004–05*	*% Change*	*1999–2000*	*2004–05*	*% Change*
ST	378.8	391.4	+3.3	676.1	713.6	+5.5
SC	413.2	421.5	+2.0	624.9	612 8	–1.9
OBC	459.9	472.4	+2.7	715.2	679.0	–5.1
UC	545.4	553.0	+1.4	975.1	983.2	+0.8
ALL	465.4	469.4	+0.9	814.0	776.3	–4.6

Note: Price deflators used: Rural India, CPI for Agricultural Labour; Urban India; CPI for Industrial Workers. All computations use NSSO supplied multipliers. UC = 'Upper' Caste, i.e., those not belonging to ST, SC or OBC.

The simplest comparison is that of median consumption expenditure levels for the different caste groups in the two years, at constant 2004–05 prices. As a positional average immune to the distorting effect of extreme values, the median is an appropriate average to use for skewed distributions. Table 2 shows the results of this comparison, which need to be considered across two dimensions – inter-caste and inter-year.

Comparing median monthly per capita consumption expenditure (henceforth abbreviated as MPCE) gives us an initial perspective on economic hierarchies across caste. In rural India the order from bottom to top is: ST, SC, OBC and UC, which gives us the expected caste hierarchy. This holds for both the years. It is noteworthy that only the UC in rural India is above the overall (all castes) average level of MPCE in both years, with the OBC just making it in 2004–05. Comparing across the two years shows that average consumption levels have hardly changed in rural India, with the all-India average increasing by less than 1 per cent. All castes have positive changes, though these are small. Although they start with the lowest absolute level, the rate of increase is highest for the STs at 3.3 per cent, and it is the lowest for the UCs, who have by far the highest absolute levels of average MPCE.

Caste hierarchies in urban India seem to be somewhat different and also more complex. It is the SCs rather than the STs who are at the bottom here, followed by the STs, OBCs and the UCs. Here, all castes other than UCs are well below the national average of MPCE for all castes. Comparing across the two years, urban India seems to have fared badly, with average MPCE actually declining by 4.6 per cent. The median MPCE for both SCs and OBCs has declined, with the latter in particular registering a significant fall of 5.1 per cent. On the other hand, urban STs seem to have registered significant increases in average consumption levels of 5.5 per cent, and they have also moved up one rank in the caste hierarchy, being in second place after the UCs in terms of median MPCE. This is a significant finding and needs to be investigated further. What are the factors responsible for the improvement in ST median MPCE? Why are they absent in the case of the SCs and specially the OBCs? These are questions that can only be answered through detailed empirical research.

Table 3

Mean Monthly Per Capita Consumption Expenditures, by Caste Group 1999–2000 and 2004–05, by Sector, with Standard Errors of Mean

Sector	Caste Group	1999–2000			2004–05			
		Observations	Mean MPCE	SE of Mean	Observations	Mean MPCE	SE of Mean	% Change
RURAL INDIA	ST	51,977	430.52	0.97	62,548	439.12	0.93	+2.00
	SC	63,212	464.86	1.23	67,559	471.32	0.91	+1.39
	OBC	131,629	526.11	0.91	153,423	544.98	0.86	+3.59
	UC	127,393	641.14	1.11	114,147	668.86	1.52	+4.32
	ALL	374,853	539.69	0.57	398,024	549.96	0.59	+1.90
URBAN INDIA	ST	14,916	842.15	5.25	16,220	869.74	6.67	+3.28
	SC	28,235	742.97	2.64	29,373	731.96	2.72	–1.48
	OBC	63,660	871.13	3.22	74,623	850.45	2.18	–2.37
	UC	117,905	1225.17	3.15	84,479	1282.20	3.78	+4.66
	ALL	225,143	1034.76	1.99	204,789	1031.53	1.96	–0.31

Note: The MPCE distribution has been slightly trimmed by dropping top 10 and bottom 10 values. MPCE is in rupees at constant 2004–05 prices; price deflators used: Rural India, CPI for Agricultural Labour; Urban India: CPI for Industrial Workers. All computations use NSSO supplied multipliers. UC = 'Upper' Caste, i.e., those not belonging to ST, SC or OBC.

Although it is a robust and useful average, the median is not amenable to further statistical analysis. In particular, where sample survey results are concerned, estimates of sampling error are not available for the median. In order to address this issue, Table 3 reports on the mean MPCE, along with the standard errors of the mean, for each caste group. The last column of this table shows the percentage change in the mean MPCE between 1999 and 2005.

For rural India, Table 3 confirms the impressions conveyed by Table 2: like the medians, the means of MPCE for all caste groups, as well as for rural India as a whole show a positive change, although the magnitude of this change is rather small. The UCs have registered the largest increase in mean MPCE at 4.3 per cent, while the SCs have the smallest at 1.4 per cent. However, for both years, the caste hierarchy retains the same order by mean as by median MPCE – the STs are at the bottom, followed by the SCs, and OBCs, with the UCs on top.

For urban India, the picture presented by Table 3 is once again very close to that in Table 2. It is clear that urban India has not done very well across these five years, with mean consumption levels showing a small decline for the sector as a whole. The OBC and SC mean MPCE has declined, but the UC mean shows a significant gain of almost 4.7 per cent while the STs too have gained by about 3.3 per cent. Table 3 also confirms the extraordinary showing of the ST category, which is ranked second in terms of mean MPCE in 2005, having moved one rank up from the 1999 level.

Table 4

Change in Mean MPCE between 1999–2000 and 2004–05

Sector	*Levels of Confidence*	*Mean MPCE 2004–05 is significantly HIGHER than Mean MPCE 1999–2000*	*Mean MPCE 2004–05 is significantly LOWER than Mean MPCE 1999–2000*
RURAL	99.9%	ST OBC UC ALL	
	99%	ST SC OBC UC ALL	
	95%	ST SC OBC UC ALL	
URBAN	99.9%	UC	OBC
	99%	UC	OBC
	95%	ST UC	SC OBC

Table 4 summarizes the implications of the standard errors; it allows to see at a glance which caste groups have registered a statistically significant increase or decrease in mean MPCE across the two surveys. As expected, almost all caste groups, as well as the all-castes grouping register an increase. The only exception are the SCs whose mean MPCE for 2004–05 is *not* significantly higher than the 1999–2000 figure at the 99.9 per cent level of confidence.

Urban India presents a sharp contrast: only the UC group has statistically significant increases in mean MPCE, and it is joined at the 95 per cent confidence level by the STs. The OBCs have significantly lower mean MPCE in 2004–05 at all confidence levels, but are joined by the SCs at the 95 per cent level. It is noteworthy that the all-castes mean MPCE for 2004–05 is neither significantly lower nor higher than the 1999–2000 figure at all confidence levels.

Though they are indispensable as readily understood summary measures, averages also suppress a lot of information by making a single number represent an entire distribution. The representative claims of the mean or even the median are greatly weakened when the distribution in question is a skewed one, as is the case with consumption expenditure. Therefore, it is necessary to go beyond averages to look at the 'shape' of the distribution itself, to see how different sections of it have been affected during the period in question. This is attempted in the next section.

Comparison of Percentiles of Consumption Expenditure

This section takes a disaggregated look at the MPCE distribution for each caste group by looking at five percentiles – 5th, 25th, 50th (the median), 75th and 95th. Thus, instead of a single value in the middle of the distribution (like the median or mean), we are now looking at five values spread along its full range. Table 5 shows the five different percentiles for each caste group and for rural India as a whole for the two surveys.

Except for the STs and SCs, other caste groups as well as rural India as a whole show the greatest gains in the highest percentile, i.e., the 95th. The same percentile shows small declines for both STs and SCs, implying that the top of the distribution has remained stagnant across these five years for these castes.

Table 5
Percentiles of Monthly Per Capita Consumption Expenditure Distribution by Caste Groups, 1999–2000 to 2004–05, Rural India

Percentiles of MPCE	*Year of Survey*	*MPCE (in 2004–05 Rupees) of Different Caste Groups*				*Rural India (All Castes)*
		ST	*SC*	*OBC*	*UC*	
p5	1999–2000	204	230	257	288	249
	2004–2005	199	243	267	289	253
	% Change	–2.70	5.38	3.90	0.46	1.66
p25	1999–2000	293	324	357	419	355
	2004–2005	299	334	366	417	360
	% Change	1.93	2.89	2.58	–0.42	1.27
p50	1999–2000	379	413	460	545	465
	2004–2005	391	422	472	553	469
	% Change	3.13	2.09	2.57	1.38	0.77
p75	1999–2000	509	542	610	753	628
	2004–2005	520	546	623	763	630
	% Change	2.17	0.72	2.12	1.30	0.39
p95	1999–2000	814	844	987	1283	1057
	2004–2005	803	844	1038	1361	1084
	% Change	–1.39	–0.02	4.87	5.74	2.45

Note: % change is calculated with 2004–05 as base; MPCE data for 2004–05 (61st round) as per "Mixed Recall Period" of Planning Commission Expert Committee, which is roughly comparable to 1999–2000 (55th round). UC=Upper Caste, i.e., all those who are not included in ST, SC or OBC groups. Percentile values shown in cells are rounded to the nearest integer, but percentage change is computed on the accurate un-rounded values.

The large amount of information contained in Table 5 is better assimilated through a graphical presentation. Figure 1 shows the percentiles of MPCE for different caste groups for each of the two surveys. Because they are drawn to the same scale, it is possible to get a sense of both inter-year features as well as inter-caste features of the MPCE distribution. The placement of the caste curves of percentiles remains the same across the two surveys, showing that the UCs are clearly the best off, with the OBCs next, followed by the closely bunched curves for the SCs and STs. The gap between the UC and OBC curves is bigger than the gap between the OBC curve and those for the SCs and STs. Generally, the inter-caste difference at each percentile tends to increase as we move from the lowest (5th) to the highest (95th) percentile. The curve of each slope increases (i.e., it becomes more steep) as we move to higher levels of MPCE, with the segment connecting the 75th to the 95th percentile being the steepest.

Figure 1

Caste and Consumption Levels, Rural India, 2000–05

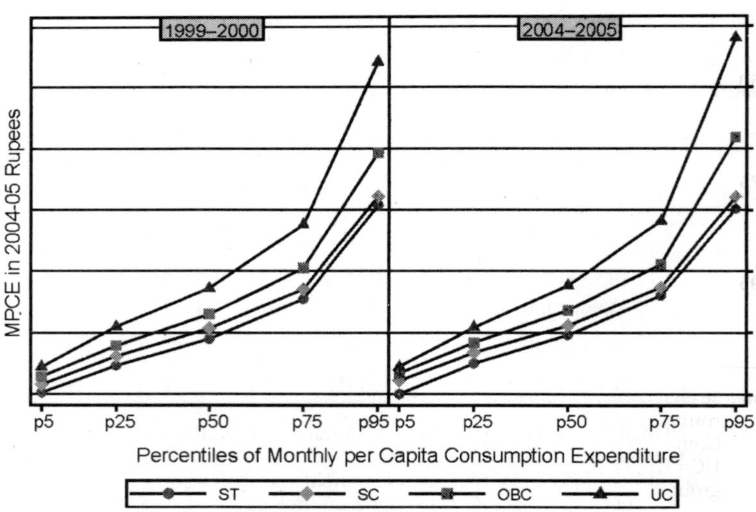

Source: Computed from NSSO 55th and 61st round data.

The situation in urban India is very different from that of the rural India, as Table 6 demonstrates. It is immediately striking that so many of the percentiles for so many caste groups as well as for urban India as a whole show a decline between 1999 and 2005. For the poorest of the poor at the 5th percentile, these five years have led to lower levels of consumption in *all* caste groups. In fact, for the SCs and OBCs, all percentiles except the 95th register a decline in consumption levels; the same is true of urban India overall.

Table 6
Percentiles of Monthly Per Capita Consumption Expenditure Distribution by Caste Groups, 1999–2000 to 2004–05, Urban India

Percentiles of MPCE	*Year of Survey*	*MPCE (in 2004–05 Rupees) of Different Caste Groups*				*Urban India (All Castes)*
		ST	*SC*	*OBC*	*UC*	
p5	1999–2000	297	323	356	410	366
	2004–2005	294	297	337	403	346
	% change	–0.9	–8.9	–5.8	–1.8	–5.8
p25	1999–2000	477	470	521	664	567
	2004–2005	490	446	504	643	540
	% change	2.6	–5.4	–3.4	–3.3	–5.1
p50	1999–2000	676	625	715	975	814
	2004–2005	714	613	679	983	777
	% change	5.3	–1.9	–5.3	0.8	–4.8
p75	1999–2000	1004	887	1028	1463	1230
	2004–2005	1094	856	997	1560	1227
	% change	8.2	–3.7	–3.1	6.2	–0.3
p95	1999–2000	1890	1521	1850	2798	2351
	2004–2005	1892	1615	1910	3171	2511
	% change	0.1	5.8	3.1	11.8	6.4

Note: % change is calculated with 2004–05 as base; MPCE data for 2004–05 (61st round) as per "Mixed Recall Period" of Planning Commission Expert Committee, which is roughly comparable to 1999–2000 (55th round). UC=Upper Caste, i.e., all those who are not included in ST, SC or OBC groups.

Figure 2 highlights the implications of Table 6. The placement of the caste curves shows the UC far above all other castes, with the ST and OBC curves being almost indistinguishable from each other, with the SC curve at the bottom. The ST and the OBC have slightly higher consumption levels than the SC throughout the distribution. However, it is clear that the ST and OBC are nevertheless much closer to the SC than to the UC curve. It is also striking that the caste gap at each percentile rises sharply as we move up the distribution, with the upper half showing much more divergence after nearly identical starting points for the 5th percentile. The steep upward slopes in all curves between the 75th and 95th percentiles is notable, the most prominent being that for the UCs, whose curve distances itself more and more from all other curves as we go up the distribution. In fact, Table 6 tells us that the 95th percentile consumption expenditure level for the UCs is *more than double* than for the 75th percentile in 2004–05! Figure 2 also underlines a fact presented in Table 6, namely, that the only really significant gain in consumption levels across the two surveys is for the 95th percentile of the UC caste group – the respective percentile markers for all other castes being more or less at the same level in the two years.

Figure 2

Caste and Consumption Levels, Urban India, 2000–05

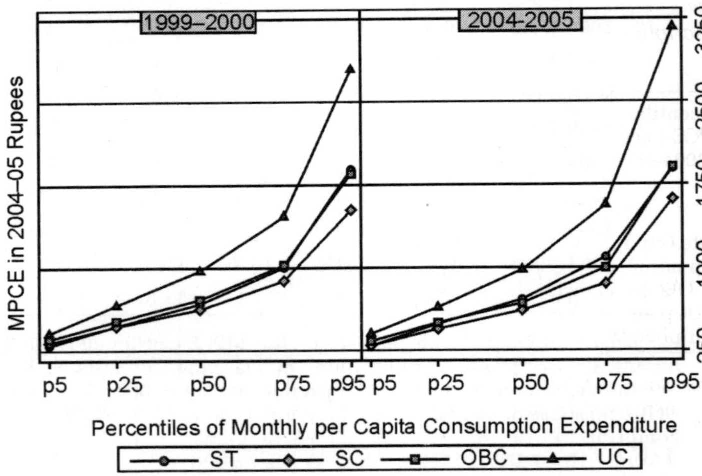

Source: Computed from NSSO 55th and 61st round data.

Comparison of 'Caste Gap' Relative to the Upper Castes

Although Tables 5 and 6 in combination with Figures 1 and 2 do give us some sense of the relative standing of different castes vis-á-vis each other, it is necessary to directly examine the extent of caste inequality and its trend over the period covered by the two surveys. In order to do this, a Caste Gap Index (CGI) is computed, which is simply the difference between the rupee values of consumption expenditure of UCs and the other castes expressed as a percentage of the UC consumption expenditure level for that percentile. Thus, for each percentile p,

$$Caste\ Gap\ Index = \left(\frac{UC_p - (ST, SC, OBC)_p}{UC_p} \right) \times 100$$

CGI also allows us to directly measure caste inequality in a simple and readily interpretable manner. Computing such an index for different percentiles along the distribution allows us a disaggregated view of caste inequality in different class segments.

Table 7
'Caste Gap' Index of Monthly Per Capita Consumption Expenditure, Rural India

Row Description	*Caste*	*NSSO 55th Round, 1999–2000*					*NSSO 61st Round, 2004–05*				
		p5	*p25*	*p50*	*p75*	*p95*	*p5*	*p25*	*p50*	*p75*	*p95*
Percentiles of MPCE in rupees at 2004–05 prices	ST	204	293	379	509	814	199	299	391	520	803
	SC	230	324	413	542	844	243	334	422	546	844
	OBC	257	357	460	610	987	267	366	472	623	1038
	UC	288	419	545	753	1283	289	417	553	763	1361
Caste Gap Index: UCp minus (ST, SC, OBC)p divided by UCp and multiplied by 100	ST	29.2	30.1	30.5	32.4	36.6	31.1	28.3	29.3	31.8	41.0
	SC	20.1	22.7	24.2	28.0	34.2	15.9	19.9	23.7	28.4	38.0
	OBC	10.8	14.8	15.6	19.0	23.1	7.6	12.2	14.6	18.3	23.7

Note: Computed from NSSO unit level data. p = percentile. Caste Gap Index is expressed in percentage points.

Table 7 (on rural India) presents the rupee values (rounded to the nearest integer) of the five percentiles of MPCE for each caste in the first four rows for ease of reference, followed by the CGI in the last three rows. There is no index for the UCs since they form the reference group. CGI rows show that for all three castes, the index rises steadily as you read from left to right, i.e., as we move from the bottom to the top of the MPCE distribution. (The only exception to this is for the move from the 5th to the 25th percentile for the STs in the 61st round.) This serves to underline the unsurprising fact that caste inequality increases with levels of affluence and tends to be highest at the top of the class pyramid. It is noteworthy that the OBCs are generally not very far from the UCs, while the

STs are generally far below the UCs, with differentials of 30 per cent or more all along the spectrum.

Figure 3

Caste Gap Relative to Upper Castes, Rural India, 2000–05

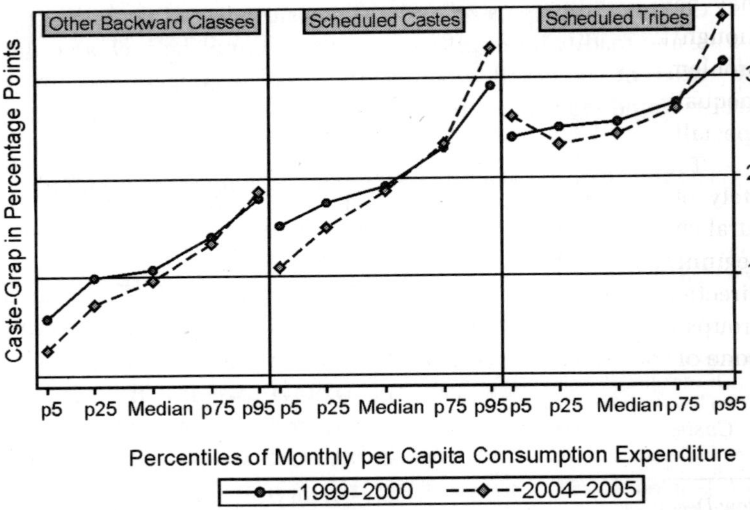

Source: Computed from NSSO 55th and 61st round data.

Figure 3 presents the CGI data from Table 7 in graphical form, where it can be more easily grasped. First, the upward slope of all three curves (the ST curve being a partial exception) shows that inequality rises with consumption expenditure levels. Secondly, the positioning of the curves for each of the three caste groups shows the degree to which they are behind or below the UC consumption levels. Thus, the OBC curves are the lowest, with the poorer end of the distribution showing differences that are in single digits, and the upper end peaking under 25 per cent. The STs have the highest curves, showing that even at the bottom end of the consumption spectrum, they are very far behind the UCs. It is noteworthy that the ST curves are above the OBC curves and do not overlap at all, highlighting the fact that the minimum CGI of the STs is above the maximum for the OBCs. One peculiar aspect of the ST curve is the apparent decrease in levels of inequality in the middle of the distribution, particularly for the 2004–05 curve. A third notable feature brought out by Figure 3 is that, by and large, the 2004–05 curves tend to be below the 1999–2000 curves except in the top quarter of the distribution. (The STs are once again a partial exception here.) This indicates that inter-caste inequalities may have declined slightly between the 55th and 61st rounds, though this must be treated as a tentative conclusion given the problems of comparability between these rounds. However, inequality increases sharply from the 75th to the 95th percentiles, specially so for the STs and SCs.

Table 8 presents the CGI data for urban India. It is immediately obvious that inequality levels are higher compared to the rural sector. Moreover, unlike in rural India where the OBCs were beginning to catch up with the UCs, or seem to be heading in that direction, there is not much to choose between the three caste groups in urban India. Although the SCs are clearly the worst off, none of the three is dramatically different from the others.

Table 8

'Caste-Gap' Index of Monthly Per Capita Consumption Expenditure, Urban India

Row Description	*Caste*	*NSSO 55th Round, 1999–2000*					*NSSO 61st Round, 2004–05*				
		p5	*p25*	*p50*	*p75*	*p95*	*p5*	*p25*	*p50*	*p75*	*p95*
Percentiles of MPCE in rupees at 2004–05 prices	ST	297	477	676	1004	1890	294	490	714	1094	1892
	SC	323	470	625	887	1521	297	446	613	856	1615
	OBC	356	521	715	1028	1850	337	504	679	997	1910
	UC	410	664	975	1463	2798	403	643	983	1560	3171
Caste Gap Index: UCp minus (ST, SC, OBC)p divided by UCp and multiplied by 100	ST	27.6	28.2	30.7	31.4	32.5	27.0	23.8	27.4	29.9	40.3
	SC	21.2	29.2	35.9	39.4	45.6	26.3	30.6	37.6	45.1	49.1
	OBC	13.2	21.5	26.7	29.7	33.9	16.4	21.6	30.9	36.1	39.8

Note: Computed from NSSO unit level data. p = percentile. Caste Gap Index is expressed in percentage points.

Table 8 also shows that, on the whole, urban caste inequalities seem to have worsened between 1999 and 2005. This is immediately confirmed by Figure 4, which shows that (despite the usual anomalies associated with the ST group) the curves for 2004–05 are clearly above the curves for 1999–2000. Once again, the ST curves are distinctive, showing a significant decline in inequality in the bottom three-quarters of the MPCE distribution; it is only with the 95th percentile that the 2004–05 curve rises above the 1999–2000 curve. For both the SCs and the OBCs, the curves for the two surveys diverge significantly in the top half of the distribution. As the worst off group in urban India, the SCs show the greatest range of inequality, the curves stretching from around 20 per cent at the bottom of the distribution to almost 50 per cent at the top. It is sobering to realize that in 2005, the consumption levels of even the richest (95th percentile) among the urban 'lower' castes are 40–50 per cent lower than that of their UC counterparts.

Figure 4

Caste Gap Relative to Upper Castes, Urban India, 2000–05

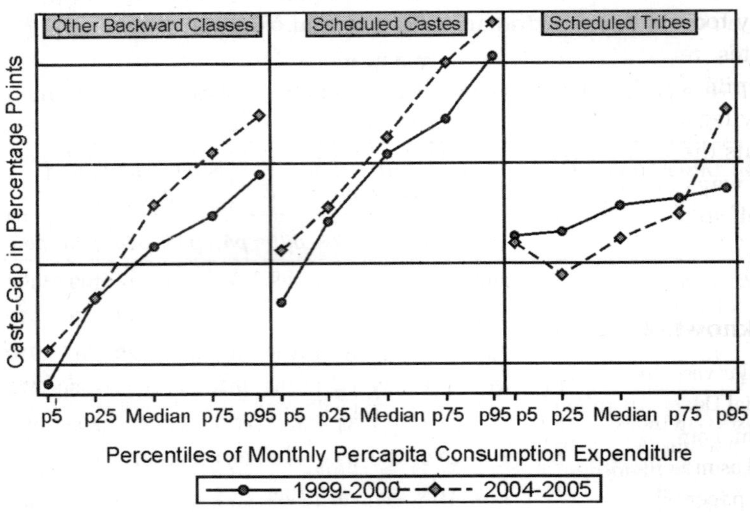

Source: Computed from NSSO 55th and 61st round data.

Conclusion

Despite the limitations of such an exercise, as pointed out in the beginning of this paper on data issues, it is clear that macro data provide a useful, even indispensable vantage point from which to study caste inequalities. In keeping with the trend towards socio-cultural contextualization of economic institutions and processes, it is necessary to consider the social identities of the poor or the disadvantaged as much as the privileged sections of our society. Such an exercise offers useful prophylaxis against the dominant ideologies of caste which tend to treat it as problem located within the 'lower' castes.

As the data in this paper amply demonstrate, caste continues to be an important dimension of economic inequalities. Although we have as yet only two data points, preliminary trends suggest that urban inequalities are worsening, though there may be a slight improvement in the rural situation, particularly at the lower levels of the MPCE distribution. Rural OBCs and urban STs are well worth studying further, particularly because they seem to be following a distinctive trajectory. However, rural STs and urban SCs are the worst off groups in contemporary Indian society and they too must be studied further. It is remarkable that the 'upper' castes remain so distinctly privileged relative to other castes despite six decades of a modern constitution that outlaws caste privilege. Rather than remaining trapped within a perspective that treats the upper castes as being 'caste-less', we need to understand the ways in which caste privilege has secularized and modernized itself so that it can be nurtured by other means.

Acknowledgements

Earlier versions of this paper were presented at seminars at the Council for Social Development and the Indira Gandhi National Open University, New Delhi. I am specially grateful to Debal Singha-Roy and Prashant Trivedi, as well as members of the audience at both venues. The statistical analysis for this paper was partly facilitated by a Faculty Development Grant from the University of Delhi, which is also gratefully acknowledged.

Notes

1. Despite the complications that beset all aggregative caste groupings, the term 'upper caste' is in my opinion a better one than

the vaguer term 'other castes'. The latter is a product of the dominant (i.e., upper caste oriented) ideology that treats the upper castes as 'caste-less' while highlighting the caste identities of the so-called lower castes.

2. Comparison of the 2001 Census figures for population share of STs and SCs with the 61st round of the NSSO for 2004–05 shows the following: NSSO estimates of ST population are very accurate, with the rural figures being 0.16 per cent points less and the urban ones being 0.6 more than the census. However, NSSO SC population share estimates exceed census figures by more than 3 per cent (rural=3.41, urban=3.27). See S. Deshpande, 2008. Dalits in the Muslim and Christian Communities: A Status Report on Current Social Scientific Knowledge, National Commission of Minorities, Government of India, January, p. 21. Table 3 for details.
3. See the press release of the Planning Commission entitled 'Poverty Lines for 2004–05' of March 2007.
4. Price indices are taken from the Labour Bureau, Shimla, website at http: //labourbureau.nic.in/The CPIAL price deflator for January 2000–January 2005 is 341/307, while the corresponding CPIIW deflator is 526/431.

3

Violence, Aspirations and Migration in Post-liberalization Rural India

Conflict and Change in a Strife-Torn Village

RAVI KUMAR

What once used to be called Central Bihar has drawn distinct nomenclatures to justify its situation, ranging from the 'flaming fields of Bihar' to the 'zone of extremist violence'. The situation in the area, which used to comprise of Gaya, Patna, Nawada and Bhojpur districts primarily, reached such a level that the state government, with its myopic understanding of the crisis, had not stopped, till recently, carving out districts, as smaller units equipped to deal with violence, in the hope of reducing violent conflict. The conflict or violence, as different voices of society tend to term it, has not been merely a result of an atrocious caste relation but a combination of the social, economic and political factors. In fact, they have been enmeshed with each other to such an extent that it would be difficult to separate them. Treating the conflict as a consequence of only one of such factors will be myopic and deficient. There have been efforts to look at such violence from different viewpoints, the dominant discourse tends to look at it as an issue of law and order. The liberal faces of capital tend to locate it in terms of a problem that could be easily located through within system reforms (Bandopadhyay, 2006). There have been efforts to reject the demand for a systemic change outrightly by them as well (Kumar, 2008). Such an approach, if analysed closely, rejects the politics of resistance based on class as well as the understanding that locates the problem as embedded in the mode of production and therefore resorts to a mobilizational politics to resolve it.

The situation in Bihar has, in the recent past, especially since the 'assertion' of the backward castes, has seen certain significant developments. While, there have been significant changes in terms of shifts in land ownership pattern (Sharma, 2005), there has been a drastic reduction in the nature of radical left movement as well as the counter-mobilization against it in the areas referred to as Central Bihar. This paper makes an effort to understand, through ethnographic data of a village, as to how these two changes have occurred and are intrinsically linked with the combined process of pauperization of people dependent on agrarian economy, rising aspirations and absence of required investment in agriculture that could generate the possibility of holding back migration. These factors have seen specific surge since the onset of liberalization in the country. Another significant aspect that the paper compels us to ponder over is the different ways in which opening up of the economy and its related developments affected different states. Bihar has been affected in its own way. In a certain sense it also tells us how a village, in its own context of violence, has been responding to the economic processes set in motion by liberalization while the state furthered the argument of high growth etc.

Great number of studies on migration is there. The causes of migration have also been discussed at length through quantitative data provided by agencies such as National Sample Survey Organization (NSSO). However, there has been a need to look at how changes happen in a village situation, especially when it is in throes of a violent crisis. The issue of migration has been studied by many social scientists.

The crisis has further been thrown open by the rising aspirations and the declining productivity in agriculture in states such as Bihar where fragmentation of land holdings, combined with the poor infrastructure and low investment, aggravated the agrarian crisis. The cost in agriculture across the country has gone up while the returns have been in negative. This has created adverse conditions for farmers leading even to suicides (Rao and Suri, 2006).

Only those are able to survive and flourish who can sustain the consequences of high cost and low return. This has been noted in context of other states where the linkages between neo-liberal policies and the agrarian distress have been amply recorded. Scholars have argued how in such cases the worst affected are the small farmers, as they are more vulnerable to crop losses and price declines (Mohankumar and Sharma, 2006). Optimization of surplus from agriculture or other economic activities have been quite evident in rural Bihar. While they have failed to take off due to the absence of necessary infrastructure that the economy would require, there have been theoretical arguments to show how this desire for surplus accumulation led to violence in the area. Caste remains as a powerful ideological instrument in the village society that allows the sustenance of hegemony of particular castes and how it has also been expression of conflict between the entrenched economic interests and the upcoming economic interests (see Kumar, 2007 for details). Even in the village where study was carried out while one could find diversification into different occupations – for instance, opening of dairy by some Bhumihars – there have been also use of extra-coercive means to accumulate surplus (see Chandra and Khandelwal, 1990) to elaborate how use of such means could result in violent conflict. Hence, there has been obvious economic reason for the friction. Social hegemony also becomes an expression of this. Recently, things have altered as well, as village economy becomes insufficient for the new aspirations (generated by the recent invasion of market in an unprecedented manner) and migration takes place. The village economy and society finds itself at an interesting intersection of violence (furthered by an effort to maintain hegemony by the landed or even those who aspire to be part of that landed gang on the one hand and by the resistance capacity of the SCs/landless on the other, who are better organized now). This paper makes an effort to understand how this intersection comes into being and how does it express itself in social, political and economic terms.

Conflict, Structure and Society

Central Bihar has been in conflict since early 1980s, involving different radical left groups, gangs of landlords and private armies constituted by the landed gentry of different castes over a period of time. This conflict has been intrinsically about social structures and the situations – economic, social and political – emanating out of it. Efforts have been made to typify the Bihari society and economy. In fact, not only in Bihar but in the country as a whole debates have taken place around how to understand the society and economy and how to classify its mode of production. It has been termed as semi-feudal because of the overwhelming role played by caste in the social and economic organization of society.[1] Others looked at how caste has been "affected by economic differentiation (Omvedt, 1992: 131) and how, in fact "the existing class/caste complex also provides a fertile ground for capitalist farmers to use casteism to appeal to their kin among the middle peasants and labourers, to divide the rural semi-proletariat, and to attack its Dalit and adivasi sections ... who are often most militant" (ibid.: 133). There are still others who look at the caste–class correlation as existing even today (Louis, 2002: 26–27). And, the movement of the radical left political formations try to explain the atrocious tendencies of landlords in terms of feudal remnants or traits of semi-feudal Bihari society. Some scholars have tried to argue on lines of characterizing the Bihari society and economy as semi-feudal by stating that

> while this sort of 'semi-feudalism' became the characterizing aspect of Bihar's agrarian social structure, the slow but inevitable process of commercialization broke the isolationist, self-contained village whose peasantry had until then stoically borne exploitation and oppression. Economic unification led to the evolution of a general policy whose features were instability, disequilibrium and unrest. The socio-political placidity which had been caused by economic stagnation was broken by the changes in the economy of the state of Bihar became witness to an era of agrarian tensions, unrest and movements which, though endemic, were limited in their scope and arrested in their development like the economy itself. (Das, 1982: 45)

Prasad (1994: 178) furthers the semi-feudalism thesis and goes on to argue that due to the semi-feudal mode of production the exploitation of the poor peasantry intensified in Bihar after mid-sixties. The significance of caste was recognized by the CPI (ML) in its early days when it was found appealing to the caste feelings without even critically reflecting on what kind of implications it would have as Omvedt seems to argue above. CPI (ML) in one instance appeals to the Kurmi peasants that their caste has been "known as honest, hard-working and brave" but some "arch-reactionaries and their goons" belonging to the same caste were endangering the respect that people had for the caste (CPI (ML), 1986, p. A–20).

This debate has been very vital to understand the society and, therefore, for not only strategizing movements but also setting their agenda. The issue of structure has been a vital aspect of this debate. Structure, which can be looked in terms of differentiations across class or caste, also experiences transformation. This transformation may not be necessarily about breaking down of structures but it may also imply certain form of mobility in economic terms experienced within each caste, if that is understood as the primary basis of stratification, or across class if latter is taken as the fundamental division in society. The battle in Central Bihar in a certain sense is interwoven with the issue of structures and the changes experienced by it. The reasons for conflict remain more or less same despite the fragmentation of land holdings as the Dalits are still largely landless agricultural labourers and the issue of social oppression remains omnipresent. However, there have been significant changes in the nature of conflicts as market comes in, pauperization happens, and newer aspirations are generated, resulting in migration towards urban centres in search of better opportunities as well as to supplement their income. The liberalization of Indian economy only fomented this process as the benefits of the process lured the masses and a sharp difference in terms of development of infrastructure remained between the urban and rural centres, especially when it came to states such as Bihar. In fact, Bihar as a whole remained on the peripheries of this development process. It could not, as a state, proceed towards becoming a party to the post-liberalization development process. Whatever changes occurred – in terms of changing attitudes or the lifestyle – they were attributable to migration. This failure to become part of the liberalization and then neo-liberal agenda was deep rooted in the socio-political landscape of the state, where the stage after the OBC assertion was missed by the then dominant political elite and which has been set in motion in a more vigorous fashion after Nitish Kumar took over as the Chief Minister.

This is not so say that the new agenda of capital could not find entry in the state (because a tiny state is too weak to resist it). It is also important to point out that the all required conditions were well prepared which triggered the changes at political level for the new process to begin. The changes mentioned in this paper also require to be looked at from this dimension. In other words, the decline in the mobilizational strength of the radical left in particular and left in general in the state need to be located within the framework of these changes. This paper intends to locate the sharpening of the conflict between the landless agricultural workers and poor peasants and the landed segment/interests through ethnographic study of a village and how it gradually lost its sharpness due to changes brought about by the onset of the liberalization process which increased the cost of agricultural production and also generated the need for further surplus generation.

The changes in the politics of radical left movements as well as its counter-forces such as Ranvir Sena (a militia of upper castes/landed segment) are taking place at the level of villages where they flourished. Jehanabd, for instance, no longer remains the same 'flaming fields of Bihar'. While these changes have not been analysed in detail, in fact, not even paid enough attention, there are efforts at delegitimizing the existence of marginalization at grassroots level. This delegitimization is done by ignoring existence of socio-economic situations which actually result in such a crisis. The movement, whether armed or unarmed, are reflections of deep-rooted discontent in society. They become mirrors of structural inequality in many cases. Once such movements fall silent, they need to be read as indications of some profound change, which in many cases may imply a silent victory of the ruling class ideology and politics. These changes become, more so for us, interesting because of the two simultaneous developments: (1) while the radical left forces seem to be weakening in many of the areas which they considered as their bastion; and (2) there seems to be a consistent and well planned strategy to delegitimize their existence by branding them as terrorists or equating them with any other form of law and order problem. These two developments, if analysed critically, become necessary for the neo-liberal capital to expand without hindrance because the notions of a harmonious, non-conflictual order (within an essentially inegalitarian and hierarchically structured society) become important for stability of a system because it provides and unhindered expansionist possibility of its interests.

The paper, which is based on years of observation in a village and its surrounding areas, also tries to bring forth an account of evolution of conflict in a village and district, which has not been used very frequently as a method to understand the violent conflict in the area. The other aspect which this paper intends to highlight is the need to look beyond the current trend of characterizing the conflict in Central Bihar or elsewhere in India as a law and order problem. The paper reaffirms the socio-economic and political character of the conflict and tries to argue how the delegitimation process of struggles and the efforts to construct new discourses towards that process are flawed.

The nature of radical left activism in the Jehanabad district has been consistently changing. The issues raised by them as well as the nature of their activism have also experienced significant changes. However, not much attention has been paid to these changes which so profoundly affect the existential aspects of the organizations active in the area. Rather, a general consensus is being built by the Indian state about their characterization as "threats to internal security". And, there is hardly any reflection on the construction of this discourse which aims at destroying the basis of movements as well as hides the reality that lies in the belly of this emerging tiger economy. In fact, the standpoint of the UPA itself has changed drastically from the days it came to power. The CMP of UPA posted on the website of the Prime Minster's Office says that

> The UPA is concerned with the growth of extremist violence and other forms of terrorist activity in different states. This is not merely a law-and-order problem, but a far deeper socio-economic issue which will be addressed more meaningfully than has been the case so far. False encounters will not be permitted. (p. 10)

The Prime Minister, later on and quite contrarily, changed his understanding of the problem, which should be considered quite too appropriate for the head of a neo-liberal state and for a person who has been instrumental in furthering and facilitating the interests of capital. Not very surprisingly, while addressing the Chief Ministers on the question of internal security, he remarked:

> I have said in the past that left-wing extremism is probably single biggest security challenge to the Indian state. It continues to be so and we cannot rest in peace until we have eliminated this virus.
>
> We need a coordinated response to this challenge. The answers to the problem are well known. We need to cripple the hold of naxalite forces with all the means at our command. This requires improved intelligence gathering capabilities, improved policing capabilities, better coordination between the Centre and the states and better coordination between states and most important, better leadership and firmer resolve. Improving policing capabilities requires better police infrastructure, better training facilities, better equipment and resources and dedicated forces. (Singh, 2007)

Why this should not have come as a surprise is that a general consensus *within* the ruling class was taking shape, which considered the anti-systemic struggles as detrimental to the development and security of the Indian state and society. Hence, it has been no surprise that L.K. Advani of BJP also took a somewhat similar stand when he said that "when the threat is so menacing as this, I am both dismayed and alarmed at the failure of the UPA government to educate the people of India about the ideological basis of left-wing extremism, its nature of operation, its international connections and the crimes against humanity perpetrated by it around the world". He goes on to say that "communist extremism not only endangers India's national security and our democratic system, but also our precious cultural and spiritual heritage. The rabidly anti-Hindu propaganda of naxalites must be noted in this context" (Advani, 2006).

Therefore, it becomes interesting to understand and analyse the developments that were taking place at the ground level as organically linked to the larger consensus that was being developed in favour of a neo-liberal economy. While the representatives of the India's ruling class were articulating the ideological need to tackle radical left mobilizations, the movements themselves were gradually disintegrating due to various reasons at the sites of struggle. This was the most appropriate expression of momentary triumph of the neo-liberal ideology and ethos which sought to retain the structured inequality in society while generating the hope and possibility that upward mobility through hard work (i.e., by serving the system in a more diligent fashion) was possible. It (i.e., the neo-liberal economy), due to its inherent character, was also producing side-effects of extreme pauperization and marginalization. These two factors produced an unprecedented migration towards urban centres. The conflict, by no means, remained in the village society because of the asymmetries emanating out of production process but those asymmetries were not getting expressed in the mobilizational politics of the radical left. In other words, the status quo seemed to be triumphing and the questions of exploitation are looking for newer forms of expression.

Evolution of the Peasant Movement in Central Bihar

Central Bihar, prior to the bifurcation of the state, was comprised of Patna, Gaya, Aurangabad, Jehanabad, Nawada, Bhojpur, Rohtas, Nalanda and Muger districts. Within these districts Jehanabad experienced a much proliferated war between the radical left and the private armies of landed class. Once again, Jehanabad has been bifurcated into another district called Arwal. The village, where the study is being carried out, falls now within this district.

The Central Bihar, especially the region comprising Patna, Gaya, Bhojpur and Jehanabad, has been the centre of protest and the history of peasant movement goes back to the pre-independence days when Swami Sahjanand Saraswati led the peasants of the area against the exploitation unleashed by *zamindars* (landlords). He evolved from being a leader of peasants, fighting primarily for the rights of tenants, to that of a leader who believed in the ultimate insurrection by the poor and working people. He summed up his aims as following in his autobiography:

> I believe in giving in the hands of the wage labourers only, and taking away from the others, the control of state .... We have to take it by force through struggle. That is the only way we will be

able to sustain it. Receiving it easily (without a fight) will result in losing it again and that is the absolute truth. This kind of achievement is, in my mind, akin to property of dreams …

… I do not want bookish knowledge. Sole knowledge of books ends up in deceiving oneself. I want a struggle and the struggling masses for the cause. I renounce the struggle for independence that does not include the class (economic) struggle. (And) I want to convert the war of independence into a class (economic) war. I want social, economic and political revolution and this cannot be attained in any other way. I will, thus, support only those people (who believe in such a struggle). (Saraswati, 2000: 293)[2]

The issue of discrimination and oppression by the hegemonic social and economic groups, such as, the Bhumihars, constituted the agenda of other socio-economic and political formations like Triveni Sangh (formally constituted in 1934 as representative of Kurmi, Koeri and Yadav castes primarily) as well. Their participation in the elections of 1937 as a separate identity after Congress refused to give them tickets revealed their power in the region. The Triveni Sangh emerged in a region which was already witness to organization of peasants and, therefore, the question of what led to the emergence of another political formation has often been debated. One of the views has been that an alliance between the Kisan Sabha and the Triveni Sangh could not be forged because of the ominous presence of Bhumihars in the Sabha (Pinch, 1996). The Sabha has been criticized on grounds that it vocalized largely a pro-Bhumihar stance of the *young* Swami Sahjanand Saraswati against the Brahmin dominance. The scholars who worked on him have not paid much attention to his evolution as a political persona, which culminates into his pieces such as *Maharudra ka Mahatandav* (see Saraswati, 2000 for details).

The other view believes that "while most of the anti-feudal movement led by Kisan Sabha before independence was successful on the economic agenda (like unsettlement of permanent settlement), they could not absorb the 'social aspirations' of the backward class tenants" (Gupta, 2002: 3; also see Gupta, 1994: 202). Though this view also narrates how the backward castes were economically benefited by the Triveni Sangh and in fact most of its support base came from the section which would be immensely benefited by agro-capitalism, which led to substantial accumulation, after the laying down of railway tracks along Patna in pre-independence India (ibid., pp. 3–4). Even Pinch indicates towards the emergence of class antagonism with the popularisation of Triveni Sangh. And, the Congress felt that it would fracture unity against the British rule. "The electoral power of this union was clearly demonstrated in 1937, as was its potential for class formation. ... nationalist politicians, anxious to minimize the growth of class antagonisms that would not only threaten the fragile unified opposition to British rule but also their own super-ordinate status, worked successfully to co-opt Triveni Sangh as part of an undifferentiated "backward class" component of the Indian National Congress" (Pinch, 1996). Pinch, though, fails to explain as to how was Triveni Sangh fostering class antagonism, which the Congress feared.

Two very distinct developments emerged in form of Kisan Sabha and Triveni Sangh: while the Kisan Sabha allowed the inclusion of the *zamindar* elements from the upper castes and also gave substantial importance to their opinion against the tenants and poor peasantry (and this was evident when Swami Sahjanand parted ways with Congress which represented the landlords of the state), the members of Triveni Sangh were quite easily co-opted into the Congress fold as important backward caste leaders (see Pinch, 1996). The tension between tenants, poor peasants and workers and landlords remained despite these developments. And it was obvious in villages such as Kasauli (where this study has been going on) where after being denied donations by the money-lender-landlord Sahjanand stopped going to his family members and rather used to stay with others. Swami Sahjanand Saraswati emerged as a very vocal opponent of landlordism in the area. These were indications of a persistent simmering conflict in Central Bihar.

The rule of Congress and the virtual hegemony of the landlords never allowed the emergent elite from the backward castes a share in power until the formation of Karpoori Thakur government in 1970s. The landless agricultural labour coming from Dalit castes were also, meanwhile, playing an important role and they had strong political representation as well in the form of

Communist Party of India (CPI). In fact, one of the reasons for absence of a formation in the state, which could call itself exclusively representing the Dalits, has been their support to the different communist parties at different junctures in Bihar's political history.

By 1960s the CPI was organizing landless agricultural labourers in Jehanabad district. Lands were being captured by the landless to build hutments. In 1969 the *aam gair majarua* (government land), *bhoodan* lands still being controlled by landlords, land exceeding the *hadbandi* (ceiling) and *maalik gair majarua* lands were captured by them. The landlords of the local society, who otherwise controlled and cultivated these lands, were provoked by such moves. Meanwhile, they faced another challenge as the landless agricultural workers started raising demand for minimum wages. Strikes for payment of minimum wages began in villages which was a completely new phenomenon during this period. Hence, between 1960 and 1980, the landless agricultural labourers were involved in everyday movement on issues of land and wage led by the CPI. Such movements were witnessed in villages such as Bhuapur, Khajuri, Khadasin etc. The lands exceeding the ceiling and being cultivated by the landlords in Koil, Pahleja, Gandhar Math, Sakri, etc., were captured by the landless under the leadership of CPI. In many of the instances the workers were successful whereas in many others it led to fierce conflict. The results in both the cases were similar – the class antagonism aggravated. By 1980, the CPI (ML) Liberation, represented through the front organization of Indian People's Front (IPF) as well as the Mazdoor Kisan Sangram Samiti (MKSS)[3], a front organization of CPI (ML) Party Unity, had started organizing the landless agricultural labourers as well as peasants in the area. Capturing land was one of the landmarks of the radical left movement, apart from raising the issue of *izzat* (dignity). This was also seen in the village where the study has been carried out. It was also observed that in villages such as Kasauli, these organizations were also making members among the Bhumihar peasants, with land holdings as big as even 10 bighas. In fact, some of the Bhumihars who later became office bearers of Ranvir Sena were active members of IPF or

MKSS at some point of time as revealed by Abhinandan Sharma of Kasauli.

The growing tension indicated towards an uneasy calm which led to an unsaid and informal alliance across middle/rich peasantry in Patna and Jehanabad area. This was visible in the results of State Assembly as well as parliamentary elections. Gun-totting, representatives carrying image of a powerful leader, were elected from most of the constituencies around early 1980s. Sardar Krishna from Arwal, Jagdish Sharma from Ghosi, Ramjatan Sharma from Makhdumpur, Abhiram Sharma from Bela and Poonam Devi from Masaudhi were some of the MLAs, whereas 'King' Mahendra was elected from Jehanabad parliamentary constituency. A clear-cut political message was sent to the struggling masses about the nature of political power and clout that the landlords and middle and rich peasantry enjoyed. Caste was 'sacrificed' by the landed interests in this battle against the landless and poor peasantry. The youth of the landed segment was infused with a new arrogance and sense of 'power' after such political victories and they started moving around with firearms in villages threatening the landless and poor peasants. A process of prolonged armed conflict seemed to be in offing. What many describe as dialogic process was gradually losing its relevance as groups started considering each other as intolerable enemies. Firearms became the new instruments of resolving conflicts.

MKSS started organizing landless and poor peasants into *dastas* (armed groups) and amassed huge arms and ammunition apart from funds, which were collected through forcible fund collection drives from landlords as well as middle and rich peasants. The confidence and arrogance generated among the landed segment youths conflicted with simultaneous growing sense of power among the landless generated through the fact that even they possessed the same instruments of power – the guns – but, additionally, they also had an organization and ideology. On 19 April 1986 around 23 members/sympathizers of MKSS were killed by police in Arwal while holding a meeting before block office in what was described as the modern-day re-enactment of Jallianwallah Bagh. Around the same period (of mid-1980s) the different private armies such as Brahmrishi Sena, Savarna

Liberation Army, Lorik Sena, the Yadav Gang of Ramanand Yadav, Raja Yadav Ramashish Yadav and Rajdeo Yadav started unleashing a series of attacks on landless, who were primarily Dalits. *It is important to observe that it was not a battle between two castes but between the landed, who belonged to different castes such as Bhumihars, Yadavas, Kurmis etc., and the landless and poor peasants.* A situation wherein violence emerged as the paramount instrument of struggle became the part of everyday life.

The nature of activities of the radical left was also changing. The *modus operandi* of their armed struggle involved identifying individuals who have been notorious in the area and killing them. If one looks at the record of incidences in the area, s/he finds that the massacres (collective killings) were being undertaken by the landlords. However, all this changed when the Maoist Communist Centre (MCC) killed 32 members in 1992 belonging to Bhumihar caste in Bara village bordering Gaya and Jehanabad districts. A look at the list of massacres in the district reveals that this was the first time that such an action (of mass murder) was committed by the radical left forces. A battle line which reflected similar attitude, in terms of action (of killing people en masse), from both the camps emerged. The insecurity among people, a constant feeling of fear among those who tried to remain non-partisan or even those who were participating in the struggle, had now increased to new heights. *It must be mentioned that by now the assertion of landless in terms of their right to life with dignity had resulted in great transformation. Their women were not being taken for granted by the Bhumihars in Kasauli, for instance, or the manner in which they were addressed before also changed a great deal due to the fear that even they were empowered by the gun.*

The violence was to grow into more serious form of conflict. On 1st December 1997, Ranvir Sena massacred 61 landless agricultural workers (from Dalit caste) in Bathe village of Jehanabad. The power of the Sena seemed to be increasing and the radical left felt the need to inspire confidence among its support base as well to send a strong message of its power to the rival camp. Hence, on 10th January 1998, in retaliation, they massacred nine people from landed class (Bhumihars) in Rampur Chauram, a stronghold of Sena. While the violence was growing intense and politically vulgarized, it extended beyond class enemies and also took form of caste wars, e.g., attack on Bhumihar villages or Dalits. The Bathe incidence had initiated a series of massacres. After Rampur Chauram, on 25th January 1999, in Shankar Bigha, 23 people from Dalit caste were killed by Sena. On 10th February 1999, the retaliation by Sena resulted in killing of 12 people from Dalit caste in Narayanpur. The next month, on 18th March 1999, 34 people from Bhumihar caste were killed by MCC in Senari. On 16th June 1999, Mianpur was witness to a massacre of 39 people belonging to Yadav caste by Ranvir Sena. Ranvir Sena consolidated itself after the Senari massacre. In fact, the massacres by both the camps were being used as instances of existential tactics of survival and expansion. For instance, this was also the time when MCC, which had substantial presence in Gaya district, made its presence felt in Jehanabad too. Villages such as Rampur Aiyara and Jhunathi had seen the penetration of Ranvir Sena in the aftermath of this series of massacres. In fact, the Sena came to be so dexterously organized at this point of time that they started using women as tools in their struggle. This has been a controversial development. The fact-finding missions, however, criticized police for the brutalities against women (PUCL, 2001). Whereas, an interaction with the locals did reveal that the womenfolk had, in many cases, started shielding the Sena cadres by engaging in violent retaliation against the raiding police forces using sticks, pelting stones etc., in direct confrontation. These incidences got massive media coverage in the state. The media portrayed it as a new development in violent conflicts where women were seen as becoming active members of the Sena.[4] There have been also some studies trying to look at the way the insecure and weak image of women changed after their participation as active agents in violent conflicts (Björkert, 2006). In retrospect, however, as of now, no such development as women cadre building in Ranvir Sena is visible in Jehanabad district. What we come across is sharpening of conflict in the district till 2001. The conflict has been on a decline for the last six years or so. An effort is being made here to understand how this decline happens with the help of observations from a village which has been in centre of conflict, namely, Kasauli. For last six years or so the conflict has subsided. When we say it has subsided, it is largely in terms of the political strength of the contending forces. Some violent incidence may have occurred as the compactness of an organization fizzled out and unemployed, criminalized youth started assuming roles of self-proclaimed commanders and collecting donations (which have been largely extortions) from the villagers. It is these people, whom the respondents identify as having the potential to execute the murders/massacres. At another level, the conflict may break out again in an organized form because the issues of wage and land are still important. No doubt, the fragmentation of landholdings has happened and a change in land ownership pattern has also been witnessed wherein the 'backward castes' have an increased share of land (Sharma, 2005). Even in Kasauli the lands sold by the Bhumihars have been bought by the Yadavas of nearby villages. Dalits or the landless labourers who comprised the chunk of support for the radical left still remain landless and the payment of even minimum wage still remains a burning issue. These have been the situations which encouraged the conflicts to proliferate and it may raise its head once again. However, there is one major transformation that has happened. The market has penetrated deep inside the rural hinterland and, hence, so have the aspirations for a better life. Consequently, migrations have happened and the support base of the Ranvir Sena, the youth, has shifted to cities in great number as the figures from Kasauli indicate.

Kasauli – the Mini-narrative of Socio-political Conflict

The village was under the Jehanabad district before its bifurcation into Arwal district. It is a *savarna*-dominated village where the Bhumihars have been dominant caste. It has an interesting political history because a conference of the Forward Bloc was organized in the village around the time of India's independence. Later on CPI developed a strong organization in the village, though the blocklevel president of Congress during the decade of 1980s came from this village. CPI, which was organizationally strongest, had memberships from Bhumihars as well, who had a history of frequent entries and exits from the local unit. The party, besides playing an important role in getting homestead land for the Dalits, led a movement for wage and encouraged the Dalits to vote in elections which was otherwise hegemonized by the Bhumihars. Because of these reasons the party remained active with some members even till the 1990s though the neighbouring villages had shifted politically towards MKSS and CPI (ML) Liberation.

Nearly 50 per cent of the villagers are landless agricultural workers and of these the greater chunk came from the Mushar caste. The Dalits, in general, are primarily landless, whereas the Bhumihars do not have a single landless household. The village has people from around eleven different castes such as Bhumihars, Brahmins, Mushars, Chamars, Dusadhs, Dhobis etc. At one level, the everyday act of the CPI members in the village in terms of eating and sitting together with Dalits on different occasions, helping them in moments of medical emergency, assistance of administrative nature at the block level, etc., had created an environment of relative peace in the village. The strike for wage in the village and the decision that the workers were not tied to any particular peasant family for work[5] were also led by CPI. However, there were many instances, which remained to be addressed. For instance, the cases of misbehaviour with women from Dalit caste, the usage of demeaning language and the persistent sense of being placed higher up in social and economic hierarchy remained some of the most vital issues to be dealt with. There were also incidences of Bhumihar men going to the Mushar hamlet and misbehaving with their women or the youth conversing with the Dalit workers with usage of informal 'you' even when talking to the elderly (such as 'tu') and many a time abusing them. The issues of dignity being raised in the nearby villages were reaching Kasauli agricultural labourers as well.

Two incidences became significant catalysts in the village, which allowed radical left an entry. A member of CPI, belonging to the landed Bhumihar caste, forcibly captured the buffalo of Chaturi Ram, a Dalit. The CPI failed to take up the issue and in absence of any opposition to this incidence Chaturi went to MKSS for help. Around the same time, the same Bhumihar peasant wanted to buy a very valuable piece of agricultural land from a widow at his own price. But, the land was bought by Pujan Sav (of backward caste) of the neigbouring village. The Bhumihar peasant started forcibly cultivating the land. Pujan made many offers for compromise and settlement of the dispute but it proved in vain. Annoyed with this development, Pujan also went to the MKSS for help. These developments took place around 1985. CPI was faced with crisis as the landless workers started questioning their way of functioning.

The Bhumihar peasant was killed brutally by MKSS. This was an incidence in which the landless labourers or even the peasants of neighbouring village reacted. Prior to this, and even after that, many incidences took place which reflected the nature of atrocities committed by the Bhumihars. A close look at the incidences occurred since 1980 has revealed that Bhumihars have raped Dalit women, have beaten mercilessly a backward caste youth for eating mangoes from the mango orchard of a Bhumihar and no action was taken, and even murdered a backward caste person, besides committing many other acts of abuse and insult in the everyday life. Everything went unnoticed because they were crimes committed against Dalits or backward caste members. The murder by MKSS was a message to the landed segment of the population from the hitherto oppressed segment. *Jan Adalats* by the radical left were being set up and complaints against the Bhumihars were heard. In some of the cases false charges were also put up against them (e.g., Binod Sharma and Ramsajivan Sharma of CPI). This incidence also lent a serious blow to the CPI's image. In another complaint the *Jan Adalat* found some lumpen Bhumihar youth guilty of stealing the pumpset used for irrigation of another peasant and also found Govardhan Sharma, a 'respected' peasant, guilty of keeping it in his house. The conviction of Govardhan Sharma was unacceptable to the Bhumihar peasantry of the village. They united shedding their differences. This happened easily also because the MKSS activities were already being seen as attempts to mobilize the landless against them.

Apart from the above, looting the harvest of peasants (class enemies), forcible extraction of donations from rich peasants/ landlords, looting of the firearms, imposing fines for bad behaviour etc., and intentionally grazing cattle in the newly cultivated fields were some of incidences which had also created a sense of insecurity among the Bhumihars. In fact, an interview with a cadre of People's War, who moved with the *dasta* (armed group) and as its part went for many campaigns revealed that every member of the MKSS was supposed to pay five kilos of *Aghani* and five kilos of *Chaiti* (i.e., paying five kilos of grains in the months of *Aghan* and *Chait*, both being Hindu months). The *dasta* move around villages where it has members. In the *dasta* one member is such who can read and write and everybody else is supposed to follow him. This member was part of many campaigns involving looting property of landed peasants, forcible take over of paddy from a peasant's field, etc. Such incidences were becoming common and the Bhumihars of Kasauli developed a feeling of powerlessness against the earlier feeling when the balance of power was tilted completely in their favour. By 1990s they were feeling the pressure for a counter-agenda against the radical left.

There were primarily three left organizations in the village by 1990s, CPI being the weakest. However, it was also interesting to note that the IPF also found supporters among the Bhumihars. Some of the Bhumihars, who could not be assertive in the village politics or some of the lumpen elements, who were later murdered (such as Aakash and Manoj Sharma) became members of IPF. Their membership generated an image of being in company of powerful and they did gain some importance at local level. But these trends also created possibilities for lumpen activities and they started bullying, stealing and looting.

Emergence of Ranvir Sena

The challenge to the hegemony of landed Bhumihars by the newly found voice of landless and oppressed and the gradual degeneration of many of the radical left cadres into lumpen activity, especially who became part of the movement to become 'powerful' through association with guns, generated tremendous discontent among the landed. More than the later, the former reason was creating discomfort to the Bhumihar peasantry. Cases of refusal to work, demand for better wages and the constant reminders to treat Dalits as humans created a feeling as if the control was slipping out of Bhumihar's hands. They created grounds for justifying how unfair were moves of the radical left, and some can be termed as such. For instance, one Bhumihar peasant narrates his own experiences about his pumpset being stolen and he got it back once he went and confronted the people who had engineered the act. He narrates how, in an unjustified manner, the workers went on strike in 1983, on the very day he was going to sow the rice saplings. Though the workers worked in his field once he confronted them about the unjustified way of striking work on the very day when everything was ready for sowing. The next day there was a meeting of the peasants and they decided that they would work with their family labour but not meet the demands of the workers for increase in wage. However, Radheyshyam Sharma, one peasant, agreed to increase the wage and the plan fell flat.

The district by late 1990s was already in throes of a violent crisis. The intervening period of 1997–99 seemed like the one gearing up for a larger civil war kind of situation. The situation in Kasauli was also ripe for proposals to constitute the Ranvir Sena. Hence, some youths came up to Abhinandan Sharma and asked for his help in the formation of Sena. In the month of September 1999 Brahmeshwar Mukhiya alias 'Mukhiyaji', the founder and chief of the Sena, came to the village and Sena unit was formally constituted. Senior Bhumihar members were made office bearers. Abhinandan Sharma later acted as the spokesperson of the Sena and remained very close to Mukhiyaji. For two years the Sena worked quite well in the village, the cadres were visiting the village regularly and a message was also transmitted to the landless workers about the militant posture of the Bhumihars. Though no massacre took place in the village but the tension ran so high that police camps were set up in the village and overall around seven murders took place in the course of this conflict. Between 1999 and 2004 police raids happened and Abhinandan Sharma went to jail for 25 months on charge of murder of a villager and for his involvement in a massacre. The youth of the village which had started participating actively also suffered at the hands of police. Some of them were arrested and brutally tortured, while some others ran off to cities. This was also the time after arrest of Mukhiyaji in 2002 of fragmentation of the Sena and the predominance of lumpen youth with arms in the Sena, which had started making it unpopular. There has been a lull in tension since then.

The Changing Village Economy: Migration Leaves only Elderly

The land ownership pattern in the village had been tilted in favour of the Bhumihars whereas the Dalits were primarily landless labourers. Some members of the Bhumihar families shifted to cities when they got government jobs but the majority still remained in the village and even those worked outside in cities such as Patna, Ranchi and Bokaro would frequently visit the village. The children of these families started studying in the urban centres and were getting disconnected with the village life – the greatest shock for a villager being they could not even recognize their own plots of lands as their absentee landlord parents could. When the violence was at its peak a great number of people started migrating to not only bigger cities such as those mentioned above but also smaller towns such as Jehanabad and Paliganj. One evident reason was an effort to get out of the situation which was shattering their desire to accumulate whatever possible surplus from agriculture. Another important reason was the message of urban prosperity that was brought in by those who were staying outside. In fact, this had reached such a level that even an active member of the Sena, Abhinandan had sent his son to a metropolis to try his luck and he has been earning very well. He in turn took along with him many other young members from the Bhumihar community and got them jobs in the city.

The village economy was already not a very productive one. The village is not fed by any canal system. There is a traditional *pyne* but it had turned dry to the failure of the state government to take its care. Hence, economic viability of the village life became more questionable once the forceful surplus extraction through extra exploitation (less wages, extra working hours, subservience of labour etc.) was questioned by the landless workers and poor peasantry. In such a situation migration to cities appeared as a viable option. Even those who have good amount of land in the village have migrated to the cities. People who have retired from government service and can lead a comfortable life in village are living in cramped two-room flats in cities with their children in the name of sending them to a 'good' school. The trends on migration show how migration to cities became a hallmark of the village economy and society. And, the maximum migration was from the *savarna* families. Nearly 50 per cent of the family members have migrated.

It shows that the highest percentage of family members who migrate out of village belong to those sections who can afford to sustain themselves in the cities. Therefore, the *savarna* caste, which ranks better than Dalits in land ownership, has the largest migrants. The community, which is numerically ranked next to the Bhumihars – the Mushars has the least migrated population.

The migration from the village to towns or cities has been multifaceted. There have been three kinds of people who shifted to cities:

1. There are some families in the village whose youth has joined the government service in Patna and Delhi.
2. There is another lot which has made full advantage of the changing economy in terms of becoming part of the share management companies in Delhi which take care of people's investments in market. This section has attracted some youths from Kasauli and they are part of the new market economy or have been co-opted in the techno-rational capitalism of modern times as any other citizen of the country. They have aspirations to increase their income to all possible limits and this is reflected in their work ethics. They not only work for their respective companies but also act as individual self-employed agents after the office hours so that their income can be increased. There are some who started small-time businesses, such as roadside general stores etc., in the neighbouring Jehanabad town. These youths were not active members of the Sena *dastas* (armed patrolling/attack groups) but had the potential to be involved in its activities had they remained in the village. One family have their son working in Dubai and they have constructed a big house in Patna and the obvious representations of money have held the villagers in awe. Hence, an increase in income through migration, better jobs or diversification of occupations is something that many villagers see as an option for their children.

3. The third kind of youth that have shifted to the cities are those who were active members of the Sena, moved around in their *dasta* and some of them had also spent substantial time in jail. They in the beginning left the village in order to evade police and after the jail experience to remain away from the whole affair. However, once they shifted out and got engaged in some self-employed occupation, they have not gone back to the village. Some of them worked as security guards in Delhi for a brief period of time because they have also been people who did not have any education. After working for some time as security guards they went back to Bihar finding the work very demeaning for a Bhumihar. One of them thereafter started working as a part-time construction contractor. Another Sena activist, after running away from village, went to Patna, joined an upper caste criminal gang, was involved in a crime, spent two and half years in jail and is now in wood supply business in Jehanabad. Some of the villagers said that those who went out do not want to come back even if their economic condition in cities is deplorable because they have developed a liking for the city life.

The everyday necessities of life, the rising cost of living and the never ending aspirations of family members have compelled the Bhumihar youth to look for options outside the village. Agriculture was not generating the kind of surplus that they required because of high cost of cultivation, growing assertion of the landless workers and fragmentation of land holdings. Hence, agriculture as a source of livelihood became the last option. They retain land as their hereditary property, or as a source of additional income.

Conclusion

We find that violent conflict in the village began as an innate part of the local socio-economic dynamics. This has been a replication of the conflict that has been haunting Central Bihar for over two and a half decades now. There are also always certain incidences which act as catalysts of change and which bring over ground the subterranean tensions. In the case of Kasauli, the entry of the radical left organizations can be attributed to the two incidences in which the Bhumihar peasants were playing like tyrants with the Dalits as well as the backward castes. But, the real reasons were the underlying tensions that have been accumulating due to the approach of the landed class in economic as well as social terms. The issues of wage, capture of *gair mazarua* lands, retaining lands exceeding the ceiling etc., were economic issues whereas in social terms the issues ranged right from the usage of a demeaning language in the everyday life to the treatment meted out to their women. The assertion of the landless and the socially oppressed began when the radical left entered the village. The landed could not accept the challenges that were posed to them. And, the Ranvir Sena gave them an opportunity to avenge the asserting landless. It was an opportunity that the Bhumihars saw to rein in the landless. And, by reining in, they meant not allowing them to raise voices for better wage or continue as attached labour and accept the atrocities with ease. CPI which preceded these formations failed to play the role that it was expected to as a representative of the working masses. The political strategy of the party was generally of compromise and peaceful co-existence and, consequently, its support base – the Dalits – deserted it and even the peasants left it because it could not become a militant representative of the landed upper castes in the village. Murders committed. People had stopped coming out of houses beyond 4 PM as was the scene in the whole district. An omnipresent fear of violence loomed over the village. Meanwhile, both the radical left as well as the Sena developed their own internal contradictions and weakened. The lumpenization of the cadres was one of the reasons why many Dalits stopped playing active role in the People's War, for instance and the similar developments plagued the Sena after a strong central leadership declined. Another significant reason for the lull in terms of violence or political activism has been large-scale migration and the shift towards an aspiration-oriented marketized lifestyle. The backward castes, meanwhile, emerged as new landed gentry as they (especially Yadavas from neighbouring villages) started buying chunk of the land sold by the Bhumihars. Though the violence has not taken place but there are still dangers of its eruption.

The violence or the conflict that stayed in Kasauli has had certain significant consequences or in other words it provides certain important lessons. One of the consequences of the series of massacres has also been the complete demolition of dialogicity as a strategy in movements. While one of the activists, when interviewed, retorted by saying that "when you are being killed, you cannot think about being dialogic". He was true because if a soldier is asked about his reactions about relevance of dialogue while in battlefield he cannot react in any other way; there were others in Kasauli who said that "we had situations of conflict earlier as well but the villagers used to resolve them peacefully. Now, there is no space for dialogue or peaceful resolution. A situation came in 1990s when gun was the only medium of resolving the crisis".

The other significant observation which emerges is about the role played by the richest in the landed segment. They have physically remained outside the conflict (and therefore out of physical danger) because they have properties in cities and can flourish there but at the same time they also remain important part of the conflict being owning land in the village. No damage has been done to their economic interests, whereas there are many whose children became active members of the Sena and who cannot even imagine having income both ways – from cities and from the land. Those participated most vocally were the Bhumihars owning land between 5–10 bighas.

Lastly, a major change in the life of landless and socially oppressed happened. They can speak out against the Bhumihars. But, the movement for wages or for land is no more part of their agenda because the organization either does not take it up or has weakened. The ideological element of struggle has been lost.

But where does one go from here? A member of CPI (ML) Liberation from Ekwari said, in reference to a criminal Bhumihar peasant who has returned from jail, that he has started acting the way Bhumihars were in habit of doing – getting drunk and abusing the Dalits. There is a possibility that any day he could be killed. In Kasauli, the members of People's War said that Abhinandan Sharma has duped a leader of People's War and in this situation of calmness there is always a possibility that he may be killed any day (remember that because of his role in Sena there is already a hidden anger among Dalits). In the panchayat elections that were held in 2006 the Bhumihars of Kasauli had put up a candidate, who was an active but very shrewd worker of Sena (he needed to have good relation with the Dalits because of moneylending business). His cousin who happens to have criminal antecedents and is wanted by police was working for him. He would still go to the Mushari (the hamlet of Mushars) with other members of the Sena and abuse them and threaten them of massacres. These actions have not been liked in past. And, there is no guarantee they will be liked now. The only possibility is that there may not be massacres but pick-and-choose murders as People's War declared after Operation Jail break. However, given the dominance of lumpen elements, one may still expect outsiders (*dasta* of Sena comprising of people from outside the village) to initiate violence because with 50 per cent of Bhumihars migrated and Kasauli appearing to be bearing an aged look not much physical or moral support can be expected from here.

This situation also leaves us with questions such as how do we understand the participation of poor peasantry from the Bhumihar community within class framework when they fight against the landless and poor though their own condition may not be much different? How significant will be the variable of caste while understanding this conflict especially when we see that the backward castes emerge as the new landlords in the village? What kind of movemental framework is required to resolve the problems that confront the poor, landless Dalits? Will market, desire to be co-opted within the world of endless aspirations, provide an interlude for the conflict to stop till the unfulfilled desires again resurface? The framework of struggle may be different then.

Notes

1. Dev Nathan in an interview in Seldon (1992, pp. 304–05).
2. Translation mine.
3. Towards late 1970s Vinayan along with two residents of villages Bhanwar Sikaria and Bhawani Chak, namely, Jangbahadur Singh and Vishnudeo Singh formed the MKSS.
4. This is also reported in a website http: //jagdishpur.blogspot.com/ 2007/12/ranvir-sena-bhojpur-districtbihar.html, accessed on 12th November 2007.

5. Earlier, the agricultural labourer was tied to a family according to the economic capacity of the family in the sense that the family of the worker will work for that particular Bhumihar family first in priority before working for any other peasant family.

References

Advani, L.K. 2006. Press statement issued by L.K. Advani at a press conference in Bilaspur (Chhattisgarh), April 23, available at http://www.bjp.org/Press/april_2006/apl_2306_p.htm, downloaded on 9th January 2008.

Bandopadhyay, D. 2006. "A Visit to Two 'Flaming Fields' of Bihar", *Economic and Political Weekly*, December 30, pp. 5302–04.

Björkert, Suruchi Thapar. 2006. "Women as Arm-Bearers: Gendered Caste-Violence and the Indian State", *Women's Studies International Forum*, 29(5), September-October, pp. 474–88.

Chandra, Navin and Ashok Khandelwal. 1990. "Agrarian Question and Agricultural Labour in India", in V. Chandramowli (ed.), *Labour Landscape*, Delhi: Sterling Publishers, pp. 193–209.

CPI (ML) August 1986. Report from the Flaming Fields of Bihar, CPI (ML); Calcutta.

Das, Arvind N. 1982. "Peasants and Peasant Organisations: The Kisan Sabha in Bihar", in Arvind N. Das (ed.), *Agrarian Movements in India: Studies on 20th Century Bihar*, London: Routledge, pp. 40–87.

Gupta, Shaibal. 2002. *Subaltern Resurgence: A Reconnaisance of Panchayat Election in Bihar*, Crisis States Programme Development Research Centre, London: London School of Economics.

——. 1994. "Socio-Economic Roots of Peasant Movement in Central Bihar", in Kaushal Kishore Sharma, Prabhakar Prasad Singh and Ranjan Kumar (eds.), *Peasant Struggles in Bihar, 1831–1992: Spontaneity to Organisation*, Centre for Peasant Studies, Patna: Janaki Publications, pp. 191–209.

Kumar, Ravi. 2008. Indian State enumerates "Development Challenges in Extremist Affected Areas", *Radical Notes*, July 25, available at http://radicalnotes.com/journal/2008/07/25/indian-state-enumerat-sdevelopment-challenges-in-extremist-affected-areas/, accessed on 12th August 2008.

Louis, Prakash. 2002. *People Power: The Naxalite Movement in Central Bihar*, Delhi: Wordsmiths.

Mohankumar, S. and R.K. Sharma. 2006. "Analysis of Farmer Suicides in Kerala", *Economic and Political Weekly*, April 22, pp. 1553–58.

Omvedt, Gail. 1992. "Capitalist Agriculture and Rural Classes in India", in Berch Berberoglu (ed.), *Class, State and Development in India*, New Delhi: Sage Publications, pp. 82–138.

Pinch, William R. 1996. *Peasants and Monks in British India*, Berkeley: University of California Press, available at http: //ark.cdlib.org/ark: /13030/ft22900465/, accessed on 2nd August 2007.

Prasad, Pradhan H. 1994. "Poor Peasant Movement in Central Bihar", in Kaushal Kishore Sharma, Prabhakar Prasad Singh and Ranjan Kumar (eds.), op. cit., pp. 175–90.

PUCL Bulletin. 2001. Police Atrocity against Women of Senari, Jehanabad on 27.7.2000, http: //www.pucl.org/reports/Bihar/ 2001/jehanabad.htm accessed on 10th March 2006.

Rao, P. Narasimha and K.C. Suri. 2006. "Dimensions of Agrarian Distress in Andhra Pradesh", *Economic and Political Weekly*, April 22, pp. 1546–52.

Saraswati, Swami Sahjanand. 2000. *Mera Jeevan Sangharsh*, Delhi: Granthshilpi.

Seldon, Mark. 1992. "The Naxalite Legacy and the Political Economy of Contemporary India: An Interview with Dev Nathan", in Berch Berberoglu (ed.), op. cit., pp. 295–329.

Sharma, Alakh N. 2005. "Agrarian Relations and Socio-Economic Change in Bihar", *Economic and Political Weekly*, March 5, pp. 960–72.

Singh, Manmohan. 2007. PM's Speech at the Chief Minister's Conference on Internal Security, December 20, available at http: //pmindia.nic.in/speech/content.asp?id=632, downloaded on 10th January 2008.

Part II
Development and the Marginalized

4

Chap
Work
Post

NEETH

Develop
equated
solution
gender
having
would
Accordi
women
is often
lation
relatio
theory
and in
new forma
restruct
women

general
of wome
towards
the Indi
assume

4

Changing Dimensions of Women's Work and Gender Inequality in the Post-reform Period

NEETHA N.

Development within the framework of economic reforms is often equated with growth rates which are highlighted as the only solution to all the problems – be it poverty, unemployment or gender, class and caste. Higher economic growth, apart from having its trickle-down effect, is assumed to bring in synergies that would finally shake the earlier structures and relationships. Accordingly, it is assumed that a simple correlation exists between women's work and women's status. Thus, an important issue that is often highlighted in the context of economic reforms is the translation of labour market changes into defining or redefining gender relations and empowerment of women. The supporters of this theory see current development as one which has opened up new and increased opportunities for women, with women entering into new forms and sectors of work that are highly market-oriented and remunerative – whether the link is seen through the expansion of women-oriented sectors or through the cost-differential dimension.

Well within this framework as well as much within the general understanding of women's status, increased participation of women in economic activity has normally been seen as a step towards enhanced autonomy and equality of women. Apart from the individual gains, women's entry into the labour market is assumed to bring in changes even at the household level – be it education or nutritional status of the household. Work is thus an important lens through which one could get an understanding of the impact of reforms. The changes in work participation rates, patterns of work and sectoral/industrial divisions are some of the indicators which could give one an understanding of how reforms have impacted this central variable. This paper analyses women's work since the 1990s and explores the emerging patterns in women's employment and work and its implications in terms of social status of women.

Women's participation in employment has always been much low, partly due to the definitional issues as well as their absence conventionally recognized categories of work. Level of participation in economic activity in a population crucially depends on how work and worker are defined. In the definition followed by the major statistical data systems a person is a worker if he/she is engaged in any "economically meaningful activity". This definition excludes many women from the boundary of production as they concentrated in the subsistence sector largely for household use/consumption. Thus, a large section of women are rendered invisible and hence do not even figure while estimating worker participation rates.

Employment since 1993–94: Broad Trends and Patterns

Though the initial response to deregulation largely took the established understanding of expanding opportunities for women, doubts were raised on its actual impact with growing evidences of employment stagnation and increasing informalization of the workforce. Further, it has also been argued that the changes associated with reforms – technological changes, industrial relocation and the shift from subsistence production to market orientation – have unleashed forces that have pushed women to a marginalized and discriminated position in the labour market. In this context, the effect on female employment – be it feminization, defeminization or marginalization – has been a central issue that has caught much attention.

The Census of India gives population projections for various years for both the sexes separately for rural and urban areas. The projected data as on January 1, 2005 is used to calculate workforce estimates applying it to the segment-wise workforce participation rates as given by NSSO. The estimates for 2004–05 are compared with that of previous rounds of data[1] both for principal status as well as usual status workers. From Table 1 it is clear that the first important change in employment relates to aggregate workforce itself. Quite contrary to the 1990s, which saw a quite dramatic deceleration in aggregate employment generation, which fell to the lowest rate recorded, the period between 1999–2000 and 2004–05 shows a revival of aggregate employment growth, with male–female workforce increasing sharply.

Table 1

Trends in Workforce Across Various Years (00)

Categories	*Usual Principal Status (UPS)*			*Usual Status (UPSS)*		
	1993–94	*1999–00*	*2004–05*	*1993–94*	*1999–00*	*2004–05*
Rural males	1826513	1916993	2148785	1877438	1950044	2192965
Rural females	747223	796118	919227	1047390	1030474	1242096
Total rural	2573736	2713111	3068012	2924827	2980518	3435062
Urban males	635879	756367	894457	645795	763739	907684
Urban females	134342	157962	201015	172091	187664	247174
Total urban	770221	914329	1095472	817886	951403	1154858
Total males	2462392	2673360	3043242	2523233	2713784	3100649
Total females	881565	954080	1120242	1219480	1218138	1489270
Total	3343957	3627440	4163484	3742714	3931921	4589919

Source: 1993–94 and 2004–05: Calculated using census segment-wise population projections and NSS segment-wise Worker Population Ratios.
1999–00: Calculated using population figures taken from Sundaram (2001) and NSS segment-wise Worker Population Ratios.

This recovery in employment is all the more important for women as the earlier period showed a near stagnation in the number of female workers and an absolute reduction in the number of rural female workers by usual status. The 2004–05 figures show a substantial increase in absolute number of women workers not only in rural areas but also in urban areas, with a larger increase in rural areas. However, the recovery is not only confined to female workers and in fact male workers show a much better recovery in terms of absolute number increases.

Volatile Workforce Participation Rates

The declining work participation rate of women during nineties has been the issue which has received much attention in the present era of globalization and its gendered implications in the country. In line with increased workforce figures, the participation rates show significant improvements for both urban and rural areas for both the sexes in early years of last decade. The data show some recovery after a substantial decline in women's participation rate during 1993–94 and 1999–2000, to reach the level of 1993–94, though as per principal status the rates have gone much higher than the 1993–94 rate (Table 2). For females, participation rates show about 3 percentage point improvement over the previous period for both rural and urban areas. It is true that there has been increase in male participation rates though the rate of increase is less than that of females. The rural–urban disaggregation shows that the rates have improved in both rural and urban areas almost at the same rate as women while for men the increase is largely in urban areas.

Table 2
Workforce Participation Rate in NSSO Rounds

Rounds	*UPS*			*UPSS*		
	Male	*Female*	*Total*	*Male*	*Female*	*Total*
			Rural			
1993–94	53.8	23.4	39.0	55.3	32.8	44.4
1999–2000	52.2	23.1	38.0	53.1	29.9	41.7
2004–05	53.5	24.2	39.1	54.6	32.7	43.9
			Urban			
1993–94	51.3	12.1	32.7	52.1	15.5	34.7
1999–2000	51.3	11.7	32.4	51.8	13.9	33.7
2004–05	54.1	13.5	34.6	54.9	16.6	36.5
			Total			
1993–94	53.2	20.6	37.5	54.5	28.6	42.0
1999–2000	52.0	20.3	36.5	52.7	25.9	39.7
2004–05	53.6	21.5	38.0	54.7	28.7	42.0

Source: Various rounds of NSSO data.

The workforce participation rates raise two issues of concern with regard to female employment. Firstly, the increased participation rate of women in rural areas during a period of crisis are largely led by agricultural regression and by no imagination could be seen as a positive outcome.[2] Secondly, a comparison of the participation rates across principal and usual status shows that the increased participation of women in both rural and urban areas is largely accounted by the increase in women workers in the subsidiary category. A quarter of women workers in this category are either non-workers or unemployed by principal status but undertake work in part. In rural areas about 26 per cent women workers enjoyed subsidiary status while in urban areas this was less at 19 per cent. In comparison only a negligible proportion of men are subsidiary workers which clearly points to social compulsions, especially that of domestic responsibilities which still limit women from taking up full-time work.

The increased number of women in subsidiary category, especially in rural areas in the context of the alarming agrarian crisis, means that they do not have opportunities for long-term regular employment. It is not only the proportion of women in subsidiary activity which is a matter of concern but it is also the increase in this category of workers which clearly reflects struggle to make both ends meet by a large number of women. However, to understand this change and its implications, one has to analyse the issue at further disaggregate levels which could reveal important insights into the dynamics of the processes at work and push more and more rural women to employment.

Continuing Dependence on the Unorganized and Primary Sector

A woman's class and social origin determines her status in the labour market, if she participates in it. This is reflected in the concentration of women in the unorganized sector. Of the total women workers in 2004–05, 91 per cent belonged to the category of unorganized sector workers and 95.9 per cent were unorganized workers (including workers in organized sector with conditions of work similar to that of unorganized sector workers).

Table 3

Proportion of Women in Unorganized Sector and Unorganized Workers

	Unorganized Sector Workers		*Unorganized Workers*	
	1999–00	*2004–05*	*1999–00*	*2004–05*
Total male	83.3	84.0	89.3	90.7
Total female	91.4	91.3	95.6	95.9
Rural female	95.0	94.5	98.0	98.0

Source: NCEUS Report, 2007.

Unorganized workers, whether self-employed or wage are labourers, largely unrecognized as workers legally and hence are vulnerable to exploitations. For women workers in the informal sector the double burden of combining the tasks of production and reproduction is even arduous, given the precarious conditions of work in the unorganized sector. A higher work participation rate in such a context is more likely the result of economic hardships than the availability of opportunities.

The prospects of the manufacturing sector in India to absorb women workers have been debated extensively in the literature on women's employment, given the socio-cultural context of the country. Along side, emphasis has been given to the prospects of service sector jobs in terms of growth in GDP and employment.[3]

The trend in female employment becomes all the more puzzling if one turns to sectoral shares. The sectoral changes in employment show a large increase in the number of women in the primary sector, though in terms of share in female employment the sector shows a decline. However, the sector shows an increase in the share of female workers in total primary employment by almost 3 percentage points. The rural–urban also division shows increased number of women in primary sector in both the areas leading to increased female share in total primary employment. Further, in urban areas, the share of primary sector remained almost stagnant unlike the earlier period contrary to the expected shift away from agriculture as economy develops.

Table 4

Broad Sectoral Distribution and Shares Across Male and Female Workers – UPSS

(per cent)

	1993–94			1999–00			2004–05		
	Male	*Female*	*Total*	*Male*	*Female*	*Total*	*Male*	*Female*	*Total*
					Rural				
Primary	74.80	86.51	79.00	71.86	85.60	76.60	67.10	83.52	73.04
	(60.76)	(39.24)	(100.00)	(61.42)	(38.58)	(100.00)	(58.63)	(41.37)	(100.00)
Secondary	10.50	7.89	9.57	11.98	8.70	10.84	14.90	9.89	13.09
	(70.44)	(29.56)	(100.00)	(72.30)	(27.70)	(100.00)	(72.66)	(27.34)	(100.00)
Tertiary	14.70	5.59	11.44	16.17	5.70	12.55	18.00	6.59	13.87
	(82.47)	(17.53)	(100.00)	(84.32)	(15.68)	(100.00)	(82.80)	(17.20)	(100.00)
Total	100.00	100.00	100.00	100.00	100.00	100.00	100.00	100.00	100.00
	(64.17	(35.83)		(65.47)	(34.53)		(63.82)	(36.18)	
					Urban				
Primary	10.28	25.27	13.43	7.39	18.02	9.49	7.00	18.38	9.44
	(60.44)	(39.56)	(100.00)	(62.59)	(37.41)	(100.00)	(58.28)	(41.72)	(100.00)
Secondary	33.23	32.07	32.99	31.87	29.03	31.31	33.50	32.17	33.21
	(79.56)	(20.44)	(100.00)	(81.74)	(18.26)	(100.00)	(79.26)	(20.74)	(100.00)
Tertiary	56.49	42.66	53.58	60.74	52.95	59.21	59.50	49.45	57.35
	(83.26)	(16.74)	(100.00)	(82.39)	(17.61)	(100.00)	(81.53)	(18.47)	(100.00)
Total	100.00	100.00	100.00	100.00	100.00	100.00	100.00	100.00	100.00
	(78.98)	(21.02)		(80.31)	(19.69)		(75.58)	(21.42)	

Source: NSSO employment and unemployment data, various rounds.

Note: Figures in parentheses refer to female share in total employment in the given sector.

The female shares show an increase in primary and tertiary sectors in rural areas with the primary sector showing maximum increase of around 3 percentage points between 1999–2000 and 2004–05, which needs to be seen in the light of its declining share in the previous period. In urban areas also the share of women workers in the primary sector shows a drastic increase from 37.41 per cent to 41.72 per cent. The female share of employment in the secondary sector stagnated, while that of service sector increased though at a much lower level compared to that of primary sector. Thus, the trend in sectoral distribution seems to dispel some of the existing understanding of female employment changes with the opening up of the economy – a sharp shift away from primary to service sector employment. This becomes all the more critical in the context of an increasing trend of projecting service sector, especially the ICT-driven ones, as an engine of growth and as a source of employment, especially for women.[4]

Employment Expansion through Increased Self-employment

To understand the dynamics of women's employment much closely, the distribution of women workers across various categories of employment as well as sectors is examined. The first and foremost of the changes is the unprecedented increase in self-employment for both male and female workers, accounting for about half of the workforce. Self-employment has of course always predominated over wage employment so far as women are concerned because of the predominance of peasant agriculture. However, as can be seen from the Table 5, till 1999–2000, there was a consistent decline in the proportions of self-employed for both men and women. However, a reversal can be seen between 1999–2000 and 2004–05, whereby the share of self-employed increased dramatically from 55.6 per cent to 61.04 per cent for females. Though the shares have also up gone up for men, the increase has been much lesser than that of female workers.

The rural–urban division shows that the increase in self-employment is largely a rural phenomenon. The share of women self-employed rose drastically from 57.3 per cent in 1999–2000 to 63.7 per cent in 2004–05, thus accounting for nearly

Table 5
Percentage Distribution of Employment by Status (UPSS)

Employment Status and Year	*Rural*		*Urban*		*Total*	
	Male	*Female*	*Male*	*Female*	*Male*	*Female*
Self-employed						
1987–88	58.6	60.8	41.7	47.1	54.3	58.9
1993–94	57.7	58.6	41.7	45.8	52.9	56.7
1999–2000	55.0	57.3	41.5	45.3	52.8	55.6
2004–05	58.1	63.7	44.8	47.7	54.21	61.0
Regular employees						
1987–88	10.0	3.7	43.7	27.5	18.6	6.9
1993–94	8.5	2.7	42.0	28.4	17.0	6.3
1999–2000	8.8	3.1	41.7	33.3	14.0	7.3
2004–05	9.0	3.7	40.6	35.6	18.25	9.0
Casual labour						
1987–88	31.4	35.5	14.6	25.4	27.1	34.2
1993–94	33.8	38.7	16.3	25.8	30.1	37.0
1999–2000	36.2	39.6	16.8	21.4	33.2	37.1
2004–05	32.9	32.6	14.6	16.7	27.54	30.0

Source: Various rounds of NSSO data.

two-thirds of all jobs in rural areas. In non-agriculture sector, workers classified as self-employed are actually home-based workers. The industries where home-based production dominates include handlooms, beedi, artistic metalware, agarbatti and so on. A significant proportion of home-based workers are also unpaid family workers. Many of the activities undertaken by home workers are conducted within a value chain and are sometimes connected globally – and garment industry is the best example. Between home workers at one end and retailers at the other end, and with a row of intermediaries in between, the wages that home workers get are mostly a small proportion of the price of the commodities in the market. Seasonality of work and wages is yet another issue that home workers face largely.

But it is also remarkable for urban workers, -who have increased from 45.3 per cent to 47.7 per cent. What needs to be noted is the corresponding fall in share of casual labour from 39.6 per cent to 32.6 per cent in rural areas and from 21.4 per cent to 16.7 per cent in urban areas. The share of regular women workers in the urban areas also shows a substantial increase which would indeed be a sign of a positive and dynamic process if it is also associated with increasing share of women in sectors which have better conditions of work. In the context of the definition of regular employee[5] followed by NSS this category is bound to capture a large number of workers who may not have even minimum conditions of work but some regular work. In 2004–05, 54 per cent of the regular women workers were hired by private households mainly for domestic purposes.

Overall the aggregate data suggests that across the ten-year period between 1993–94 and 2004–05, women's employment in India was marked by volatile shifts and major fluctuations in work participation rates in both rural and urban areas as well as across employment categories. In the first half of the decade when the overall proportion of self-employed declined, women's work participation rates also fell quite sharply. In contrast, the second half of the decade registered a sharp increase in the share of self-employed and women's work participation rates recovered from their earlier levels.

Self-employment and Unpaid Labour

One of the most striking features of self-employment is the extremely high share of unpaid work by women that may be found in both rural and urban areas. In fact, if one removes unpaid women workers from the category of self-employment, it appears that wage employment is the overwhelmingly predominant form of paid work among women in India. Typically time spent on unpaid economic activities is found to decline as with market penetration, monetization of work is supposed to do away with unpaid labour. Shockingly, the recent major increase in self-employment among women in rural areas has been accompanied by an actual drop in the proportion of own account workers and employers and a marked increase in the share of women's unpaid labour.

Table 6
Paid and Unpaid Work in Self-employment, 1993–94–2004

	50th (1993–94)		*55th (1999–2000)*		*60th (2004)*	
	Rural	*Urban*	*Rural*	*Urban*	*Rural*	*Urban*
Own account worker	25.24	51.69	25.38	53.15	24.73	48.45
Employer	1.53	1.80	0.75	0.89	0.95	1.74
Worked as helper in household enterprise (unpaid family worker)	73.23	46.51	73.87	45.96	74.33	49.81
Total	100.00	100.00	100.00	100.00	100.00	100.00

Source: NSSO, employment and unemployment data, various rounds.

While the share of own account workers and employers among self-employed rural women declined from 26.73 per cent in 1993–94 to 22.9 per cent in 2004, the share of unpaid workers increased from 73.27 per cent to 77.10 per cent. This in effect means that the rising share of self-employment among these women workers is essentially an expression of the mobilization of women in unpaid work. Clearly, the sharp slow down of the rate of growth of agriculture in GDP and declining returns to agriculture is reflected in the incapacity of agricultural incomes to pay for casual hired labour even when required. The thinner spread of agricultural incomes is being expressed in the substitution of casual labour by the unpaid labour of women. In other words, rural women are working more for less income.

The picture in relation to unpaid work is somewhat different in urban areas. Here, although the absolute number of unpaid women workers in self-employment continues to increase, their proportions show a marginal decline, with a corresponding increase in the share of own account workers. On the face of it, this appears to reflect a progression from unpaid to paid self-employed work by women but as is commonly known the nature and location of women's entry into the market for labour and products are generally in the lowest and often in the below subsistence categories. A large part of such own account workers are home-based workers including persons working under the putting out system, viz., where a part of production which is 'put out' is performed in different household enterprises and not in the employers establishment. It is well acknowledged that this is one of the most exploited and low-paid categories of workers – an aspect that the macro data sets on employment cannot reveal.

Industrial Distribution of Workers

In the context of the above broad trends, it is pertinent to look at the changes at the disaggregate level across various industrial sectors/sub-sectors as it could reveal important insights into the processes that are under way. Increased share of women in sectors where the conditions of work are better would mean entirely different process when compared to a situation where women are pushed to sectors which are known for drudgery and poor conditions of work. The process becomes all the more different when one takes into account the conditions under which women take up work. For many women, labour market participation is an outcome of poverty and livelihood, which have strong implications on their sectoral concentration, nature of work and bargaining position.

With agriculture accounting for close to three-fourths of all women workers in India, development in agriculture remained the most important factor influencing women's employment. A long-standing feature of women's employment in the country has been the persistent and substantially high concentration of women in agriculture. This is reflective of the fact that for most women, urbanization and the pattern of industrial development did not mean expanding opportunities for employment. It is for this reason that even within urban India, agriculture, which is elsewhere peripheral to the urban context and urban employment, continues to account for a far larger share of the female workforce than one would expect.

As evidenced by the fall in the share of primary sector, the share of agriculture has more or less stagnated with a small decline over the period (Table 7). The share of the mining and quarrying also shows a decline, leading to an overall decline in the share of primary sector as has been discussed earlier. But, what is striking is the huge increase in the absolute number of women engaged in agriculture during the period 1999–00 and 2004–05 by around 1.7 million women workers. This, when taken in contrast to the decline in the number of women in the earlier period, points to the

Table 7

Distribution of Female Workers Across Various Industrial Categories – UPSS Total

Industrial Category	*1993–94*			*1999–2000*			*2004–05*		
	1	*2*	*3*	*1*	*2*	*3*	*1*	*2*	*3*
Agriculture, forestry and fishing	945357	77.44	39.48	912023	74.88	38.74	1079652	72.42	41.63
Mining and quarrying	5222	0.43	19.51	3842	0.32	17.14	4221	0.28	16.52
Manufacturing and repair services	120987	9.91	29.14	123355	10.13	28.24	174039	11.67	31.05
Electricity, gas and water	516	0.04	3.71	375	0.03	3.61	494	0.03	4.07
Construction	16482	1.35	13.61	20343	1.67	11.66	28024	1.88	10.75
Trade, hotels and restaurants	39376	3.23	12.84	52325	4.30	12.78	61208	4.11	12.31
Transport, storage and communication	3285	0.27	3.06	4408	0.36	3.01	5945	0.40	3.19
Finance, insurance, real estate and business services	4489	0.37	12.07	4692	0.39	9.61	9152	0.61	11.72
Community, social and personal services	84987	6.96	26.35	96587	7.93	28.94	128026	8.59	33.93
Estimated workers[6] ('00)	1220700	100.00	32.59	1217950	100.00	30.94	1490759	100.00	32.47

Source: NSSO employment and unemployment data, various rounds.

Notes: 1. Absolute number of workers ('00); 2. Sectoral share in total female employment; 3. Female share in total employment.

direction of changes that are happening in the economy. This is not to say that only agriculture registered increase in absolute number of women. All the sectors do show increase in absolute number of women. However, the intensity of the biased nature of employment shifts is evident from the fact that of the 2.7 million increases in women workers across all the sectors, 1.7 million is in agriculture. On account of this increased number of women in agriculture, the female share of the sector shows substantial change during the last two periods with the share increasing by about 3 points.

This strikingly sharp increase in the number of female workers and their increasing share in total agriculture employment need to be analysed against the backdrop of the ongoing agricultural crisis. In the context of declining wages and shrinking agricultural incomes, there seems to have been no alternative left to rural households than trying out all possible ways of survival.[7] The entry of a large number of women into the labour market could thus be mainly an outcome of desperation. The increased share of women in agriculture thus seems to be the resultant of the known trend of shifting of burden of subsistence agriculture onto women in the context of its declining economic condition. In the absence of any other alternative source of employment, such desperation would add only to the number of underemployed in agriculture, further lowering productivity.

The industrial sector, including repair services, shows increase in both absolute numbers as well as its share. Female share in total industrial employment also shows an increase from 28.24 per cent in 1993–94 to 31.05 per cent in 2004–05, as against the earlier period which showed a decline. This definitely shows a break from the previous period of stagnation and declining share of female employment and thus marks some degree of positive change. However, to arrive at any firm conclusions, there is a need to look at rural–urban division and specific sectors that have contributed to this increase in female employment in manufacturing.

Construction industry, which accounts for a considerable proportion of women workers, has almost stagnated over the period while in absolute terms there has been some increase. The female share in construction employment shows a decline, which is an indication of replacement of female workers with mechanization of construction work. The most important change that needs to be highlighted, and which is quite reverse of the trend observed during the previous periods, is the decline in the share of women engaged in the trade, hotels and restaurants, though in terms of absolute number there is an increase. In the category of community, social and personal services, the substantial increase in the number of women seems to indicate a process of feminization of the sector with the female share in total employment increasing at around 5 percentage points. Here again, there is a need to explore sub-sectoral patterns to understand its actual implications for female work as wide variation exists among these sub-sectors in terms of wages and other conditions of employment.

Urban Employment Expansion through Low-paid Work

In the 1990s, there has been a precipitous fall in women's employment in urban agriculture reflected both in the reduced number of women in agriculture and also in its share in female employment and total agricultural employment. However, during the period between 1999–2000 and 2004–05, the number of women engaged in agriculture shows a sizeable jump, surpassing the number of women registered even in 1993–94 (Table 8). This increase is reflected in the rising share of the sector in women's total employment as well as in the sharp increase in the female share in total agricultural employment. The female share has increased by about 5 percentage points exceeding even the 1993–94 shares by more than 2 percentage points. The increased dependence on agriculture in urban areas though goes beyond the conventional understanding of urban development and employment, the direction of change in other sectors does help one in broadly positioning these changes.

Among other sectors, interestingly, the big shift for urban women workers has been in manufacturing, the share of which has increased by about 4 percentage points. The female share in total manufacturing employment also shows an increase on account of a substantial increase in women urban workers by around 1.4 lakh workers. Construction industry shows decline both in terms of its share in female employment and also in the share of female

Table 8

Distribution of Female Workers Across Various Industrial Categories – UPSS Urban

Industrial Category	*1993–94*			*1999–2000*			*2004–05*		
	1	*2*	*3*	*1*	*2*	*3*	*1*	*2*	*3*
Agriculture, forestry and fishing	42506	24.68	42.24	33029	17.62	39.95	44986	18.18	44.83
Mining and quarrying	1033	0.60	10.95	751	0.40	9.85	494	0.20	5.71
Manufacturing and repair services	47669	27.67	22.66	45039	24.02	20.84	69703	28.17	24.63
Electricity, gas and water	516	0.30	6.25	375	0.20	5.79	494	0.20	6.37
Construction	7056	4.10	13.67	9008	4.80	11.94	9393	3.80	10.11
Trade, hotels and restaurants	17381	10.09	9.58	31715	16.92	12.38	30155	12.19	10.61
Transport, storage and communication	2237	1.30	3.45	3378	1.80	4.08	3460	1.40	3.44
Finance, insurance, real estate and business services	3442	2.00	12.02	4692	2.50	12.01	7910	3.20	12.87
Community, social and personal services	50423	29.27	30.73	59489	31.73	32.07	80826	32.67	37.41
Estimated workers ('00)	172263	100.00	21.02	187476	100.00	19.69	247421	100.00	21.42

Source: NSSO employment and unemployment data, various rounds.

Notes: 1. Absolute number of workers ('00); 2. Sectoral share in total female employment; 3. Female share in total employment.

workers in total construction employment reflecting a process of defeminization which could be largely attributed to the mechanization boom in the sector.

Within the service sector, the share of trade in female employment which rose sharply during the period between 1993–94 and 1999–2000 absorbing part of displaced workers from agriculture and manufacturing during the period seems to have lost its importance in the later period. This has resulted even in an absolute decline in the number of female workers. The share of trade in total employment of women fell sharply from 16.92 per cent to 12.19 per cent during the period with female share declining from 12.38 per cent to 10.61 per cent. The category of community, social and personal services though shows only a small increase in share, the female share in total employment shows a dramatic increase from 32.07 per cent to 37.41 per cent, which is brought out by the substantial increase in the number of women workers by around 2.1 lakh. Since the category comprises of various sub-categories, the dynamics of the sector and its implications for women's overall employment would be clear only from a sub-sectoral analysis. Thus, while the share of both agriculture and manufacturing in urban women's employment showed a decline between 1993–94 and 1999–2000 it was partly cushioned by the increase in trade, absorbing part of the displaced workers. However, as has been seen earlier, women are found leaving the sector to take up employment elsewhere.

At the overall level, the trends in women's employment during the period are somewhat puzzling. On the one hand, more and more women are found moving to agriculture alongside an increase in their number in manufacturing and personal and community services. This broadly denotes a positive development with some signs of women getting entry to some forms of employment. However, sectoral shifts – with women moving out of agriculture and taking up trade-related activities in the initial period followed by a further crowding into agriculture and other service industries – point to a desperate situation where women are trying out various possibilities. This suggests that female employment is largely driven by survival options and thus is far from being a positive labour market outcome. These trends are thus

Table 9

Distribution of Women Workers Across Various Sub-sectors of Manufacturing

Categories	*No. of Female Workers ('00)*				*Share to Total Female Employment in Manufacturing*			
	UPS		*UPSS*		*UPS*		*UPSS*	
	1999–2000	*2004–05*	*1999–2000*	*2004–05*	*1999–2000*	*2004–05*	*1999–20000*	*2004–05*
Division 15: Manufacture of food products and beverages	3475	3417	4129	4202	9.4 (14.62)	6.72 (16.42)	9.17 (16.69)	5.99 (19.15)
Division 16: Manufacture of tobacco products	7898	7237	9196	9145	21.37 (71.98)	14.23 (73.40)	20.42 (74.35)	13.03 (71.99)
Division: 17: Manufacture of textiles	8372	11860	10697	19280	22.65 (24.10)	23.32 (24.61)	23.75 (28.83)	27.46 (34.07)
Division: 18: Manufacture of wearing apparel; dressing and dyeing of fur	3633	11257	4504	16066	9.83 (23.37)	22.13 (29.36)	10 (27.85)	22.89 (36.61)
Division: 24: Manufacture of chemicals and chemical products	3159	4422	3566	4696	8.55 (26.58)	8.7 (33.64)	7.92 (28.83)	6.69 (33.89)
Estimated workers	36963	50857	45039	70197	100 (17.89)	100 (19.42)	100 (21.04)	100 (24.51)

Source: NSSO employment and unemployment data, various rounds.

Note: Figures in parentheses refer to female share in total employment in the given sector.

indicative of growing labour market uncertainty and volatility rather than steady improvement in female employment.

In order to understand the processes that are under way, a further sub-sectoral analysis is done, for both principal and usual status workers which could help in understanding the nature of employment created. The data is restricted to only those sectors which account for considerable share of women workers. Primary sector though important is largely accounted by agriculture and hence the sub-sector analysis is not attempted.

In manufacturing the trend of falling share of food products and tobacco continued with the share of food products and tobacco reducing further to 6 per cent and 13 per cent in 2004–05 (Table 9). In the case of tobacco there is even an absolute reduction in the number of women. The whole upward movement of manufacturing is largely limited to just two sectors, viz., garment-making and textiles. Textiles account for the largest share of manufacturing (27.46%), registering an increase of about 4 percentage points. Garment-making shows the highest increase of about 12 lakh women workers, raising its share from 10 per cent to 22.89 per cent of total manufacturing.

Overall, the sub-sectoral analyses of manufacturing do not suggest any major shift in female employment. The substantial difference in the number of workers across principal and usual status, especially in sectors which show a boom in female employment, suggests the possibility of the revival of the subcontracting/putting out system where women are employed largely as piece rate workers. Such systems of employment are known for its ad hoc character and low pay and hence to see this as a very positive outcome is questionable.

The disaggregate analysis shows that the decline in trade is largely accounted by the drastic reduction in the share of retail trade, which fell down from 81.55 per cent to 70 per cent by usual status (Table 10). The decline in absolute number of women is quite sharp with more than 4 lakh women seen moving away from the sector, with female share of employment showing a decline. The sudden decline in the number of women engaged in trade, after a sudden boom, points to the instability and volatility of such employment in general and for women in particular.

Table 10

Distribution of Women Workers Across Various Sub-sectors of Trade

Categories	*No. of Female Workers ('00)*				*Share to Total Female Employment in Manufacturing*			
	UPS		*UPSS*		*UPS*		*UPSS*	
	1999–2000	*2004–05*	*1999–2000*	*2004–05*	*1999–2000*	*2004–05*	*1999–2000*	*2004–05*
Division 52: Retail trade, except of motor vehicles and motorcycles; repair of personal and household goods	20377	18694	25710	21257	78.66 (11.31)	70.99 (10.04)	81.55 (13.65)	69.92 (11.09)
Division 55: Hotels and restaurants	3791	5226	4129	6179	14.63 (13.82)	19.85 (14.91)	13.10 (14.97)	20.33 (16.72)
Estimated workers	25906	26333	31528	30402	100.00 (10.46)	100.00 (9.54)	100.00 (12.32)	100.00 (10.66)

Source: NSSO employment and unemployment data, various rounds.

Note: Figures in parentheses refer to female share in total employment in the given sector.

This means that incomes from petty retailing were neither stable nor financially viable for many forcing them to shift to other sectors in search of employment. What seems to have happened is that people who are out of the workforce through shifts in the traditional occupations have tried alternative sources of livelihood and because of different reasons petty retail trade is often seen as an important source of employment for poor women, who are uneducated and lack specific skills. The perceived relative skill required for entering into retail trade, especially small vending, is not much as compared to other categories of work. The self-employed nature of the occupation makes the entry of poor and vulnerable groups into the occupation easier, which is furthered by the requirement of a very low capital investment. Hotels and restaurants show increase in both absolute number of women as well as share, as has been during the earlier period.

Community and personal services do seem to have some of these displaced workers – suggesting a movement of women from trade to community and personal services (Table 11). Further, the category of community and personal services disaggregated across major categories clearly shows signs of segregation. The inability of the public administration sector to absorb more and more workers is visible in the declining share of women in this sector and an almost stagnant figure in terms of absolute numbers. Education, as always has been the case, accounts for majority of female workers in this category. The data shows substantial increase in the number of female workers though the share has not registered much increase. The decline in the share of female teachers as principal status workers is noteworthy reflecting a tendency of increased presence of part-time workers which could be largely seen as a resultant of privatization of the sector.

Health and social work sector also seems to have declined in terms of its importance in its share of women. What seems to be quite interesting is the sharp increase in the share as well as number of women engaged in private household employment. The more than doubled share of the sector has positioned the sector next to and almost close to education. In terms of absolute numbers too the increase has been quite substantial from 9,75,900 to 26,20,000 during the period. For the first time the category of

Table 11

Distribution of Women Workers Across Various Sub Sectors of Community and Personal Services

Categories	*No. of Female Workers ('00)*				*Share to Total Female Employment in Manufacturing*			
	UPS		*UPSS*		*UPS*		*UPSS*	
	1999–2000	*2004–05*	*1999–2000*	*2004–05*	*1999–2000*	*2004–05*	*1999–2000*	*2004–05*
Division 75: Public administration and defence; compulsory social security	7266	7639	7319	7662	13.18 (10.74)	9.87 (12.68)	12.30 (10.83)	9.48 (12.76)
Division 80: Education	19271	24926	21206	28672	34.96 (46.84)	32.21 (45.51)	35.65 (48.45)	35.47 (47.74)
Division 85: Health and social work	6792	8644	6944	8898	12.32 (37.14)	11.17 (39.45)	11.67 (38.41)	11.01 (40.55)
Division 93: Other service activities	11373	5628	12573	7415	20.63 (41.46)	7.27 (25.69)	21.14 (44.05)	9.17 (30.57)
Division 95: Private households with employed persons	9004	24926	9759	26200	16.33 (61.55)	32.21 (75.85)	16.40 (64.11)	32.42 (75.62)
Estimated workers	55129	77391	59489	80826	100.00 (30.45)	100.00 (37.58)	100.00 (32.07)	100.00 (37.63)

Source: NSSO employment and unemployment data, various rounds.

Note: Figures in parentheses refer to female share in total employment in the given sector.

private households with employed persons has been sub-categorized and data was collected across sub-activity classifications within that. The data shows that women are largely employed as housemaids/servants accounting for about 70 per cent in this category, with female share as high as 87 per cent (Table 12). The gender-based segregation is clear across the categories, with women accounting for all who report as governess/baby sitters and their complete absence from categories such as gardener/ watchman and so on.

Table 12

Distribution of Women Workers Across Various Sub-sectors of Private Households with Employed Persons

Categories	*No. of Female Workers ('00)*		*Share to Total Female Employment in Manufacturing*	
	2004–05		*2004–05*	
	UPS	*UPSS*	*UPS*	*UPSS*
95001-Housemaid/servant	17824	17973	70.97 (86.83)	69.81 (87.04)
95002-Cook	676	729	2.71 (100.00)	2.83 (100.00)
95003-Gardener	0	38	0.00 (0.00)	0.00 (0.00)
95004-Gate keeper/chowkidar/watchman	0	64	0.00 (0.00)	0.00 (0.00)
95005-Governess/baby sitter	497	526	1.99 (100.00)	2.83 (100.00)
95009-Others	5929	6869	24.33 (61.97)	24.53 (63.90)
Total estimated workers in the category 'private households with employed persons'	24926	26200	100 (75.59)	100 (76.23)

Source: NSSO employment and unemployment data, various rounds.

Note: Figures in parentheses refer to female share in total employment in the given sector.

From the data it seems that employment in domestic sector appears to be the only available option for many of the disadvantaged groups or sections that are faced with limited opportunities. The wages and other conditions of work in the sector are one of the lowest, with the sector being even out of the minimum wages purview in many states. The growth of the sector is indicative of as to how women are affected by the development process.

To wrap up, at the overall level, the analysis reveals that the increased participation rates of women in urban areas is not necessarily a positive phenomenon as it has not made much structural changes in women's employment. The trend seems to suggest a highly regressive tendency with women getting concentrated in the lower rungs of the labour market. Further, with reduced family incomes and rapid impoverishment, it is quite likely that more and more women, who are entering into the workforce seeking employment, take up different tasks at different points of time which could fluctuate in quantum, depending on the opportunities available such as petty trade – adding to fluctuations in such categories of work.

Pressure on Agriculture with Volatile Rural Non-farm Employment

Agriculture occupies a central position as far as rural employment is concerned. The excessive dependence on agriculture shows a continuation during the period though there has been some degree of diversification of employment. The data shows that though there has been a small decline in the proportion of women in agriculture, non-farm activities account for only about 17 per cent of the workers. The increase in the number of women engaged in agriculture is alarming with about 1.5 million additional women joining the sector thus pushing women's share in total agriculture employment by about 3 percentage points. This crowding of women in agriculture in this context of a deceleration in agricultural growth and productivity would only mean that the already low income from agricultural production is shared by many hands, further aggravating the rural crisis, which has been highlighted earlier. Sectoral shifts are relatively lower in other sectors with manufacturing, trade, and community social and personal services, showing marginal increases in its share when the two time periods are compared.

Part of the overall crisis of rural employment is because non-farm employment has not been expanding to absorb additional job seekers. The stagnation in other sectors is partly due to the crisis in agriculture since the declining returns from agriculture spill over to other sectors in the form of shrinking demand.

Table 13

Distribution of Female Workers Across Various Industrial Categories – Rural

Industrial Category	*1993–94*			*1999–2000*			*2004–05*		
	1	*2*	*3*	*1*	*2*	*3*	*1*	*2*	*3*
Agriculture, forestry and fishing	902850	86.11	39.36	878994	85.30	38.70	1034666	83.22	41.50
Mining and quarrying	4190	0.40	24.17	3091	0.30	20.90	3726	0.30	22.07
Manufacturings and repair services	73317	6.99	35.81	78316	7.60	35.49	104336	8.39	37.59
Electricity, gas and water	0	0.00	0.00	0	0.00	0.00	0	0.00	0.00
Construction	9427	0.90	13.56	11335	1.10	11.44	18631	1.50	11.11
Trade, hotels and restaurants	21995	2.10	17.56	20609	2.00	13.45	31052	2.50	14.57
Transport, storage and communication	1047	0.10	2.47	1030	0.10	1.62	2484	0.20	2.89
Finance, insurance, real estate and business services	1047	0.10	12.24	0	0.00	0.00	1242	0.10	7.49
Community, social and personal services	34564	3.30	21.81	37097	3.60	25.02	47200	3.80	29.27
Estimated workers ('00)	1048437	100.00	35.83	1030474	100.00	34.53	1243338	100.00	36.18

Source: NSSO employment and unemployment data, various rounds.

Notes: 1. Absolute number of workers ('00); 2. Sectoral share in total female employment; 3. Female share in total employment.

Manufacturing seems to have absorbed some proportion of the increasing women workers, with the share showing a marginal increase. Unlike the trend observed in urban areas, where there has been a substantial decline in the share of women in trade, rural areas show a stagnant picture with a small increase. Community, social and personal services also show a marginal increase. Overall this reveals that there have not been substantial changes across major industrial categories of women workers in rural areas.

In the backdrop of the above trends, to get a better understanding of the dynamics of rural female employment, the critical segments of non-farm employment such as manufacturing and personal and community services are analysed at further disaggregate level for the last two rounds. Here again, the data is restricted to only those sectors which account for more than 2 per cent of women.

The traditional sectors of rural women's employment such as food products and tobacco show a decline in their share as has been the trend in the past. The most important feature of the changing employment in manufacturing is the huge increase in the number and share of women engaged in the manufacturing of wearing apparels as in the case of urban areas (Table 14). The number of women engaged in textiles has also increased though the share shows an overall stagnation. The increase in the share of wearing apparel is particularly sharp when subsidiary workers are also taken into account – which indicates the possibility of large-scale subcontracted – putting out home-based work in the sector.

Yet another sector which has shown dramatic increase so far as women's employment is concerned is that of community and personal services. The sub-sectoral data shows a declining share of public administration in women's employment in this category, reflecting the shrinking of government jobs (Table 15). Education is found to occupy the most important position in terms of its share in total employment followed by private households with employed persons. Education shows further signs of sex-based segregation with female share increasing sharply over the period from 29 per cent to 38 per cent. The growing share of women in education could be linked to the individual and family aspirations resulting

Table 14

Distribution of Women Workers Across Various Sub-sectors of Manufacturing

Categories	*No. of Female Workers ('00)*				*Share to Total Female Employment in Manufacturing*			
	UPS		*UPSS*		*UPS*		*UPSS*	
	1999–2000	*2004–05*	*1999–2000*	*2004–05*	*1999–2000*	*2004–05*	*1999–2000*	*2004–05*
Division 15: Manufacture of food products and beverages	7961	8273	10305	9937	13.16 (24.45)	10.59 (26.97)	13.16 (31.43)	9.88 (28.93)
Division 16: Manufacture of tobacco products	19107	21142	25762	26084	31.58 (78.25)	27.06 (68.91)	32.89 (78.58)	25.93 (75.93)
Division: 17: Manufacture of textiles	12738	16546	16488	21116	21.05 (36.12)	21.18 (41.49)	21.05 (39.51)	20.99 (47.29)
Division: 18: Manufacture of wearing apparel; dressing and dyeing of fur	2388	8273	3091	13663	3.95 (29.34)	10.59 (29.96)	3.95 (34.57)	13.58 (39.78)

Source: NSSO employment and unemployment data, various rounds.

Note: Figures in parentheses refer to female share in total employment in the given sector.

Table 15

Distribution of Women Workers Across Various Sub-sectors of Personal and Community Services

Categories	*No. of Female Workers ('00)*				*Share to Total Female Employment in Manufacturing*			
	UPS		*UPSS*		*UPS*		*UPSS*	
	1999–2000	*2004–05*	*1999–2000*	*2004–05*	*1999–2000*	*2004–05*	*1999–2000*	*2004–05*
Division 75: Public administration and defence; compulsory social security	3981	2758	4122	2484	11.90 (11.29)	6.67 (9.99)	11.43 (11.52)	5.26 (9.04)
Division 80: Education	10350	18385	11335	21116	30.95 (27.25)	44.44 (35.25)	31.43 (29.25)	44.74 (38.42)
Division 85: Health and social work	3184	4596	3091	4968	9.52 (29.34)	11.11 (29.96)	8.57 (34.57)	10.53 (36.16)
Division 93: Other service activities	12738	6435	14427	7453	38.10 (29.34)	15.56 (20.97)	40.00 (30.25)	15.79 (24.11)
Division 95: Private households with employed persons	1592	7354	2061	8695	4.76 (58.68)	17.78 (59.92)	5.71 (69.15)	18.42 (63.28)
Estimated workers	33437	41365	36067	47200	100.00 (22.41)	100.00 (27.52)	100.00 (25.21)	100.00 (30.53)

Source: NSSO employment and unemployment data, various rounds.

Note: Figures in parentheses refer to female share in total employment in the given sector.

from the social acceptability of sector. The maximum increase in share has been for private household with employed persons, which registered a three-fold increase in its share during the period – indicative of a desperate entry of women into paid work. Working conditions of domestic workers in terms of wage earnings and other benefits are one of poorest and an overwhelming majority of domestic women workers, nearly 84 per cent in urban areas and 92 per cent in rural areas, were found to get wages below the minimum wages of Rs 66 per day (NCEUS, 2007).

On the whole, the broad pattern indicates that the changes in the non-farm sector do not show any signs of long-term employment changes but are reflective of the continuing volatility and uncertainty in non-farm employment. Thus, in an overall term, rural female workforce seems to be highly disadvantaged with further signs of segregation into the lower rungs of the economy.

Women as Unpaid Care Workers and Rising Social Inequalities

Apart from women's role in the conventionally defined productive work, the reproductive or household work assumes particular significance in any discussion on women's work. The only data available to look at this aspect of work is the time use data collected by CSO. The data distinguishes three broad categories of activity based on the standard international system of accounting – SNA, extended SNA and non-SNA. The SNA activities include primary production activities like agriculture, animal husbandry, fishing, forestry, processing and storage, mining and quarrying; secondary activities like construction and manufacturing; and tertiary activities such as trade, business and other services. Extended SNA activities include household maintenance, care for children, the sick and the elderly, and community and voluntary work. Learning, personal care and self-maintenance, and social and cultural activities are categorized as non-SNA activities. Activities covered under SNA are much broader what these actually mean and hence there will be a difference in workforce estimates. Despite these limitations, analysis across these broad categories of SNA and extended SNA would give insight into the division between 'economic' work and unpaid care work. This becomes extremely important in the context of a large proportion of women (about 54%) reporting to have worked from their homes during 2004–05 (NCEUS, 2007)

An overview of the distribution of participants (those from whom time disposition data was collected) in terms of their participation in a day in only SNA, only extended SNA (care work) or in both are given below. The pattern is important from a gender perspective as women generally participate in both SNA and care work in larger numbers than men.

Table 16

Percentage Distribution of Participants in Only SNA, in Extended SNA and in Both SNA and Extended SNA

Rural		*Only SNA*	*Only ESNA*	*SNA and ESNA*	*No SNA or ESNA*
Combined states	Male	43.8	5.1	40.6	10.5
	Female	2.6	19.1	73.5	4.7
Urban					
Combined states	Male	32.3	9.0	41.7	17.0
	Female	1.7	49.7	41.5	7.1

Source: Time Use Statistics, unit level data, 1999.

The gender difference is striking. While a large proportion of men did only SNA activities, very few women belonged to this category. For rural females, while 'both SNA and extended SNA' accounted for the largest proportion, in urban areas women engaged in 'only extended SNA' constituted the largest share.

Table 17

Average Daily Time Spent on SNA and Unpaid Care Work – Age 10 and Above

		Rural				*Urban*			
State		*Male*		*Female*		*Male*		*Female*	
		Hour/ minutes	Parti. rate	Hour/ minutes	Parti. rate	Hour/ minutes	Parti. rate	Hour/ minutes	Parti. rate
Combined States	SNA	7.6	84.4	4.4	76.1	8.1	74.0	3.2	43.2
	ESNA	1.2	47.7	5.5	92.6	1.1	50.7	6.1	91.2

Source: Time Use Statistics, unit level data, 1999.

What is to be noted specifically is that a large proportion of women were active in both SNA and extended SNA activities, unlike men, and that the female–male difference in SNA was much smaller than that in extended SNA. Apart from whether an individual participated in SNA/ESNA or both, what is more important for the issue under study is the time spent on these activities.

Women spent a significantly larger proportion of the day in unpaid care work and the male–female difference was very sharp, irrespective of rural/urban difference. In rural areas, women spent about 5.5 hours in a day on unpaid care work while men spent only 1.2 hours of their day on such work. The male–female difference was slightly more in urban areas with women spending about 6.1 hours daily and men almost the same time as their rural counterparts.

These women perform a number of activities that help households to supplement their income. But these are not included into the realm of economic activity and thus do not get reflected in workforce participation rate. What is important to note in this context more than monetization of such work is the non-recognition and lack of appreciation of such work which is reflected in the lack of public and social policies. There is increasing understanding of how housework is an aspect of family life most resistant to change. Occupational demands and expectations continue to be based on the assumption that the worker is an individual who is relatively free of domestic and family responsibilities. Withdrawal of the state from education, health, food provision and other social sectors are bound to increase the pressure on women as women may have to put in more time as care givers.

As per the 61st round of employment and unemployment data among women in the prime age group 15–59 years, 53 per cent in urban and 65 per cent in rural areas reported that they were engaged in domestic duties by principal status. Many women who report themselves as principally engaged in work report some economic activity, which would fetch the household some additional income. Such participation, if nominal, or is a borderline case of economic activity, would not be reflected in the usual indicators of employment. Therefore, a set of probing questions are put to all the members of the household classified as 'engaged in domestic duties' according to the usual principal status regarding their participation economic activities.

Between the period 1993–94 and 2004–05 the proportion of women with domestic work as principal status reporting subsidiary economic activity has increased which, though shows increased opportunities for women, also mean increased pressure on women. Further, the kinds of activities that women take up as additional work do not in any case suggest the possibility of opportunities rather one of survival, forced by the economic hardships. The activities that these women are mostly engaged in free collection of goods and fuel, household poultry and dairy, sewing, tailoring, weaving, grinding of food grains etc.

Even in the event of economic pressure, the social pressure on women to remains within the boundaries of households and the pressure of house work is evident from the proportion of women who showed willingness to take up economic work provided such work is done at home. Of the 56.8 per cent women reporting domestic duties, 35.7 per cent in rural areas and 29.4 per cent in urban areas showed willingness to do work if it could be done at home.

Other social indicators also reflect the inequality that women are subjected to. Adverse sex ratio remains an important issue after many decades of intervention suggestive of a continuing discrimination against women by their own families. The decline in the child sex ratio, which is reported from all states of the country, unlike its presence in selected pockets, as has been the case earlier, indicates the fact that the structural issues are deep-rooted which work against the interest of women at large. Undernutrition is described as a characteristic feature of the condition of women and girl-children in most parts of India. It is well known that intra-household distribution of food tends to discriminate by gender, usually because of self-denial by women and girls. As per the NFHS survey, the prevalence of anaemia for ever married women has increased from 52 per cent in 1998–99 to 56 per cent in 2004–05.

Violence against women is a good indicator of status of women in society. There is increasing evidence to show that all women, regardless of age, class, caste and community, are vulnerable to violence – marriage, a joint family, education, economic security and social status do not provide any real protection. The National Crime Records Bureau collates and publishes data on crime against women annually, which shows that crimes against women have been increasing at a higher rate (Table 18).

Table 18

Incidence of Crimes Against Women in India (1990–2005)

Crime Head	*1990*	*1995*	*2000*	*2005*
Rape	9518	13754	16496	18359
Kidnapping and abduction	11699	14063	15023	15750
Dowry death	4836	5092	6995	6787
Cruelty by husband and relatives	13450	31127	45778	58319
Molestation	20194	28475	32940	34175
Sexual harassment	8620	4756	11024	9984
Importation of girls	—	191	64	149
Sati Prevention Act	—	1	0	1
Immoral Traffic (Prevention) Act	—	8447	9515	5908
Indecent Representation of Women (Prohibition) Act	—	539	662	2917
Dowry Prohibition Act	—	2814	2876	3204
Total	68317	109259	141373	155553

Source: Crime in India, various rounds, National Crime Records Bureau, Ministry of Home Affairs, Government of India and past volumes.

Of all the crimes against women, dowry deaths is such a violence, which is closely linked to the social custom, and reflects the attitude of the society. The number of rape cases and the trend over time are clear indicators of the overall status of women. The latest NFHS round also confirms the increasing violence against women. The survey finds that traditional gender norms, particularly those concerning wife beating, are still strongly entrenched. Further, earning for the family may raise their status to some extent, but does not necessarily give them greater autonomy in family – which would be adversative to empowerment. NFHS data suggests that majority of married women do not have the final say on the use of their own earnings or all other household decisions which they were asked about. This means that the structural issues of gender inequality, i.e., patriarchal norms and values, still remain.

Conclusion

The analysis provided in the paper suggests that the growing socio-economic crisis is locking vast sections of women workers into a downward spiral resulting in a deepening of gender-based inequality. The phenomenal increase in the number of workers in the category 'private households with employed persons' further shows the signs of distress-driven employment growth. The sectoral and sub-sectoral trends thus point to the fact that the increase in participation rate of women is more an outcome of the search for livelihood options than an actual labour market expansion. Thus, though the visibility of women as workers has increased, in the context of gender segregations and unfair production relations, they are still victimized.

Further, the employment choice for women needs to be seen both in the context of alternatives or in the absence of such alternatives. The burden of supporting the family is increasingly falling on women as men are involuntarily unemployed or choose what kind of job they would take up and thus are voluntarily unemployed (Neetha, 2004). The survival needs of the family often has its toll on women with household work and reproductive responsibilities still entirely seen as women's work outside the sphere of production. This, given the asymmetrical power relations and division of labour in the private sphere, implies that women are doubly disadvantaged. Further, women's employment needs to be seen from the point of potential for challenging and destabilizing social inequalities and the extent to which they merely express and reproduce those inequalities. Thus seemingly one could argue that there have been changes in the economic roles of women, but it cannot be labelled as their empowerment.

Notes

1. For 1999–2000, the population figures are taken from Sundaram (2001) and for 1993–94 are calculated using the census population projections as on January 1994. The segment-wise population figures are applied to NSSO segment-wise worker-population ratios to arrive at workforce estimates.

2. The agrarian distress is reflected in the spate of farmers' suicides in many parts of the country, especially in states like Maharashtra, Andhra Pradesh and Kerala. The crisis is perceived as an outcome of the integration of the economy to the world in a context of worldwide recession. With the removal of quantitative restrictions and freer global trade, not only are those developing countries' farmers engaged in growing exported cash crops suffering, but the livelihoods of millions of food grain producers are also being undermined as a result of imports of exceptionally low-priced foreign grain. It is argued that the agrarian crisis is likely to persist as long as the present policies of openness to the world market continue, as global conditions of trade in primary commodities are likely to remain unfavourable (Patnaik, 2005).
3. In the Approach Paper to Tenth Five-Year Plan (2002–07) of the Planning Commission, service sector has been projected as the most potential sector in terms of employment. The paper calls for the promotion of specific service sectors jobs which are women-friendly and gender-neutral such as IT and ITES.
4. In this context, though the trends and patterns of employment in specific sectors like ICT are important, the same is not attempted in this paper. For a detailed discussion of this aspect, see Neetha (2006).
5. The category includes persons working in other's farm or non-farm enterprises (both household and non-household) and getting in return salary or wages on a regular basis. The category not only includes persons getting time wage but also piece wages or salary and paid apprentices, both full-time and part-time.
6. Total workforce estimates may vary slightly across tables as they are derived from adding up sectoral estimates, calculated from the proportions across industrial categories as given in the published data.
7. Between 2000 and 2004, with the deepening of agrarian crisis, wage employment in agriculture seems to have become scarce with the number of agricultural labourers falling steeply by almost 10 million (see Neetha and Mazumdar, 2006).

References

Chandrasekhar, C.P. and Jayati Ghosh. 2006. "Working More for Less", *Macro scan*, November 28, http://www.macroscan.org/the/employment/nov06/emp171106Employment_ Growth.htm

Ghosh, Jayati. 2002. Export Oriented Employment for Women and Social Policy, Paper No. 6, UNRISD, Geneva.

Government of India. 2006. National Family Health Survey (NFHS–3), 2005–06, Vol. I, Ministry of Health and Family Welfare, Government of India.

National Commission on Enterprises in the Unorganised Sector. 2007. Report on the Conditions of Work and Promotion of Livelihoods in the Unorganised Sector, National Commission on Enterprises in the Unorganized Sector, Government of India.

Neetha, N. 2004. "Making of Female Bread Winners: Migration and Social Networking of Women Domestics in Delhi", *Economic and Political Weekly, Review of Women Studies*, 39(17).

——. 2006. Women's Employment and Sunshine Sectors: Scope, Potential and Concerns in the Context of ICT Sector in India, paper prepared for National Productivity Council, New Delhi.

Neetha, N. and Indrani Mazumdar. 2006. Globalisation and Women's Work: Trends in Women's Unpaid Labour in India, paper presented in the International Seminar on "A World in Transition: New Challenges to Gender Justice", GADNET-CWDS, December 13–15, New Delhi.

Patnaik, Utsa. 2005. Global Capitalism, Deflation and Agrarian Crisis in Developing Countries, Paper No. 15, UNRISD, Geneva.

Sundaram, K. 2001. The Employment-Unemployment Situation in India in the 1990s: Some Results from the NSS 55th Round Survey (July 1999-June 2000), Working Paper 89, Centre for Development Economics, Delhi School of Economics, Delhi.

Standing, Guy. 1999. "Global Feminization through Flexible Labor: A Theme Revisited", *World Development*, 27(3).

5

On Deepening Poverty of the Masses including Deprived Social Groups in Rural and Urban India under Economic Reforms

UTSA PATNAIK

India is widely projected abroad as a shining success story of economic reforms, an important 'emerging market' for northern goods and services, and an attractive destination for investment – all this in view of the high annual GDP growth rate which has been averaging 6 to 7 per cent, second only to China. This portrayal of a dynamic economy is indeed partially true, and it carries benefits for a small well-to-do minority, but it is entirely misleading as regards the welfare implications for the majority of the population. A high growth rate by itself conveys no information at all either about the composition of this growth or its income distribution effects.

Agriculture and industry, the material productive sectors supporting together over four-fifths of the population, have gone into stagnation or decline as regards their contribution to GDP and to employment growth in the country. There is a severe depression in agriculture in particular for over a decade, marked by falling per head real incomes. Unemployment rates in both rural and urban India have been rising, and average food grains absorption within the country has declined to a historic low comparable to the colonial period, with the brunt of the increased hunger being borne by rural India. For a decade now there is unprecedented agrarian distress manifesting itself in rising farm indebtedness, loss of assets including land, and many thousands of farmer suicides in excess of normal numbers. Official figures and claims of decline in rural poverty, which are also reproduced in World Bank publications, are misleading as they are based on a logically incorrect method of poverty estimation. Correct estimates show poverty to be high and increase in the depth of poverty during the period of economic reforms.

An observer of Indian society and economy today would not be able to avoid a sense of deep unease as a kind of dualism becomes more blatant. On the one hand, there is a visible real estate and share market boom, while on the other hand many thousands of farmers in excess of 'normal' numbers, are committing suicide.[1] Similarly, while on the one hand there is fast burgeoning consumption of more varied high-protein diets and of modern consumer durables and electronic goods by urban middle classes, on the other hand food grains absorption in rural India is today lower than before World War II, and the depth of hunger is growing with declining energy intake for the majority of the population in villages and more recently in towns as well.

The one sector of the economy which has been expanding rapidly is the services sector. While a small segment is high-income Information Technology (IT)-enabled and financial services, but the bulk remains low-income personal and catering services for the benefit of the small minority of rich Indians – a minority which has enjoyed rapid rise in real incomes under reforms. There is also rising income inequality of a very specific and disturbing kind: on the one hand, there is an absolute decline in real incomes for the vast majority of the population, and very rapid rise in real incomes for a small minority, which has fed the real estate and tourism boom, fast growing demand for high-end consumer durables and electronic goods by this minority which is seeking to emulate northern lifestyles; on the other hand, for the majority of the population, it has meant higher unemployment, indebtedness, land and other asset loss and hunger, in short, growing immiserization.

The rapid changes in India's economy and society are the direct outcome of neo-liberal economic policies and trade liberalization. India started implementing reforms and opening up of free trade from 1991, after taking an extended financing facility from the IMF of $5 billion following the temporary difficulties created by the first Gulf War. The sum borrowed was small and soon repaid, but it was the entry point for the international financial institutions' agenda pushing for a complete reversal of the strategy followed up to that date, of Nehruvian *dirigiste* planned development, in which the state had been a major investor, banking had been nationalized, and public sector enterprises had been set up in a range of industries.[2]

The basic question is – why should rapid growth under neo-liberal reforms and trade liberalization, advised by the Bretton Woods institutions and under the WTO discipline, be accompanied by agricultural depression and acute distress in particular regions, and why should there be an adverse impact on food security and poverty? The answer to this question, at one level, is complex but at another level it is quite simple. It can be summarized as follows: the core of neo-liberal reforms, advised by the international financial institutions, is expenditure-deflating policies which are applied in the main to the population in the unorganized sector – the peasantry. These macro-economic deflationary policies lead to rising unemployment and falling incomes. Second, the peasantry is exposed to global demand patterns with trade openness, and the structure of land use starts to change away from crops and towards greater exports for supplying the consumption needs of foreign populations. At the same time, trade openness also means that the peasantry is exposed to the volatility of global prices, which in their downward phase ruin small producers exporting cash crops.

Declining Food Grains Output and Availability under Reforms

A severely adverse impact on our food security, following adoption of greater trade openness in India, was to be expected on the basis of the past and current experience of present-day developing countries and I have been warning of this outcome since 1992. That is indeed what has happened: 8 million hectares of land have been diverted away from food grains production mainly to export crops within a total gross sown area, which is stagnant or

Table 1

Decelerating Growth Rates of Agricultural Output

Period	*Food grains*	*Non-food grains*	*All Crops*	*Population*
1980–81 to 1989–90	2.85	3.77	3.19	2.1
1990–91 to 2000–01	1.66	1.86	1.73	1.9
2000–01 to 2006–07	0.34	n.a	n.a	1.7

Source: Government of India, Ministry of Finance, Economic Survey, 2001–02, p. 189 for first two lines. Last line calculated taking initial 2000–01 and terminal (advance estimate) 2006–07 food grains output figures from Economic Survey 2007–08 (both were near-normal rainfall years). Note that slowing down of output growth is much steeper than slowing down of population growth entailing fast falling per head output.

somewhat declining, and the end-use of grain is also changing with a higher share going as animal feed, industrial use and bio-fuels. Yield rise having slowed down, has not compensated for area decline and the growth rate of food grains output has halved in the 1990s compared to the 1980s and has become about half of one per cent in the years since 2000 (Table 1). Per capita grain output has

Chart 1

Food grains Output and Availability Per Capita in Kilograms per Annum, Triennial Average Centred on Specified Years, 1990–91 to 2004–05

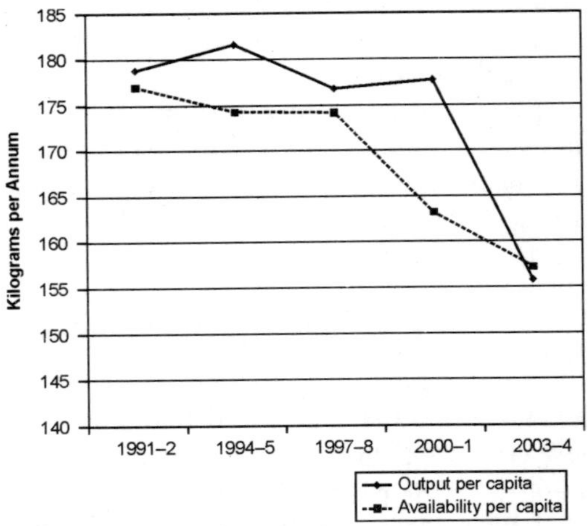

Note: Output is Net Output = 0.87.5 times Gross Output
Availability = Net Output + Net Imports – Net Addition to Public Stocks. Both variables divided by total population for per capita values. Chart updated to 2004–05 from Patnaik (2007b).

been declining more steeply than before and has touched a historic low of 155 kg per head annual average in the triennium ending 2004–05 (Chart 1). This is the same level as 50 years ago during the First Plan, and actually lower than the average during 1937–41 which was 157 kg. Forty years of effort to raise food grains output per capita to a peak of 182 kg, by the early 1990s, have been wiped out in the subsequent dozen years of neo-liberal reforms.

As Chart 1 shows per capita availability fell even faster than did output between 1998 and 2002. The large gap between the two trends reflects the fact that by July 2002 public food grains stocks of 64 million tonnes had built up, 40 million tonnes in excess of the norm of buffer stock for that time of year. The reason was the severe contraction in purchasing power of the mass of the mainly rural population, which we will discuss a little later. At the same time private grain exports also rose. Unlike every previous short episode of per head domestic output decline, which had been always compensated by net imports and drawing down of stocks to maintain domestic availability, this long period was highly abnormal in seeing the opposite – as per head output declined, more stocks built up and more was exported, reducing availability more and more to a historic low.

The Indian government ignored the real reason for the lower absorption which was loss of purchasing power and demand deflation, and wrongly argued that the problem was 'over-production'. It put the blame on allegedly 'too high' minimum support price to farmers which gave 'the wrong signals' leading to a higher output than the market demanded. Instead of putting back purchasing power and food into the hands of the poor, which the situation demanded, it proceeded instead to export 22 million tonnes of grain out of stocks during 2002 and 2003, besides freezing procurement price and reducing public procurement. All these disincentives have led farmers to cut back on food grains output, which became stagnant and hence fell so steeply in per capita terms after 2002, that imports became necessary to meet the minimum needs of the public welfare programmes.

There can be no more deplorable stories of incorrect policies increasing hunger than the Indian government's handling of the food security question in recent years. By its obtuse attack on the viability of farmers and the purchasing power of the masses, it has succeeded in taking India back to near-stagnant grain output and to deepening undernutrition. Specialization in primary products and their export always leads to an attack on the food security of the poor. The ability to raise productivity (crop yields) and so maintain domestic food availability, even with a stronger export thrust, is crucially dependent on more investment in irrigation, high yielding crop varieties and extension services. Far from rising, however, all these suffer actual reduction in the present era of neo-liberal reforms because the core of such reforms is deflation – the reduction in public expenditures advised by the international financial institutions. Public investment in agriculture was already declining in the 1980s but the decline has become steeper in the era of economic reforms after 1991. Plan development expenditures including on irrigation, vital for the primary sector, was nearly 4 per cent of Net National Product in the pre-reform period but halved to 1.9 per cent by 2000–01 and continues to be far below the pre-reform level in 2007–08.

Macro-economic deflationary policies advised by the international financial institutions include reduction in state expenditures, monetary austerity and high real interest rates for producers (but easy consumer credit), reduction in the ratio of budget deficit to GDP, caps on wages aided by labour retrenchment policies, and currency devaluation. All these together add up to a strongly deflationary package which has been implemented by successive Indian governments since 1991 regardless of their political composition. The pattern has been that three years or more of severe contraction, immediately after a general election is followed by two years or less, of more expansionary policies as governments try to regain electoral support eroded by the hardships they have inflicted on the people. The main target of the expenditure-deflating policies has been the unorganized sector and the main segment of this sector has been agriculture.

When public investment rates and public development expenditures in the primary sector are actually declining, there is not the slightest possibility of reconciling an export thrust from farming with maintaining domestic food grains availability. The consumption of the mass of the poor is then sacrificed to meet the demands of the external sector. (A similar outcome is seen in China under its internally-driven market reforms, where export thrust has entailed declining per capita food grains availability for the rural masses from the mid–1990s). Second, the argument is incorrect, although it is regularly put forward by economists even to this day, that specialization in export crops need not lead to greater food insecurity because the increased export earnings can be used to purchase food grains from the global market. The reality is that unit dollar prices of primary products have shown a secular declining trend, with fluctuations, since the 1960s and the current value is about one-third compared to then. A doubling, say, of volume exports, can end up in no increase at all exchange earnings if the unit price halves. Further, with over 80 developing countries competing with each other to export the same crops under Fund-Bank and WTO mandated policies, developing countries find themselves in a competitive "race to the bottom" as far as exchange earnings are concerned. Even if a country does obtain increased exchange earnings, these are most unlikely to be devoted to importing food for the poor since their effective market demand has been reduced by public policy and governments deny that hunger is increasing. There is no foreign exchange constraint in India, but increased exchange earnings are financing imported automobiles and foreign tourism by the well-to-do, not foodgrain imports for the poor.

Even though it was the agrarian crisis which propelled the UPA government to power in the 2004 general elections, the government by immediately notifying the Fiscal Responsibility and Budgetary Management Act, reiterated its commitment to a strongly deflationary fiscal stance as advised by the international financial institutions. Under the Act it is mandatory for the government to reduce the fiscal deficit, and this means further expenditure deflation. From around 6 per cent in 2001 the gross fiscal deficit as per cent of GDP has been reduced to 3.7 per cent by 2007 and further to 2.5 per cent by 2008. The irrational policy of expenditure deflation remains the Vedas and the Upanishads for the government which is firmly in the grip of the global money-lenders. The latter's economic dogmas and deflationary policies are privileged over the question of livelihoods and food security of the poor, whose worsening situation to be addressed effectively, requires exactly the opposite policy of a strongly expansionary fiscal stance. While the National Rural Employment Guarantee Act, 2005 might seem to go against this, it is to be noted that budgetary allocation to this has been paltry, a mere 10 per cent more than was being spent earlier, and this allocation was cut in the 2007 budget even though it was announced that the scheme was to be extended to more districts.[3]

The basic reason for such relentless attacks on employment and mass incomes is that cropping pattern shifts and supply shifts alone will not do the job for the advanced countries wishing to see such specialization on the part of developing countries, for desired supply shifts in modern market economies need corresponding demand shifts to succeed. An essential element of the mechanism is to reduce the purchasing power of the masses, generally the unorganized rural population, so that mass demand for basic necessities, including food grains, reduces to release land resources for growing more export crops and also for the greater diversion of food grains itself towards more commercial and industrial use demanded by the local and foreign well-to-do classes. Under the colonial system where there was direct control, such reduction in purchasing power was directly made through imposing heavy taxes and using a part of taxes to buy up export goods. Under modern conditions where there is no direct control, the same mechanism works through public expenditure deflation.

Thus, the attack comes not only on the supply side reducing output growth through reduced investment, but on mass incomes through expenditure deflation, which sets in motion the reverse multiplier effects of declining development expenditures. Every Rs 100 less of such public spending cuts incomes by a multiple of 4 to 5, that is, by between Rs 400 to Rs 500 (assuming as it is reasonable to do that only one-fifth to one-quarter of every incremental rupee earned is saved and hence three-quarters to four-tenths is spent). Public expenditure deflation has been severe in the primary sector and it is this which is the main cause of not only lowered levels of activity but associated rise in unemployment (including more severe underemployment) and decline in incomes and purchasing

Table 2
Rising Unemployment Rates in India, 1993–94 to 2004

	Males			*Females*		
	Usual status	*Current weekly status*	*Current daily status*	*Usual status*	*Current weekly status*	*Current daily status*
Rural						
2004	24	47	90	22	45	93
1993–94	20	30	56	14	30	56
Urban						
2004	46	57	81	89	90	117
1993–94	45	52	67	83	84	105

Source: Economic Survey 2005–06 (GoI, Ministry of Finance) Table 10.5. Primary source NSS Reports, 50th Round 1993–94 and 60th Round 2004. Unemployment rate is number of persons or person-days unemployed per 1,000 persons or person-days. Data relate to all economic sectors taken together.

power. Table 2 shows that rise in unemployment under every status (daily, weekly and usual) has been much greater in rural compared to urban areas. The NSS consumption expenditure data clearly indicate fall in real spending on both food and clothes in rural India between 1993–94 and 2004–05, and falling energy intake (calorie intake per head per day) in rural India. This lower real spending moreover does not reflect exactly the even greater decline in income since the data also show that in many states net asset change is negative, that is, asset adjustments are being made to maintain even the lowered consumption flow. In short, farmers are selling livestock and land owing to falling incomes and indebtedness.

Substantial Rise in Rural and Urban Poverty

During the reform period, rural poverty has been rising steeply although official figures fail to reflect this owing to the faulty official methodology of estimation. The government having implemented policies under the guidance of the Bretton Woods institutions, which have substantially reduced food security and increased unemployment and hunger, continues to pretend that rural poverty is declining, in the face of a mountain of evidences to the contrary. It is clinging to a fallacious method of estimating poverty, which is no longer based on any nutrition norm and takes the cost of the quantities consumed in 1973–74, over three decades ago, and simply updates it using a price index. The resulting 'poverty lines' by now are gross underestimates of the current cost of living and give corresponding underestimates of the population in poverty. A more detailed critique and the basis for my alternative estimates, is available in my other papers,[4] while here I give a summary of the actual trends in poverty incorporating the results of the latest 61st round consumption expenditure data relating to 2004–05.

The official rural monthly poverty line expenditure for the year 2004–05 is Rs 356 or Rs 11.8 daily, equivalent to 27 US cents at the then prevailing exchange rate. This paltry amount would have bought a single one-litre bottle of mineral water, or at the most 1 kg of the coarsest rice. But it is supposed to cover all expenditure on food, cooking and lighting fuel, clothing, shelter, transport, health and education – in short, all daily spending on goods and services for one person! International agencies like the World Bank have been promoting equally unrealistic poverty lines: the norm of one-dollar-eight-cents-a-day is deflated to the rupee equivalent of less than one-third dollar a day for India for that year, to adjust for purchasing power parity (PPP), and the national poverty percentage of 35.3 is thereby derived.[5]

Just over a dollar a day would hardly be a reasonable poverty line for the USA for it would have bought at most one litre bottle of mineral water there, just as the PPP adjusted one dollar in India, could barely buy a single bottle of water. At this very low daily expenditure level, the nutrition norm of 2,400 kcal energy intake per person obviously could not be accessed in India's villages and the actual energy intake at this level is found to be 1,820 calories. In six individual states in India, less than 1,675 calories could be accessed at the state level official poverty lines (state poverty lines vary according to the presumed differences in the cost of purchasing the same base-year basket of goods).

It is clearly not difficult to 'reduce' poverty when the consumption level, embodied in the poverty line, is lowered to such sub-human levels, for few people actually survive long below these levels – those who are there today are on their way to early death. Neither the government nor the individual academics, following the same faulty estimation method, inform the public that in practice its poverty estimates have been completely de-linked from the nutrition norm and for 1993–94 and 2004–05 corresponded to energy intake levels far below the 2,400 calories recommended by the Indian Council for Medical Research, which has been the conceptual basis of poverty studies since the first estimate in 1973–74.

The main reason the official poverty lines are so low and unable to reflect the actual current cost of accessing the nutrition norm, is because the basket of commodities, hence the quantities consumed in 1973–74 is held unchanged by the Planning Commission and this basket's cost is simply updated with a price index – the Consumer Price Index for Agricultural Labourers. There is no logical defence which can be put forward for assuming an ancient fixed consumption basket when estimating current poverty, since over time the economic environment has changed and consumers face a different set of choices altogether. As the base year of the fixed consumption basket has receded in time, the official poverty line has become cumulatively distant from the true poverty line required for accessing the nutrition norm. By 2004–05, at the all-India level, the rural consumer required Rs 790 per month or over Rs 26.3 per day to access the nutrition norm, which is more

Table 3

Rural Poverty in India, 1973–74 to 2004–05

NSS Round	*28th* *1973–74*	*38th* *1983*	*50th* *1993–94*	*61st* *2004–05*
1. Direct Poverty Line DPL, Rs	56	120	325	795
2. Official Poverty Line OPL, Rs	49.1	89.5	206	356
3. Direct Poverty Ratio DPR, %	72	70	74.5	87
4. Official Poverty Ratio OPR, %	56.4	45.6	37.3	28.3
5. Calorie Intake @ OPL	2200*	2060	1980	1820
6. Deficit of Calorie Intake from norm	–200	–340	–420	–580
7. Ratio of DPL to OPL	1.14	1.34	1.58	2.23

Source: Simplified from Patnaik (2007b). Direct poverty calculated by author from NSS reports for the years specified. Direct Poverty Line is monthly per capita expenditure required for accessing 2,400 calories and Direct Poverty Ratio is the percentage of persons below this. Official Poverty Line: a lower-than-official norm of 2,200 was applied in the base year only to calculate the direct poverty line and for later years this was using the Consumer Price Index for Agricultural Labourers.

than double the official poverty line of Rs 356 per month (below Rs 12 per day). The official estimates and the correct estimates of poverty lines and poverty ratios for the decadal intervals 1973–74 to 2004–05 are juxtaposed in Table 3 to facilitate comparison.

Chart 2

Official and Direct Poverty Lines, 1973–74 to 2004–05, All-India Rural

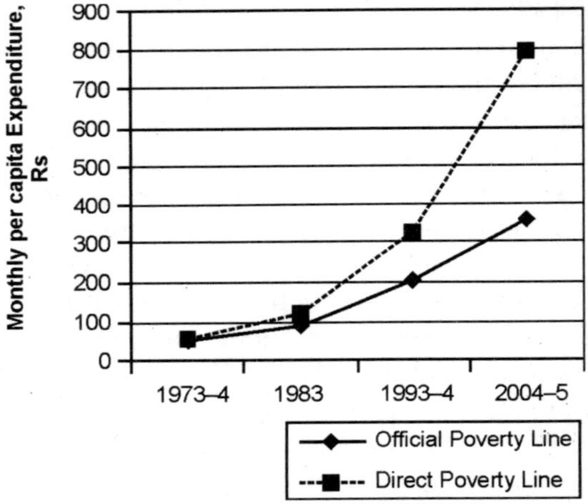

Source: Table 3, lines 1 and 2.

The initial official poverty lines in the 1970s were not too distant from the cost of accessing minimum nutrition, but with six separate episodes of underestimation between 1973–74 and 2004–05, became cumulatively distant from the true poverty lines over time (Chart 2). Accordingly, at the official poverty lines, lower and lower nutrition levels could be accessed over time (Chart 4). Clearly, one cannot make a valid comparison over time when the consumption standard is being lowered, or altered in anyway. The official poverty percentages, obtained by applying the official poverty lines, increasingly ceased to reflect the true situation of change in poverty. They showed 'declining poverty' solely because they corresponded to a progressively lower consumption standard over time (Chart 3). The decline in poverty claimed by the Planning Commission of India and by individual economists following the same method is thus quite spurious and arises from the continuous lowering of the consumption standard inherent in the official estimation method. In reality, poverty has increased, sharply so during the period of economic reforms.

Chart 3

Official and Direct Poverty Percentages Obtained by Applying the Respective Poverty Lines, All-India Rural

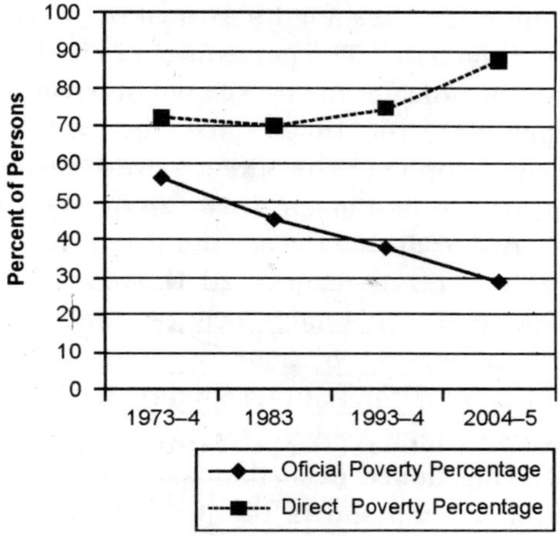

Source: Table 3, lines 3 and 4.

Chart 4

Declining Calories Intake at Official Poverty Lines, 1973–74 to 2004–05

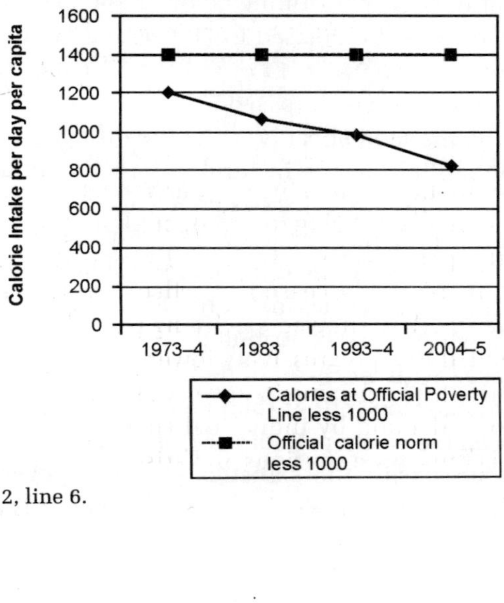

Source: Table 2, line 6.

The correct method is to take the expenditure actually required to access the nutrition norm at each point of time (these direct poverty lines can be easily obtained from the nutrition data in relation to expenditure levels which are also available every five years from the NSS, yielded by the exactly same sample the Planning Commission uses for its estimates, while ignoring the nutrition part of the data). The percentage of all persons spending below these levels indicates the true extent of poverty and these are validly comparable over time since the same consumption standard is being applied. The direct poverty estimates show a slow rise in poverty from the late 1970s up to 1993–94, and then a steeper rise thereafter during the economic reforms period.

Compared to 74.5 per cent of all persons in poverty, that is spending below the Rs 10.8 daily level required for accessing the nutrition norm in 1993–94, by 2004–05 an all-time record high of 87 per cent of the rural population spending below Rs 26.3 per day could not access enough food to reach the norm. Since the norm itself has been questioned even though it is the official one, we have also estimated and shown the proportion of persons below lower calorie intake levels (2,200 and 1,800), and in every case there is a substantial rise of population below these levels by 2004–05, indicating increasing poverty depth. By 2004–05, the proportion of persons consuming below 2,200 calories which cost Rs 19.2 to access, had increased to 70 per cent compared to below 58.5 per cent in 1993–94. In 14 out of the 15 major states in India poverty is found to have increased.[6]

Targeting the food subsidy using the official measures leaves out over 300 million people in rural India who are in reality poor but are not officially recognized as poor. In fact, targeting makes no sense where by now nearly nine-tenths of the rural population is actually in poverty, and targeting the food subsidy since 1998, has amounted in practice to the institutional denial of affordable food to the poor which has contributed to the actual deepening of poverty.[7] Faced with an ocean of deprivation, the government and Planning Commission, rather than facing up to hard reality, seem to have chosen the easier path of performing academically indefensible procedures with the statistics to claim poverty reduction. China's current official rural poverty line, which is also absurdly low at about 800 yuan per year or 2.2 yuan per day (less than a third of one US dollar), is identical to the Indian one, and its estimates of rural poverty are equally gross underestimates.

Substantial Rise in Urban Poverty over the Economic Reforms Period

Urban poverty, directly measured by counting the persons unable to access the official recommended daily allowance (RDA) of energy, also has been rising sharply during the period of economic reforms. A study of the 61st round (2004–05) data in relation to the 50th round (1993–94) with which it is stated to be comparable, inescapably leads to the conclusion that both urban poverty and poverty depth have increased over the decade and this is particularly evident in the states with the large cities – Delhi, Mumbai, Chennai and Kolkata.

Urban poverty has been usually and correctly thought of as being affected strongly by employment and income trends in rural areas. The completely landless poor in rural areas have always been foot-loose migrants, with a large component migrating seasonally to urban areas in search of work. When levels of economic activity are rising in the rural economy as a whole, employment is growing and incomes are buoyant, we would expect much less distress migration of both the landless and the land-operating to occur to urban areas and thus better prospects for urban poverty reduction. However, distress migration of petty peasant producers with owned and operated land, and of artisans, takes place in a situation of rural depression when income from agriculture and other activities falls as has been the case over the last fifteen years.

Table 4 presents the preliminary results of trends worked out for states with the largest urban centres, namely, Maharashtra, Tamil Nadu, West Bengal and Delhi. It is clear that the urban poverty estimates of the Planning Commission, using the indirect method of adjusting the 1973–74 poverty line by a price index, have produced by 2004–05 grossly underestimated 'poverty lines' which do not permit even 1,700 to 1,750 calories energy intake to be accessed by the urban consumer. The official poverty ratios are thereby no longer measuring the numbers and percentage of the poor, but only the poorest of the poor.

Table 4

Direct and Indirect Official Poverty Estimates for Selected States, Urban India, 50th Round, 1993–94 and 61st Round, 2004–05

State	*<2100*	*<2100*	*<1800*	*<1800*
	2004–05	*1993–94*	*2004–05*	*1993–94*
Direct Poverty Estimates				
1. MPCE required for Calorie Intake (Poverty Line, Rs)				
Delhi	1150	445	710	330
Maharashtra	1750	558	885	295
Tamil Nadu	1180	440	680	308
West Bengal	1165	365	515	230
All-India	1000	395	510	253
2. Percentage of Persons in Poverty				
Delhi	57.0	35.0	24.0	19.5
Maharashtra	85.0	52.5	52.0	27.0
Tamil Nadu	70.5	69.0	39.0	42.5
West Bengal	68.5	49.0	21.5	18.0
All-India	64.5	57.0	22.5	25.0
Indirect Official Estimates				
3. Official Poverty Line, Rs	2004–05	1993–04		
Delhi	612.9	n.a.		
Maharashtra	665.9	335		
Tamil Nadu	547.4	300		
West Bengal	449.3	255		
All-India	538.6	285		
4. Official Poverty			5. Calorie Intake at OPL	
Percentage	2004–05	1993–94	2004–05	1993–94
Delhi	15.2	n.a.	1710	n.a.
Maharashtra	29.0	35.0	1725	1865
Tamil Nadu	22.2	39.9	1685	1785
West Bengal	14.8	23.0	1735	1850
All-India	25.7	33.2	1835	1885

The reasons for the inability of official price indices to capture the actual rise in the cost of living have been extensively discussed in the literature. The long-term reasons are connected with increasing monetization of the economy and loss of common property resources, while the more recent reasons since economic reforms began arise from unemployment and loss of incomes, combined with sharply rising costs of utilities and health care, which forces reduction in real food expenditure for large segments of the urban population.

What the direct estimates show is that in order to access the RDA of energy (which is a modest one, only 2,100 calories daily per capita) the urban consumer needed to spend Rs 1,000 per month or nearly double the officially stipulated poverty line of Rs 539, and there has been a steep rise in the percentage of persons unable to access the RDA, during 1993–94 to 2004–05. The percentage in urban poverty has gone up from 57 to 64 at the all-India level but in the major states with the large urban conurbations, the extent of rise has been generally more except in Tamil Nadu. In Maharashtra, the percentage of all urban persons in poverty has risen steeply from 52.5 to 85, in Delhi from 35 to 57, in West Bengal from 49 to 68.5 with Tamil Nadu registering the smallest rise from already high poverty level of 69 in the earlier year. While Tamil Nadu had the highest urban poverty among these states in 1993–94, this is no longer the case by 2004–05 since Maharashtra has outstripped it while West Bengal has acquired the dubious distinction of coming very close to it.

The picture of substantial urban poverty rise during the period of economic reforms should not surprise us when we remember that the urban employment situation has deteriorated over the period and the increasing privatization of utilities and of health care has raised non-food costs substantially. Given stagnant total real expenditure, the real expenditure on food has fallen substantially even for poorer spending classes. The Consumer Price Index for Industrial Workers, as well as that for Urban Non-Manual Employees, have been used as deflators to compare the 61st round expenditure with the 50th round. The two indices move almost in tandem and there is virtually no difference in results.

There has been a substantial decline in real expenditure on food for all expenditure groups including the poorest spending classes who can ill afford it, with the overall average in urban India dropping by 12 per cent, during 1993–94 to 2004–05. Real expenditure on clothes in urban India has fallen as well. The main reason is the increased cost of medicine and health care, utilities like water, power and transport, which leaves less for spending on the other basic necessities when income is stagnant or even declining.

It is an alarming scenario indeed when 60 to 80 per cent of the urban population in states containing the major metros, including the national capital, cannot access even 2,100 calories of energy and spend enough to maintain already very low food and cloth consumption. The present policy thrust towards undermining the supply of public goods, the privatization of utilities and the increasingly higher cost of health care and medicines is going to worsen the situation if the trend is allowed to continue unchecked. Unfortunately, those who are in the Planning Commission and those who run the government are deluding themselves into believing that urban poverty is low and declining while precisely the opposite is the case – urban poverty is high and rising. Especially alarming is the situation in Maharashtra where poverty depth has risen fast with over half the population unable to access even 1,800 calories intake compared to around one-quarter in that situation a decade ago. Poverty depth has also risen in all other states studied here except Tamil Nadu, which had the highest initial poverty depth but has marginally reduced it.

Above Average Rise in Urban Poverty among Deprived Social Groups

While the average picture of poverty rise is bad enough, the position of Scheduled Castes (SCs) and Scheduled Tribes (STs), as always, is much worse than the average. As Table 5 clearly brings out, while in rural areas the ST population was worse off than the SC population at both dates, the converse was the case in urban areas where the SC population appears to be worse off than the ST population. The incidence of poverty and poverty depth was significantly higher among both social groups compared to the general population at both dates, and there has been substantial rise in poverty and increase in poverty depth among deprived social groups.

Table 5
Poverty among SC and ST Populations, 1993–94 and 2004–05

Calorie Intake	*<2200*	*<2200*	*<1800*	*<1800*
	1993–94	*2004–05*	*1993–94*	*2004–05*
RURAL				
Percentage of persons with intake below specified level				
1. ST	73.5	82.5	30.0	44.0
2. SC	70.5	79.0	27.0	33.0
3. General	58.5	69.5	20.0	25.0
URBAN				
Percentage of persons with intake below specified level	<2100	<2100	<1800	<1800
	1993–94	2004–05	1993–94	2004–05
1. ST	67.5	81.0	33.0	61.5
2. SC	75.0	87.5	39.5	66.5
3. General	57.0	64.5	25.0	22.5

Source: Calculated from using data from NSS reports 402,405,422 for 50th round 1993–94 and reports 508,513,514 for 61st round, 2004–05.

As regards higher than average incidence of poverty among deprived social groups, while seven-tenths of the general population in rural India could not access even 2,200 calories per day by 2004–05, the incidence was 79 per cent for SC population and 82.5 per cent for ST population. While 64.5 per cent of the general population could not access even 2,100 calories per day in urban India, the incidence was 87.5 per cent for SC population and 81 per cent for the ST population. Particularly shocking is the very sharp deepening of poverty among deprived groups in urban India whereas among the general population it actually shows a slight decline. Thus, the percentage of ST population unable to access even 1,800 calories rose from one-third to 61.5 per cent, while the corresponding rise for the SC population was from about two-fifths to 66.5 per cent.

The undermining of the public distribution system over the last decade, and the misconceived 'targeting' of the population where only those officially designated as 'below poverty line' are given access to affordable food grains, has undoubtedly contributed to the observed deepening of poverty among the deprived social groups. As argued here, since the Planning

Commission estimates of general poverty themselves are gross underestimates and the claim of poverty decline is false, the understanding which informs policy making at the highest level is incorrect. The entire policy thrust at the central level has been in the direction of undermining food security and increasing poverty. It is recognized by every state government by now that the estimates of BPL population are incorrect, that food grain allocations from the central pool to the states are inadequate, and that a large proportion of the poor have been excluded from the public distribution system. Only an immediate going back to a universal distribution system, combined with increased procurement and a level of issue prices which are affordable for the poor, can reverse the present situation of worsening nutrition and increasing poverty depth.

Notes

1. K. Nagaraj (2008) provides the most systematic analysis of suicide rates and their regional incidence using police records.
2. See P. Patnaik and C.P. Chandrasekhar (1995).
3. Only Rs 10,900 crore, one-tenth more than already spent under various preceding employment generation programmes which the NREGP replaced, was the allocated sum for the programme in the 2006 budget and this was cut to Rs 10,000 crore in February 2007.
4. Patnaik (2007b).
5. See World Development Report, 2006, Table A1 on p. 278, cols. 9 & 10. The Bank's global poverty line is based on the unrealistically low national poverty lines of developing countries derived from the median value of the poorest 10 countries' rural poverty lines, and this happens to be India.
6. See Patnaik (2007b) for a detailed discussion.
7. See Swaminathan (2002).

References

Nagaraj, K. 2008. *Farmers' Suicides in India: Magnitude, Trends and Spatial Patterns,* Chennai: Madras Institute of Development Studies, available on www.macroscan.org

National Sample Survey Organisation. (Available on www.mospi.nic.in)

Report No. 401. Key Results on Household Consumer Expenditure, 1993–94.

Report No. 402. Level and Pattern of Consumer Expenditure, 1993–94.

Report No. 405. Nutritional Intake in India, 1993–94.

Report No. 457. Level and Pattern of Consumer Expenditure in India, 1999–2000.

Report No. 471. Nutritional Intake in India, 1999–2000.

Report No. 497. Income, Expenditure and Productive Assets of Farmer Households, 2003.

Report No. 508. Level and Pattern of Consumer Expenditure, 2004–05.

Report No. 513. Nutritional Intake in India, 2004–05.

Patnaik, P. and C.P. Chandrasekhar. 1995. "The Indian Economy under Structural Adjustment", *Economic and Political Weekly,* November 25.

Patnaik, U. 1996. "Export-Oriented Agriculture and Food Security in Developing Countries and India", *Economic and Political Weekly,* 31(35–37), Sp. No., reprinted in *The Long Transition: Essays on Political Economy*, Delhi: Tulika.

——. 2003a. "On the Inverse Relation between Primary Exports and Domestic Food Absorption under Liberalized Trade Regimes", in J. Ghosh and C.P. Chandrasekhar (eds.), *Work and Welfare in the Age of Finance,* Delhi: Tulika.

——. 2003b. Global Capitalism, Deflation and Agrarian Crisis in Developing Countries, Social Policy and Development Programme, Paper No. 13, United Nations Research Institute for Social Development (UNRISD), October.

——. 2007a. *The Republic of Hunger and Other Essays,* Delhi: Three Essays Collective.

——. 2007b. "Neo-Liberalism and Rural Poverty in India", *Economic and Political Weekly*, July 28-August 3.

Swaminathan, M. 2002. "Excluding the Needy: The Public Provisioning of Food in India", *Social Scientist,* 30(3–4), March-April.

World Bank. 2006. World Development Report, New York: World Bank and Oxford University Press.

Part III
Culture and Religion

6

Globalization, Mass Media and Proliferating 'Gurus'

The Changing Texture of Religion in Contemporary India

SURYA PRAKASH UPADHYAY AND ROWENA ROBINSON

'The changing texture of religion' is considered to be an important part of the structural transformations in contemporary India and one worthy of closer analysis. While the mass media and the new forms of communicative technologies facilitated by globalization appear to have transformed almost all religions (if not 'religion' *per se*!), South Asian religions (like those elsewhere) have always been changing. What *is* new is that the nature of religious change itself may be changing (Babb and Wadley, 1995: 1). In this paper we will be focusing in particular on Hinduism and on contemporary Hindu gurus.

As we know, theorists of modernity had written off religion in the 1950s and 1960s (see Lerner, 1962; Eisenstadt, 1966; Inkeles and Smith, 1974). It had appeared to them to be, like other so-called 'primordial' identities, on the wane. In the modern world, it had been argued, if religion persisted at all, it would confine itself to the realm of the private. The public apparition of religion that rose in many developing and developed countries, long after modernization's last whistle, was something later theorists had to contend with (Das, 1990; Appadurai, 1997; Sacks, 1991). It is now accepted, if a little late in the day, that ethnic and religious identities rarely disappear with modernity. Rather, modernity refashions religious identities in various ways and, in fact, can lead to a resurgence of faith under particular conditions.

The last decade or so of globalization resurrected all the old debates of modernization (Appadurai, 1997; Singh, 2000). In a global economy and culture, would the world be likely to end up looking more and more similar? Will the modernist dream of one world, one market and one culture ever materialize? Or, as seems far more likely, does globalization promote particularistic identities of various kinds, enabling them to be projected onto a much larger map facilitated by modern communication technologies? The trajectory of development has shifted enormously, and religion, as Robinson (2005) has argued elsewhere, is playing a much more important role than has been imagined. That is why, most scholars have now began acknowledging that religion will have to be taken seriously even by those engaged in issues of development and structural change, for its implications spread far and wide.

Globalization is clearly implicated in this process. However, as we shall argue, some of the crucial elements in the creation of the new public Hinduism in India – and particularly in the role of mass media such as television – emerged in the period before the onset of globalization or liberalization. As such, there is no linear development from globalization to mass media and thence to the proliferation of gurus in contemporary India. Rather, the processes are far more complex and interwoven. On the other hand, they are not unconnected. Their simultaneity at a period of time is not purely accidental; clearly, globalization fed off and then fed into the new contemporary Hinduism. In this paper, we shall use the case of Asaram Bapu to analyse the place of television channels, in particular, in changing the ways in which Hinduism is experienced, shaped and spoken about in the public realm.

Television: The Afterlife of the Screening of the *Ramayana*

It was really television in the late 1980s that can be said to have marked the beginning of the transformation of the texture of modern Hinduism. In fact, if there is one occurrence that is to be held responsible for making the public representation of Hinduism legitimate in contemporary India, it would have to be the serialization of a Hindu epic *Ramayana* on national television starting in January 1987. These were the days before globalization, arrival of the Internet and before the proliferation of television channels, when one government-controlled channel – Doordarshan – held sway over the entertainment habits of a whole nation.

The broadcast of the *Ramayana* in serial form across the country suddenly made Hindu gods, symbols and values and beliefs available, accessible and legitimate. Where there had once been a veil over the public discussion of religion itself, now Hinduism was out there in the public space. While it was in politics that the slogan "Garv se kaho hum Hindu hain" was coined, the naturalness of the pride of being religiously and culturally Hindu actually seeped into popular imagination more slowly (and perhaps more enduringly) through the regular telecast of the epics and, in particular, the *Ramayana*.

Further, and even more pertinently, the *Ramayana* lent itself readily to nationalist interpretation. Ramanand Sagar's epic collapsed nation and Hindu civilization by recasting the tale as a parable of modern times. The epic became a metaphor about the Indian nation-state, projected into the ancient past. It conveyed the sense of a Hindu civilization which could be made ready for the modern age, if only the demon politicians could be dealt with. As Rajagopal (2001) points out, the introduction of Hindu epics on national television and the spread of the media itself can be linked in myriad ways to transformation in both Indian politics and the Indian economy. These changes include the dramatic rise of the fortunes of the Bharatiya Janata Party (BJP) and the spread of liberalization. The forces of the market and the media played a significant role in changing the character and texture of modern Hinduism and, in particular, forging its political *avatar*.[1]

The political life of Hinduism in the last two decades can hardly be separated from any discussion of the character of Hindu practices in contemporary India. Several scholars have pointed to this intertwining. There are a whole host of new elements in the realm of popular religion today that may have insidious and intricate linkages with right-wing Hindu politics (Robinson, 2004; see also Panikkar, 1999; Rajagopal, 2001).[2] There are also clear linkages of such trends with a liberalizing economy; these shall be explored further.

In this paper, however, the political trajectory of contemporary Hinduism will not be the main focus. The consequences of the transformation in modern Hinduism are complex and varied; all the strands cannot be tightly tied up. While there are overlaps, there are also probable divergences. What is clear is that the space of Hinduism has expanded, even while there are strong forces trying to drive it into a narrow, specific mould. In the language of economics, there is a market for Hinduism and also an increasing degree of choice in what is available on this market. It is within this context, in fact, that one may have to look at the proliferation of 'gurus' and the ways in which people embrace them or alter their allegiances.

What the televised *Ramayana* did, fundamentally, was to bring *darshan*, for the first time, into one's drawing room. There were instances of people taking off their footwear before sitting before the television. Watching the serial was treated as a form of devotion and, certainly, streets cleared and shops virtually shut down while the serial was in progress. Silence was maintained and people prostrated before the television. Whole families and often neighbours watched the serial together; in any case, television in India was at the time rarely an individual experience. A sense of the collective, a moral community, otherwise unusual within Hindu worship, was created; indeed, it was a collective that in the end merged with the nation itself. This was not entertainment; it was a religious experience for all, a form of socialization for the children and a solace for the elderly. It was a ritual, worship, and *puja* itself. When technology developed further, the elements already available till this point received a further boost.

Marketing Religion

It is clear that the new technologies have enabled the consummate marketing of religion. From television to audio- and video-cassettes and thence to VCDs and DVDs, the processes of globalization and liberalization have changed the whole experience of religion. Religious discourses and performances are now repeatable and reproducible, easily and everywhere. Faith is now readily packaged and marketed without difficulty. It is available off the shelves, is movable, technologically up-to-date and, indeed has fun. The packaging of faith has played a major role in making Hinduism pleasing in modern times. Audio- and video-cassettes, hip music albums, packaged rituals, workshops on meditation – religion is now available in easily digestible forms and clean and sanitized shortcuts. The Internet has made it possible to have virtual *darshan* and make offerings at major temples without enduring the heat and dust of actual travel.

There is a complexity to this profusion of religion available today. On the one hand, one has the increasing claims of affirmation of tradition by science. Advertisements for ayurvedic cosmetic or medical products stress their 'naturalness' and 'scientifically-proved' benefits. The concept of *kundalini*, the benefits of yoga or the ideas of *vaastu shastra* are all shown to adhere to *scientifically* valid notions of truth. The gesture constitutes a valorization of science and a privileging of tradition in the same moment. The deeply problematic nature and consequences of this attitude to science emerge in debates centring around the country's science policies (see Parthasarathy and Robinson, 2001).

There is, however, also another side to this religious profusion: increasing credulity and dependence on the supernatural and mystical. One might recollect the avidity with which modern Indians – resident and non-resident in India – came to believe in the miracle of the milk-drinking Ganesha some years ago. The dependence on cults and the manipulation of the divine often for materialistic ends signals a frantic need to latch onto certainties in the face of the destabilizing pulls of global change. Both trends feed off cultural patterns globally available: the increased curiosity of Westerners in alternative medicine, alternative science and alternative lifestyles and the interest in looking at these 'indigenous practices' more scientifically. At the end of this paper, we will try to understand some of the patterns emerging out of this profusion, indeed, as it sometimes appears, confusion!

Tele-gurus: The Case of Asaram Bapu

The term 'tele-guru' may be coined to refer to those religious and spiritual leaders whose visibility became more prominent with the telecast of their religious discourses through satellite and cable television networks. This technology enables such gurus to spread their influence across the country and even the globe. Today, there are religious discourses, referred to as *satsang* shown by mainstream entertainment channels such as Sony or Zee TV. However, there are also several channels devoted to the full-time telecast of religious discourses by spiritual gurus and teachers. Asaram Bapu was one of the early entrants on this medium. Bapu is said to have been born in 1941 in the Sindh region and spent his childhood in the village Berani in Nawab district of what is now Pakistan.

Bapu's was an affluent family. His father Seth Thaumal Sirumalani was a merchant and his mother Mangiba was a pious and religious lady. However, after partition, his family migrated to India and took refuge in Ahmedabad, where his father started in business. As is usually the case, signs of Asaram's future greatness were visible from the very outset. It is said that after his birth (his name was then Asamul), his father's business flourished and his family condition improved immensely. At the age of eleven, however, Asamul's father died and his brother became his guardian. Life became difficult. He started working in Siddhapur and maintained a daily ritual of prayer as well as spiritual striving. Various miracles came to be attributed to his interventions. After three years, Asamul returned to Ahmedabad to an austere life full of devotion. His family forced him to get married to Lakshmi Devi.

He learned Sanskrit in order to read the Vedas and other Hindu scriptures. He left home in search of the truth and went to the Himalayas. There he came under the influence of the guru Lilashah in Nainital. Lilashah tested his devotion for nearly seventy days. He then advised him to fulfil his duties as a householder. Asaram left Nainital and went to meditate on the banks of the river Narmada. He undertook the *anusthan* sacrifice for forty days.[3] One day his mother and wife came to his ashram to take him back to return home. He said that he had not completed the *anusthan* and so could not go with them. His wife and mother waited till the completion of the *anusthan*. While on the way to Ahmedabad with his wife and mother, he got off the train and came to Bombay. There, he met his guru Lilashah again. Lilashah was touched by Asaram's devotion and blessed him with the gift of self-realization.

Guru Lilashah ordered Asaram Bapu to live as a householder and start giving sermons to people. He reached Disa and settled temporarily there. There, it is said, he gave life to a dead cow and from then on people started believing in him as a *siddhapurusa*.[4] Bapu went again into the forest to meditate. When he emerged out of meditation, he felt hungry. He decided that he would not search out food; the God would bring it to him. Instantly, two farmers came with food. They urged him to come to their village and show them the path of righteousness. However, he took the food and left from there. After that, he settled down on the banks of the river Sabarmati in Ahmedabad and began preaching.

Bapu settled at his small cottage in a forest area in Ahmedabad in 1972. In the beginning, people from all walks of life would gather around the guru. There was no permanent group of people living with him in the ashram. In fact, until the mid-1970s, there were only two or three people who were living permanently in his ashram. The visitors to the ashram were largely Sindhis, among whom he slowly became popular. Usually, people came to know about him through their personal contacts. Those who could not come for *satsang* regularly started recording his sermons for their personal use.

In the beginning, Bapu used to deliver *satsang* on select days in the week. People started recording sermons only after 1975. The initiative of recording the *satsang* was taken by one of Bapu's followers. The first audio-cassette was recorded in January 1976. This was done on a simple two-in-one recording system. The voice was recorded on compact cassette. These cassettes were sold by the followers at the ashram. The practice of recording was carried on until 1980. Till the early 1980s, there was no one with any expertise in these activities in the organization. Bapu himself had not realized the importance of the technology. Gradually, Bapu's popularity among the Gujaratis grew and the number of people coming to the ashram and attending *satsang* increased. The ashram expanded and the number of permanent residents also increased. A new interest grew in the recordings of Bapu's sermons and discourses. The first public audio-cassette brought out by the ashram was called *Mai Kaun Hoon?* (Who am I?) in 1981. Before that the recordings had not been titled.

In the early 1990s Bapu's following began to grow. During the Ujjain Kumbh festival in April 1992, he delivered *satsang* for a month. Almost all the local newspapers published articles on his growing popularity. Nevertheless, the sphere of his influence enlarged once his *satsang* and preaching began to be aired on various television channels. In 1994, his sermons began to be broadcast on ATN channel. Later, when ATN TV merged with Zee TV, the latter started telecasting Bapu's morning sermons. This was later picked up by Sony TV. Sony TV expanded Bapu's audience greatly.

A year ago, religious and spiritual channels contributed to only around 1 per cent of total television viewership. In 2007, it had gone up to 2.8 per cent. Interestingly, it has almost started to match the viewership for music channels, which stands at around 2 to 2.5 per cent. It is these television channels that make it possible for the gurus to reach out to the public and in return these channels earn through advertisements at the start and the end of each telecast. There is an economic relationship here as well. To attract the growing number of viewers, religious channels are said to give prominent gurus such as Asaram Bapu or Swami Ramdev free airtime. In fact, during a general *satsang* in Ahmedabad, Asaram announced that these TV channels have paid Rs 1.75 million to the ashram for telecast of the *satsang*.

In the early days, the followers did not even have a photograph of their guru. Then, one of the devotees brought a video camera from abroad and started recording sessions at the ashram. After around 1983, VHS cassettes were produced, though the cost remained high. Even so, the production of these audio/video cassettes helped people to organize video *satsang* at public gatherings at different places. Since 2001, the ashram has started using very sophisticated and highly advanced recording equipment. With the advent of digital technology and high-speed recording systems, the ashram has started producing CDs and DVDs. Since the advancement in media technology has made these processes cheaper, it has also become possible for individuals to purchase their own copies of the sermons. The ashram now has almost 13,500 hours of recorded sermons. Besides, old audio/video cassettes have also been digitalized.

Since its inception, the ashram had brought out a bimonthly magazine in the Sindhi language named *Darvesh Darshan*. Until the 1980s, the ashram had published only a few booklets. It started publishing its magazine *Rishi Prasad* much later in July 1990. It was in Gujarati and was a bimonthly. Its Hindi version was started a year later, i.e., in July–August 1991. Now, the ashram brings it out in six languages: Gujarati, Hindi, Marathi, Oriya, Telugu and English. Along with the magazine, the ashram also brings out the edited version of its *satsang* programmes. It also started a monthly newsletter called *Lok Kalyan Setu* in July 1997.

A website has also been launched by the ashram, which is managed/updated by his followers from New Jersey in the US. The website has material on Bapu's life and activities held in the ashram. One can read the monthly magazine and listen to the *satsang* by registering online. Besides, various products of the ashram can also be purchased. Bapu also initiates people into his fold through the use of new technologies like web-casting. During Guru Purnima in 2006, the technology was employed to give *diksha* (initiation) to people in the United States.

Several booklets released by the Bapu's organization place him in the category of highly revered saints and seers such as Sankaracharya, Tulsidas, Raidas, Kabirdas, Guru Nanak, Ramakrishna Paramhansa and Vivekananda. Bapu himself practices Sanatan Dharma. His spiritual knowledge and enlightenment are not based on sudden mystical or esoteric experiences; rather they are, for the most part, attained through systematic striving and the blessing of his guru. Ecstasy or miracles are not part of his charismatic attraction. He does not claim to be God incarnate. Unlike other contemporary saints such as Satya Sai Baba or Mata Amritanandamayi, Bapu is a householder; he has a wife and children.[5] He is a 'man-in-the-world' and a 'man-outside-the-world' at the same time. "It is the ideal of his life to 'live in the world' but to do so in the light of the renouncer's philosophy" (Madan, 2001: 3). Bapu makes no direct intervention in the lives of his followers, though they believe that he does intercede in hidden and mysterious ways.

Bapu is not associated with any particular temple or pilgrimage. He is not deeply engaged in social reform or social service activities. He is also not strictly part of the bhakti tradition, which stresses the singing or recitation of *bhajans* and the emotional immersion in the divine. Rather, he is more closely associated with the dissemination of religious values and traditions in a lucid style. He describes everyday life experiences in religious terms. People are attracted by Bapu's simplicity of speech. The new media have also given an impetus to the process of dissemination of religious discourses followed by Bapu.

Satsang is a generic term that is heterogenous and includes several religious expressions. It is used for religious discourse, a way of devotion through singing *bhajans* and *kirtans*, a meritorious and auspicious act, a proselytizing mode or even listening to cassettes and watching religious videos. It includes aspects of interpersonal behaviour, ethics of profession and life, family values, morals, meditative techniques, esoteric knowledge, simplified *kathas* or the understanding of the scriptures. This movement moves through discourses rather than in the poetic manner of a Kabir, a Nanak or a Tukaram. Listening to the *satsang* has become part of the daily routine of devotees; it may even replace other rituals.

The Changing Texture of Hinduism

It is time now to turn our attention to the ways in which these shifts are altering the experience of religion, particularly Hinduism. Hinduism has been constantly changing; each age has seen its breakaway movements and also its cults, gurus and saints. Over time, many such movements seem to reproduce sameness rather than speak of something new. Nevertheless, each age also produces something novel, even if that novelty is not completely split from received traditions.

Clearly, the case of Asaram Bapu is instructive from many perspectives. First, it shows us that the media and globalization may have played an important role in expanding the domain of a contemporary guru, but this happens in stages and, often, with the gurus who are already in this business prior to the media explosion. Again, the televised *satsang* brings the guru into the home of the devotee, as with the telecast of the *Ramayana* one could have Lord's *darshan* in his/her drawing room. One may even take *diksha* from his/her home. Spatial distance is now reduced; the guru is brought closer to his followers without their physically visiting his ashram. The audience for the guru is potentially a global one. Several gurus had an international presence even before travel became less expensive and the media and the Internet made it virtually unnecessary. Nevertheless, the Internet, video conferencing, web-casting and the like have an unmatched capacity to allow the guru to enter into thousands of people's lives across the globe – both simultaneously and separately.

Asaram Bapu's organization produces a range of products apart from those related to the dissemination of his sermons. There are herbal medicinal products, a range of prayer materials (*puja samagri*) and other items. The market of religious goods has thus expanded considerably. The new pride in Hinduism, an extension, as has been said before, of many processes, also feeds this market-ability. The development of a moral community is also aided. Small or large groups hear the *satsang* together. Devotees greet each other by saying "Hari Om".

As with the serial *Ramayana*, the televised *satsang* is understood and treated as a form of worship. It may be viewed home or in a public place with a bigger group. One such group was formed in Mumbai, where a few devotees gathered together on Sunday mornings to watch Bapu's videos. After Bapu visited Mumbai in the early 1990s, the number of people coming to the group sessions increased. At present, around a hundred and fifty people come to *satsang* which includes *sandhya*, a few *kirtans* and the telecast of Bapu's teachings. Then, *Sri Asaramayan* is sung and *prasad* distributed. After this, the devotees disperse.

Devotion to Asaram Bapu and listening to his *satsang* can transform the nature of daily religious practice in the home as well. A devotee of Bapu in Lucknow described their daily routine in the following way:

> I did not believe in any Babas or gurus. I rarely visited the temple and believed that worship and prayer are not for show. I hated such people. I had the view that you get nothing from these Babas. We are both running a small company and always keep very busy with our work.

Probably, it was Saturday or Sunday. I do not remember exactly, but it was a holiday. We had had some losses in our business and we had to pay money to the bank. I was a little anxious because of that and I got up a little early. I prepared tea and started browsing channels on TV. What I saw on Sony channel, was totally new to me. I stopped browsing channels and listened to it. There was a man clad in white, just looking like a *rishi-muni*, and talking about the ill-effects of tea. I concentrated on that but I was feeling a bit relaxed at the end of the programme. It was Bapuji on TV. After that, I always tried to get up early to catch that programme. I told my wife about the *satsang* of Bapuji on Sony TV.

We both liked his sermons and the way he removed our suspicion about Babas was really indescribable. We regularized our daily routine and both of us stopped tea. We decided that we must go and visit this guruji but nobody from our group was able to tell us anything about him. However, in April 1997, Bapuji came down to Lucknow for the first time. There were big hoardings and banners everywhere in the city, featuring Bapuji and information about the schedule. So we decided to go and attend the *satsang*. When we reached there, the whole ground was jam-packed with men and women sitting in two separate blocks.

We listen to the *satsang* and did not realize how time passed. That day I was convinced that we must be initiated by a guru in order to be rid of the vicious cycles of birth and death. So, I started thinking about a guru. I did not know till then that Bapuji also gives *diksha*. We came back and decided to go again on the next day. On the second day, Bapu announced that whosoever wants to get *diksha* should purchase a bag. I rushed and bought two bags that contained a book, a *mala*, a *gomukhi* (a little pouch in which *mala* is kept), one copy of Sri Asaramayan, a small blanket to sit on, and a framed photograph of Bapuji. Bapuji described about the importance of *diksha* and the kinds of preparation necessary before getting initiated.

Since then, we both watch morning *satsang* that comes on Sony TV. We have stopped watching movies and other programmes. We have even stopped listening to film music. Now, we bring only Bapuji's *satsang* cassettes. We have kept a music system in our office and we usually play any *satsang* cassette while doing our work. We listen to *satsang* while on the way to the office or elsewhere. It is so fruitful that we need not go to any Baba or temple. Whenever we encounter any kind of problem, we just

> pray to Bapuji to resolve it and the solution comes to us while listening to or viewing the *satsang*. Sometimes it appears that Bapuji is directly guiding me.

As with all such programmes, the telecasts present the guru in frontal position, usually seated directly in front of the viewer and gazing directly at him or her. Each viewer feels that the guru is looking directly at him or her and speaking directly to him or her. Each viewer also feels a sense of unity and attachment with the guru. The narrative above shows the impact of such *darshan*. This couple has given up tea and the watching of entertainment television. A reform has come about in their daily routine. 'Tele-guru' Asaram Bapu has transformed the religious practices of people. They change their everyday lives and habits, they recite his prayers and worship items. They feel directly guided by him in their everyday lives and problems.

Thus, through the telecast of *satsang* on TV, the boundary between the public and private forms of religious practice melts. It is largely the media that has been instrumental in producing this homogeneity. As discussed earlier, people often purchased video-cassettes and organized *satsangs* locally. One such case comes from Mumbai, where a group of people started 'video *satsang*' in 1987. Every Sunday, a group of Bapu's followers gathered in the precincts of a local temple to view the *satsang* on a television donated by one of the devotees. At that time, Bapu had no ashram in Mumbai and just a few followers. As the old devotee said:

> We still keep (the television in) the same place we used to keep it earlier. We were only five people who started this video *satsang*. The selection of the temple for organizing video *satsang* was made on purpose. We wanted to spread the good messages of Bapu to the people. Also, it was inconvenient for us to do it at home. There are intermittent distractions and you cannot listen to *satsang* consciously. Also, people come to this temple in large numbers on Sunday. So, we decided to organize *satsang* at this place. When people saw this, they were startled and gradually it became so well known that people from other localities started coming. In the beginning, it was a little problematic for us, as the priest of the temple started opposing this act but we got a lot of support from people and we requested the priest either to leave the temple or not interfere in this religious programme. Later that

> priest himself became a follower of Bapu. This is the magic of our Bapuji. At the same time, *Ramayana* had started on TV, so we brought a little shift in our timings. During those days, very few people were interested in taking *diksha* from Bapu. Gradually people got interested and they started inquiring about the way to get initiated by Bapuji. It took around 5–6 years to bring Bapuji to Mumbai. Though Bapuji used to come to Mumbai for *satsang*, those gatherings were usually organized at someone's place and the halls were not big so that we could go and sit there. But when we called Bapuji to give a *satsang* in 1992–93, it was a great event. We were not expecting such a gathering. It was a three-day *satsang* programme. In the evening of the second day, Bapuji announced that he would give *diksha* and, you will not believe, thousands of people got initiated on that day.
>
> Now in this temple more than 150 people sit together and listen to Bapuji's *satsang*. We organize everything as it is done in the ashram. We do our *sandhya* together. After that we perform a few *kirtans* and then we show a *satsang* programme. After that we sing Sri Asaramayan and distribute *prasad* and then we disperse.

The public and congregational habits of worship and of listening collectively to the *satsang* gradually appear to phase out and even replace private and domestic practices. The Sunday routine at a temple, reminiscent, if not imitative, of Christian congregational worship, collapses the distance between the Mumbai locality and the Ahmedabad ashram and Bapu and his distant followers and re-constructs the temple as a place of prayer, discourse and religious participation that is collective in nature.

Conclusion

Asaram Bapu's discourse relates to self-realization, freedom from this-worldly concerns and the vicious cycle of births and deaths. He has adapted the Vedantic philosophy about the ultimate truth to apply to daily life. In his philosophy it is observable that the age-old paths that were prevalent in classical Hinduism such as *Bhakti marga, karma marga* and *jnana marga* all run simultaneously. Bapu does not hold to any particular path but talks about freedom and individual inclination to approach the Brahman.

On the whole, the age of the 'tele-guru' has led to some degree of systematization of beliefs. For a large part, the audiences of these channels and often the devotees of these cults are urban-based.

Even if this is not the case, the images and the elements of everyday life that emerge in the discourses of 'tele-gurus' are for the large part urban in character. Certainly, there is a stress on living in the world. Renunciation is not put forward as the only path to self-realization or spiritual liberation (see Appendix to this paper). There is an acceptance of the materiality of the modern world, even while devotees are cautioned on how to negotiate these and how to ensure that one is not ensnared by them.

While there seems to be, on the one hand, profusion – several gurus, individual choice, many channels, different movements or cults – there is also, on the other hand, a process of streamlining. There is a movement towards a greater degree of abstraction and an implicit, and sometimes explicit, trend towards the formal, more highly philosophical ideas of the great tradition. It may appear that great and little traditions merge; what is really happening is a sidelining of the messy, chaotic, colourful and ritualistic little tradition. The aspect of interest is not so much that the messy contours of everyday life are embraced in their full, real and ungovernable diversity but that the higher religious teachings and philosophies are put in simple words and rendered more accessible to ordinary persons.

As we saw in the case of Asaram Bapu, and this is also true of many of the other gurus of today, the ritualistic aspects of religion are stressed less, while the philosophical, meditative and introspective aspects are encouraged. This does not mean that there are no changes in everyday life or that the everyday and the spiritual life do not intertwine. In fact, the reverse is true. The discourses of today's guru seek to enmesh the everyday with the spiritual. There is a tacit recognition, as said earlier, that people have to continue with their lives and worldly responsibilities. The path of the renouncer is not expected of all. In fact, people are encouraged to do their duty, follow their *dharma* and not shirk their household responsibilities. Further, there is some emphasis on how to pray and an attempt to regulate the format. Asaram Bapu's organization sells bags containing standard prayer items – a book, a *mala*, a *gomukhi*, a copy of *Sri Asaramayan*, a small blanket and a framed photograph of the Bapu – which each person seeking *diksha* must purchase. Even so, through and along with all this, *satsang*, reflection and following the teachings of saints and *rishis* of the past (and the present) are constantly stressed.

In Weberian language, globalization and the media enable the greater rationalization and further routinization of the faith. While examples from everyday life are present in the sermons, they are general in character rather than particular. They can apply to one and to all. The choices made by individuals are structured by the range of beliefs and teachings offered by the guru. Leading one's life by the teachings of a guru and acquiring a guru are both enthusiastically encouraged by the gurus themselves. Prayer now follows a regimen directed by the guru and that too one that is often collective and congregational in character. There is an evening-out of the processes of faith; these are normalized by being reinstated in everyday life and also connected to the texts and discourses, the immanent 'presence' of the guru. The texts become accessible through the guru, but lives, practices and decisions are then moulded by the guru-interpreted texts. While persons may change gurus and there is a certain degree of individual freedom, it does appear that gurus are leading one closer towards the ideas and philosophy of the great tradition.

Notes

1. For instance, *kar sevaks* in the *rath yatra* of the BJP dressed like Ram and Lakshman in the serial. Party meetings often used backdrops painted with iconography from the serialized *Ramayana*. Sagar himself made appearances conclaves of the Vishwa Hindu Parishad (VHP) and leaders such as the BJP's Ashok Singhal thanked him (Rajagopal, 2001).
2. Bhakti geet, spiritual lessons and *bhajans*, serials on Krishna, Ganesh or Hanuman are all available for spiritual consumption. The newspapers provide columns titled 'Sacred Space' and 'Sacred Chants', 'Inner Light', 'Religion' and 'Religious Values'. There is a profusion of sacred music – some of it upbeat and made trendy – available. Since the early 1990s, popular Hindi films have been projecting a particular idea of 'Indian' and 'family values' even as these films locate themselves increasingly in spaces inhabited by the transnational Indian. A vast amount of hectic temple-building activity is taking place, leading to the radical

transformation of urban spaces. Temples are becoming larger and much more ornate. There is a stress on larger-than-life images, many of which stand *outside* temple structures. The aspects of pleasure and mystery have been ingeniously woven into temple-visiting practices with the new era of *gufa* or cave structures dotting the urban landscape. These are, of course, also attempts to re-create in otherwise crowded metropolises the sacred structure of temples in important mountain pilgrimage sites. One might suggest that for the harried urbanite, pilgrimage of a sort has been made that much more accessible. The reinforcement of particular notions of sacredness is achieved through this re-working of the traditional pilgrimage framework in the modern setting. One is also able to comprehend the greater emotional investment these temples might rouse in the believer, given their mapping on structures and sites associated with the highest religiosity available within Hinduism.

The social and cultural activism of Hindutva organizations and their effects are documented by Panikkar (1999: xxiv). He argues that Hindu communalism has worked through a large number of social and cultural organizations carefully nurtured during the last many years. The number and strength of these organizations with branches all over the country are difficult to ascertain, but they cover almost every field of intellectual and cultural activity – be it education, history, archaeology, music or media .... About twenty thousand schools under different denominations, scores of publishing outfits in almost every language, committees to write the history of each district, literary associations and drama clubs, environmental groups, women's organizations, temple renovation committees and so on are part of this network ...

Indeed, he also notes, in the same place, that unlike the political formations, which function sporadically and intermittently, and some only at the time of elections, the presence of these organizations in civil society is continuous and uninterrupted .... If today communalism is deeply embedded in social consciousness it is to a large measure due to the cultural intervention of these organizations.

Sometimes, the gurus of today also share platforms with the RSS or the BJP and, in particular, Asaram Bapu, spoken of in this paper, sometimes voices ideas and sentiments that resonate strongly with the ideology of political Hinduism. An instance is the editorial in the October 2007 issue of *Rishi Prasad*, Bapu's monthly magazine:

On 30th August 2007, the Allahabad High Court declared that the "Srimad Bhagavadgita is the essence of all religions and it has played a great inspiring role in the freedom struggle as well. Therefore, such a scripture does deserve to be accorded the exalted status of the National Religious Scripture". In support of its decision the High Court cited the Articles 51-A(B) and (F) of the National Constitution that provide for a National Flag, a National Anthem, a National Bird and a National Flower. The court observed that it is the duty of each and every citizen to follow the ideals laid down in the Srimad Bhagavadgita and protect our cultural heritage. This is not the scripture of some particular community, but instead a guiding force to all the communities and indeed the 'Scripture of India'. This perhaps is the first sign of this Supreme Spiritual Scripture of the Indian Culture, which has already earned the acclaim all over the world as the greatest scripture of humanity, winning political recognition in India. Shri S.N. Shrivastava, the Honourable Chief Justice of the Allahabad High Court who spelled out the above decision of the court, deserves to be thanked for this (http: //www.ashram.org/newweb/PDFs/Rp178%20October%202007.pdf viewed on 18.12.2007).

3. This is a kind of sacrifice involving fasting and *havan*.
4. A person who has realized the ultimate power of the physical and material world.
5. Though none speak against the life of the householder.

References

Appadurai, Arjun. 1997. *Modernity at Large: Cultural Dimensions of Globalization*, New Delhi: Oxford University Press.

Babb, L.A. and Susan Wadley (eds.). 1995. *Media and the Transformation of Religion in South Asia*, Philadelphia: University of Pennsylvania Press.

Das, Veena. 1990. *Mirrors of Violence: Communities, Riots and Survivors in South Asia*, New Delhi: Oxford University Press.

——. 1995. *Critical Events*, New Delhi: Oxford University Press.

Eisenstadt, S.N. 1966. *Modernization and Protest*, Englewood Cliffs, New Jersey: Prentice Hall.

Inkeles, Alex and David Smith. 1974. *Becoming Modern: Individual Change in Six Developing Countries*, Cambridge: Harvard University Press.

Lerner, D. 1962. *The Passing of Traditional Society*, Glencoe IL: The Free Press.

Madan, T.N. 2001. *Non-Renunciation: Themes and Interpretations of Hindu Culture*, New Delhi: Oxford University Press.

Panikkar, K.N. 1999. "Introduction: Defining the Nation as Hindu", in K.N. Panikkar (ed.), *The Concerned Indian's Guide to Communalism*, New Delhi: Penguin Books, pp. vii-xxxv.

Parthasarathy, D. and Rowena Robinson. 2001. "Science, Astrology and Democratic Society", *Economic and Political Weekly*, 36(33), pp. 3186–87.

Rajagopal, Arvind. 2001. *Politics after Television: Hindu Nationalism and the Reshaping of the Public in India*, Cambridge: Cambridge University Press.

Robinson, Rowena. 2004. "Virtual Warfare: The Internet as the New Site for Global Religious Conflict", *Asian Journal of Social Science*, 32(2), pp. 198–215.

——. 2005. "Religion on the Net: An Analysis of the Global Reach of Hindu Fundamentalism and its Implications for India", in N. Jayaram (ed.), *On Civil Society: Issues and Perspectives*, New Delhi: Sage Publications, pp. 203–17.

Sacks, Jonathan. 1991. *The Persistence of Faith: Religion, Morality and Society in a Secular Age*, London: Weidenfeld and Nicholson.

Singh, Y. 2000. "Is Globalization a Threat to Regional and Local Identities?", in Imtiaz Ahmad et al. (eds.), *Pluralism and Equality*, New Delhi: Sage Publications, pp. 239–70.

Appendix

Mata Amritanandamayi, Asaram Bapu and Satya Sai Baba on Householder Duties

[Mata Amritanandamayi (http: //www.amritapuri.org/teachings/house/holders.php) viewed on 17.12.2007]

Question: Can householders attain liberation?

Amma: Yes, but the only thing is that they must be real householders. Living in the house, they must live like ashramites. That is real grihasthashrama. While remaining in the house, they should live for God. It is possible to carry on a spiritual life while living in the world. The only thing is that one must perform actions selflessly without any attachment. One should not worry about the past or the future. Live in the present, surrendering your actions and their fruit at the feet of the Lord. Perform your duties as sincerely as possible, keeping in mind that all is entrusted by God. Be satisfied with whatever is provided by the Supreme. Anyhow, when we act with an attitude of surrender and devotion, it will bear the best fruit. But do not confuse your mind thinking of the fruit. If you perform your duties in the present, sincerely and wholeheartedly, considering it as your duty entrusted by God, then the future will become your friend. Live today with dedication then tomorrow will be your friend. Get rid of 'I' and 'mine' and consider everything as God's.

[Asaram Bapu (http: //www.ashram.org/~rp/rp_issues/main/may06.html) viewed on 17.12.2007]

Eight Characteristics of a Virtuous Householder

Maharshi Atri tells of the eight virtues or properties found in good Brahmins and virtuous householders: (1) anasuya (non-jealousy), (2) shaucha (piety), (3) mangala (good, propitious conduct), (4) anayasa (non-straining), (5) aspriha (contentedness), (6) dama (equanimity), (7) dana (charity), and (8) daya (compassion). They are briefly described below:

1. Anasuya (non-jealousy): One who does not refute or deny the virtues of virtuous ones, who praises even those with ordinary virtues and does not deride those afflicted with vices is said to have the good quality of anasuya.

2. Shaucha (piety): One who refrains from eating forbidden foods, from associating with unworthy persons and is pure in conduct (personal hygiene and righteousness) is equipped with shaucha.
3. Mangala (propitious conduct): To conduct oneself in daily life in the manner approved by noble men and scriptures and refrain from actions disapproved by them – this is termed as Mangala by learned men well versed in the esoteric significance of dharma.
4. Anayasa (non-straining): To avoid over-exertion in good or bad acts that entail too much straining of the body and do what can be done naturally and easily is called anayasa.
5. Aspriha (contentedness): To remain ever contented in whatever is attained easily and effortlessly and not coveting another's wife, is called aspriha.
6. Dama (equanimity): He who keeps no malice towards someone inflicting physical or mental pain on him nor tries to avenge his suffering, or in other words he who vexes none, nor feels vexed by anybody – the equanimity of such a person is called dama.
7. Dana (charity): When impelled by the feeling – 'it is man's duty to give charity everyday' one gives things away happily, even if he has not much in possession, it is called dana.
8. Daya (compassion): To feel the pleasure and pains of all beings of the world, animate or inanimate, including kinsmen, friends, foes and malicious ones; as one's own and to love all, beholding one's own self, the Divinity, in them– such attitude and outlook is called daya.

[Satya Sai Baba (http: //www.sathyasai.org/intro/cults.htm) viewed on 18.12.2007]

Your primary task is to discharge your duty. This does not mean renouncing worldly life or your obligations to your family. Use the opportunities confronting you as a householder to develop detachment and self sacrifice.

7

Globalization, Faith and Development Politics

P. RADHAKRISHNAN

Globalization in India is about two decades old and democratic politics (which is expected to subsume development politics) is about six decades old, whereas religion has been with it from the hoary past. Nevertheless, the mutuality and linkages among the three are close and intricate. Understanding this, in particular how globalization and politics impact religion, which is the concern of this paper, calls for placing the three in perspective.

Religions of India

India is the home of major religions of the world.[1] Of these Hinduism is the largest. The arrival of Christianity and Islam in India is traced to the early part of the first millennium and the 7th century AD respectively; but over the centuries their followers have been mostly converts from Hinduism. That apart, none of the religions of India is pristine; for as B.R. Ambedkar observed, caste being primarily the breath of the Hindus, the Hindus have fouled the air all over and everybody is infected, Sikh, Muslim, and Christian.[2] Seen from this perspective for understanding the impact of globalization and politics on religion, it is important to focus on Hindu religion.

With Hindu gods and goddesses accounting for about 330 million, which is one-fourth of India's human population, the superabundance of myths can be socially satiating and subliminal, as for instance the belief that to gaze on the phallic emblem of Shiva standing in his temple is as beneficial as a vision of every god and goddess separately.[3] This huge number is indicative of the claim of the pervasiveness of Hinduism, and of the trumped up importance of it to legitimize the superiority of the priestly class. The related phenomena manifest as belief systems, deities and other religious processes. The communities encompassing them are often interchangeably termed as sects or cults in English.

These can be noticed in the Brahminic or Sanskritic Hinduism as embodied in many well-established temples (which traditionally enjoyed the patronage of the rulers), with the right to perform rituals in them restricted to Brahmin priests; rise of Shaiva and Vaishnava sects as part of the Bhakti movements in medieval India (from about 7th century to 16th century AD), and Basava or Lingayat sect (in 12th century Karnataka) and of a parallel religion, Veerashaivism, as a protest movement against Brahminic Hinduism; rise of myths, legends and epics as in Lingam or phallic cult, Aiyappa cult (as in Sabaramila); rise of cults of the socially oppressed sections as of Teyyam in north Malabar; the non-Brahminic Hinduism of the Shudra varna,[4] which consists of numerous castes accounting for about 70 to 80 per cent of the Hindu population, the upper castes of which engage Brahmin priests for rituals, and the lower castes engage priests from their own castes, with many of the deities worshipped as alcoholic and non-vegetarian and so on.

Hindu sects or cults are indicative of many things: the complexity and diversity of Hindu religion; its transformation and even transmogrification over centuries; its pervasive hierarchy – social, spatial and in terms of other living beings such as animals, snakes and birds;[5] the cascading effects of the epic dramas Mahabharata and Ramayana on the entire Hindu religion, with their themes and characters lacing the annual and periodic festival, ritual and celebratory cycles – as for instance, the cult of Draupadi, heroine of Mahabharata, for whom shrines of the lower strata of Hindu society exist in parts of Tamil Nadu and Karnataka, and as variants in other parts of the country; the Krishna cult as in Guruvayur temple and Jagannath Puri temple; mediation of Hindu religion through scriptures as in Tantric, yogic cults; the anthropomorphic nature of rituals and worship with no living central character as cult-figure, or iconic mediator but interpretation in terms of human personal characteristics; the complex and diverse religious traditions supposedly traversing different trajectories and converging into a confluence, with the underlying notion of immortality of the soul (no death, but only metempsychosis (transmigration of souls); the resultant belief in avatars (incarnations); and so on.

Polarization

World religions such as Hinduism, Islam and Christianity, by their very nature, are distinct and mutually exclusive often with mutually incompatible beliefs and practices. While this by itself may not be sufficient reason for their polarization, in modern context their existential dilemmas and communal politics as agent provocateur result in their polarization. As Sikhism, Buddhism and Jainism emerged from Hinduism and many Hindus view them with reverence and as extension of Hinduism, the problem of polarization is much less among these minority religions.

While Hinduism, Islam and Christianity are not polarized in a pan-Indian sense, and steadfastly, there has been polarization of them from region to region and time to time. The polarization has been mostly caused by two broad contexts. The first was the introduction of adult franchise. What M.N. Srinivas said in the 1950s, that with the coming of democracy caste got a new lease of life,[6] which is being said now with greater vehemence,[7] is equally applicable to the major socio-religious communities. Central to their increasing religious activity has been the new field of adult franchise through vote-bank politics. The religious activity has taken the form of both polarization and resurgence. This may not be as true among Hindus as a whole for whom caste has been the main unit of activity, as it is among Muslims and Christians. Here polarization need not always be interpreted as oppositional. A better way of understanding it is as communal consolidation.

The second context has been communal, and mainly among Muslims and Hindus. I have discussed elsewhere the reasons for polarization of Muslims in the context of the Sachar Committee's report on Muslim backwardness. To draw upon it:

Apparently, the social, cultural and public interactive spaces in India can be very daunting for the Indian Muslims. The general sense of unease among Muslims can be seen on a number of fronts – in the relationships that exist between the Muslims and other Socio-Religious Communities (SRC), as well as in the variations in understanding and interpreting them. One aspect of this relates to patriotism. They carry a double burden of being labeled as "anti-national" and as being "appeased" at the same time. While Muslims need to prove on a daily basis that they are not "anti-national" and "terrorists", it is not recognized that the alleged "appeasement" has not resulted in the desired level of socio-economic development of the community. In general Muslims complained that they are constantly looked upon with a great degree of suspicion not only by certain sections of society but also by public institutions and governance structures. This has a depressing effect on their psyche. Many also felt that the media tends to perpetuate this stereotypical image of Muslims.[8]

The Sachar report has focused on the effect of this identity crisis on the Muslim community's visibility in public spaces, access to housing and education, gender issues in the community which are given a 'Muslim slant', as a consequence of which "the civil society and the State locate Muslim women's deprivation not in terms of the 'objective' reality of societal discrimination and faulty developmental policies, but in the religious-community space" which "allows the State to shift the blame to the Community and to absolve itself of neglect".

While the above observations are true, it is necessary to ponder over the reasons for this image trap, and how Muslims can get out of it. The reasons for the image trap are: (1) partly historical, with the trauma of partition still etched out in the social psyche; (2) partly geographical, with continued existence of a Muslim nation as India's hostile and war-mongering neighbour (though with friendly people); (3) partly religious; (4) partly political, with the steady rise of the Hindutva Frankenstein since the 1980s mainly in the Hindi-belt where coincidentally the Muslim community is concentrated; and (5) partly developmental.

While redressing the first may be a long haul, going by the present circumstances the second seems intractable. Had India's Muslim neighbour been a friendly and a democratic nation the condition of Indian Muslims would have been much better, leave alone India as a nation, and South Asia as a strategic region. The third is somewhat amenable. Many Muslims continue to live their life through religion instead of using religion for sustaining, ennobling and enriching it. As religion is integral to many cultures and cultures transcend geographic boundaries, the nature of the use of religion in modern context is an existential dilemma and has an existential dimension.

Stated differently, unlike other major religious communities, Muslims have yet to grapple with the intricate nexus between faith and development, faith and modernization, and in the present circumstances, faith and globalization, and make informed and rational amends to their belief systems and religious perspectives so as to catch up with those ahead of them and make themselves 'cosy' in the fast shrinking Lebensraum.

The fourth can get weakened only with the rapid expansion of India's secular and civil space without necessarily turning to 'strident secularism' as a counterpoise to 'strident Hindutva' which can only rebound on the nation and on Muslims in particular. Weakening of Hindutva, which is only a matter of time, is bound to boost social bonds, morale and status of Indian Muslims. As of the fifth, in understanding the status of a community, one has to be Janus-faced. The perception regarding Muslims in India today is, to a large extent, qualitatively better than what it was, say, about four decades ago, thanks to, if one may say so, the effects of development, spread of education, growth of urbanization and spread of secularism. With greater and faster development of India as a nation, in which Muslims are major stakeholders many stereotypes centering on them may get weakened and even disappear. The statement in the report that "interestingly though, in many meetings women participants emphasized that given appropriate opportunities to work and get educated, they would 'manage' all these issues" lends credence to this optimism.[9]

As Christians are a small community (2%) and relatively more advanced than others, there has not been much of polarization among them in an oppositional sense. As of Hindus, the rise of Hindutva since the 1980s is an aberration limited to a small section of the Hindus as part of Hindutva's incremental politics. Though this can be interpreted as religious polarization, it is time and context specific and has already begun to weaken.

Faith and Development Politics

The politics of religion has resulted in the mushrooming of religious structures – not so much out of devotion or for worship as for competitive communalism in the public sphere. This is true among Hindus, Muslims and Christians. This needs to be juxtaposed with the unhealthy nexus between faith and politics. The communal flare up in Baroda in 2006, when in the process of widening public roads some of the 'religious road-blocks' were removed, is one example of this. Another is the ongoing controversy over the alignment cutting across the Adam's Bridge-Ramar Sethu – the undersea ridge between Rameswaram and the Sri Lankan coast – in the Sethusamudram Shipping Channel Project (SSCP). Let me draw upon my own writing on this, which is relevant not only in the context of the Ram Sethu row but also in other contexts where faith is often a bogey for diversionary politics and short-term political gains:

> In a country where democracy and secularism are still nascent in the minds of its unwashed millions and pale before faith, what the pillars of democracy – legislature, executive and judiciary – the intelligentsia as a class, and the media at large should do is to wean people away from peripheral and superficial aspects of faith, and faith-based politics through systematic inculcation of and pragmatic approach to diversity and development. It is our failure to do this that caused demolition of the Babri Masjid on December 6, 1992. In retrospect many of us would admit that the demolition could have been averted if we had a parliament (central legislature) which was not made up at that time – as it is to a large extent even today – of politicians who (failed to carry) their faith – inevitably a cultural baggage – only within themselves as a personal matter. (Carrying their faith only as a personal matter) is precisely how the politicians could be edifying to the masses and tell them about faith "thus far, no further", that is faith is essentially a personal matter which should have no spill over and spin off effects in public spaces and should not be a matter of public insignia. The same could be said about our judiciary which has on occasions digressed instead of trying to bring to bear upon itself pragmatic secularism, secularist pragmatism, and secular and rational humanism as hallmarks of a secular judiciary. The recent pronouncement by a high court judge in his judgment that Bhagavad Gita should be made the

national Dharmashastra, which caused a furore in different parts of the country, is only part of a longer story. The same is true of the executive: the (Babri Masjid) demolition was the culmination of the drifting and dithering of the Narasimha Rao government. If the media was sensational then it is more so now on its incessant pursuit of instant hype. More so when the younger generation of the media persons (in particular of the TV channels) has hardly any sense of history and society.

As globalization comes to mean development of material and human resources at a fast pace and turning technology itself into spiritualism, those developing countries which do not chant the globalization mantra, adapt to its needs, pace, and rhythm, and harness resources for their own development, are bound to be left behind and even caught up in the eddy of a complex process of planetary dimensions. This means that we cannot afford anymore to live in the past and the present simultaneously, and if there are roadblocks on our path to development which are not of vital concern to the nation, we ought to remove them and keep going. It is from this perspective that the Ramar-Sethu row should be understood. The issue is not one of faith but of development. Those who genuinely believe Rama as real, as divine, as an avatar, and who should continue to be revered and worshipped, already have a surfeit of sites and structures in different parts of the country. Even if Ram-Sethu was a creation or legacy of Rama, it is as archaic as Rama and is only peripheral in the scheme of divine things in modern social settings; no devotee has any access to it. In an age of lebensraum religious communities have begun to give up some of their traditional belief systems and related practices and reconcile to the needs of modernity. One example is Christianity, which has in principle accepted cremation as against burial for want of space, and in some places where cremation has not yet been adopted the practice of burial itself is undergoing different forms of change for making space to the new-comers. Another example is Islam. Some of the middle-east countries have not let mosques stand in the way of their development projects. A third example is Hinduism. For want of space sections of them who practised burial in the past have switched to cremation. However, as a country India is probably an exception where sites of faith hinder development. We have any number of such sites even in the highways and bye-ways, and even if these sites are unused and totally neglected for ages they are not removed for fear of communal orgy. Far from vouching for our democratic, diversity, pluralistic and secular credentials this clearly shows our lack of political and administrative will.[10]

While the SSCP was conceived long before the advent of globalization, but as globalization is central to development politics, particularly in democratic countries like India, its relevance here cannot be overlooked.

Globalization

Globalization is a hackneyed phrase. The terminology is not yet in standard lexicons. In India, it is often equated with economic liberalization and structural transformation particularly by economists. But both these are only a part of globalization. For the purpose of this paper, two observations will suffice. The first is by James Kurth, who in *The Templeton Lecture on Religion and World Affairs* observed:[11]

> Globalisation is often described as a process: steadily progressing over time, pervasively spreading over space, and clearly inevitable in its development. But globalisation is also a revolution, one of the most profound revolutions the world has ever known. Indeed, globalisation is the first truly world revolution.
>
> *All revolutions disrupt the traditions and customs of a people. Indeed, they threaten a people's very security, safety, and even identity. The world revolution that is globalisation in some measure threatens the security of every people on the globe.* (emphasis added)

The second is by James Petras and Henry Veltmeyer:[12]

> Globalisation is at the centre of diverse intellectual and political agendas, raising crucial questions about what is widely considered to be the fundamental dynamic of our time – an epoch-defining set of changes that is radically transforming social and economic relations and institutions in the 21st century.

Despite the accelerated pace of knowledge production on and under globalization, the nature of these changes as well as of the related transformations in social and economic relations have not been understood adequately in their complexity and diversity, as many facets of globalization have only begun to unfold. However, it is possible to discern some of its features. These include increasing economic and market capitalism and increasing economic and market integration at a global level; increasing free global movement of capital, goods and services by removing national barriers, with the IMF, the World Bank and WTO as its key instruments; the rapid pace of knowledge–technology revolution; and the need for countries to be knowledge-driven and market-driven to compete and survive in the new global scenario.

Globalization, Politics and Religion

It is a truism that globalization has led to religious resurgence, newfangled religions and god business in different parts of the world. This is contrary to conventional sociological wisdom that as societies progress the significance of religions declines.

The nature and functions of religion in society have been under speculation for several centuries; the approaches to the understanding of religion – philosophical, theological, anthropological, sociological – and the related dimensions of religious ideas have been very old; and the nexus between religion and society has been very close, with wide, complex, intricate and elaborate ramifications. The religion also has been playing an important role in giving spiritual and moral sustenance to individuals, the related regulation of social life and moral order, creating and regulating cultural forms, and the integration of society. One may go with the French sociologist Emile Durkheim's postulate (endorsed by, among others, the English anthropologist A.R. Radcliffe-Brown) that "the main role (or 'function') of religion (is) to celebrate and sustain the norms upon which the integration of society depends".[13]

But globalization seems to be nullifying this important role of religion. For the success of globalization, especially in the third world, its *dramatis personae* have been using the major religions of the world as purveyors of their globalization agenda, with unprecedented flow of funds for the purpose from the master world to the third world.

The major consequences of globalization have been: transmogrification of traditional religions and belief systems; beginning of the disintegration of the traditional social fabrics and shared norms by the invasion of consumerism, cyber culture, newfangled religions, social fads, and changing work ethics and work rhythms; fast spreading anomie (in the Durkheimian sense) forcing an ever increasing number of individuals to fall back upon – for moral and social support – the easily accessible pretentious religious banalities; and attributing to religion the creation and acceleration of extremist, fundamentalist, and terrorist tendencies in the third world countries, which are intended to destabilize them, and strike at the root of their civilization, and multicultural and pluralist nature.[14]

While globalization has strengthened Brahminic Hinduism and its institutionalized sites and structures, it has weakened the religious symbols, sites, shrines, and practices of the lower strata or what may be called folk-religion. They began to decline long before the advent of globalization, as a result of modernization, urbanization, spread of education, unemployment, migration, and so on, and the small number of persons engaged in them as "performers of traditional tasks" depending on the upper castes within the broad framework of Hindu jajmani system[15] had given up such tasks for various reasons.

What is noticeable in the context of globalization is the strengthening of cultic religion among Hindus and to some extent Christians, and the related god business, which has been a booming industry in India and through India in other countries.

In this context it is important to note that religion being a creation of society, as indicated earlier, with the advancement of societies and progress of knowledge, it is expected to decline in importance; and beliefs, practices and symbols in its realm are expected to lose their legitimacy and significance. If this has not happened in religions of the past it is primarily because of the persistence of vested interests, the hegemonic groups, to oppress and exploit the rest of society through 'holy lies' as embedded in the conservatism, obscurantism and superstitions of these religions. Two illustrations will drive this point home.

One is the tottering of Vatican in the modern context on a shaky foundation with its tradition that a miracle is a prerequisite for beatification, the related controversy centring on Mother Theresa, in the context of the testimony of an illiterate 30-year-old Bengali woman, who is believed to have claimed that she was 'miraculously' cured of an 'incurable' tumour with the posthumous blessings of the Mother. The Vatican's persistence as purveyor of superstitions may be good for its own existence and persistence, and probably for the naive and gullible sections of Christianity. More so, when of late there has been increasing debate and concern in the West about celibacy, sex and priesthood among the Catholics, and increasing demand to do away with celibacy and priesthood but not sex, inasmuch as celibacy is against human nature and to release their suppressed emotions, when occasions arise the celibates may use catharsis by going for overkill in matters concerning sex.[16]

The other is the recent revelation by the Sabarimala temple authorities that Makarajyothi is a work of human hands. This has to be seen against the fact that for decades, devotees have thronged in their lakhs to Sabarimala, South India's foremost pilgrimage place, to bear witness to an annual 'miracle': On the last day of the mid-January Makaravilakku festival, the mysterious fire that gives the festival its name flashes thrice (Makarajyothi) in the forests of the Ponnambalamedu hill, across from the Ayyappa temple. All along religious scholars, temple authorities and devotees have ascribed a divine source to the phenomenon, much to the annoyance of rationalists who have repeatedly attempted to expose its real cause. The revelation has caused instant hullabaloo,[17] particularly in the media; but as religions thrive on miracles and 'holy lies', considering that Kerala is now ruled by a communist ministry the revelation may soon turn into an 'unholy lie' and the 'holy lie' will continue to prevail.

The centrality of miracles (in the sense of magic) in religions (what may be called 'magico-religions'), especially in founded religions, is commonsense. In place of miracles, and often in addition to them, religions like Hinduism, which have no founders, have legitimation myths. Miracles and myths are in fact the life-blood and life-boat of religions without which they will languish and sink. It is in this context the god business needs to be understood.

God Business

God business is not an invention of globalization. It was there long before the advent of globalization as evident from the activities of, among others, the Anandamarg, Brahmakumaris, ISKON, Kalki, Mahesh Yogi, Osho and Sai Baba. But globalization has made it a flourishing business mainly in the context of cultic religion.

Cults in modern India are organizations of persons, who are either genuine believers or religious charlatans and tricksters, engaged in god business. Known as godmen and godwomen they are claimed to be godheads in human form (incarnation or avatar). They are too numerous. While all of them are part of cultic religion, many of them are not cult material. Even then cults are legion. Their details are not properly documented and understood.

Among the prerequisites to remain active and effective in god business in India are: image-building of the cult figures as avatars; aura of divinity around them; their mystification to the followers; make-believe spiritual acts of pop religion as trade marks or USPs; close-knit organization with the cult figures at the centre, spin doctors, programme and media managers as inner core group, and performers of various other tasks as larger inner group; esoteric nature of these groups in the sense of restricted access of the larger group to the core group, and of the followers from outside to both; and the much needed followers. Implicit in these are also the cult criteria.

One issue which should engage sociologists is how and why cults emerge in a country, and only in some places. The following observations by Paul Zacharia, one of Kerala's well-known fiction writers and political commentators, on the emergence of god business in India (published in *Tehelka*, 30 June 2007) contribute to the understanding of the emergence of cultic religion, albeit in a limited sense:

> Religion makes lots of money because of the universal belief that you earn merit by giving. The best of faith-founders have stressed compassion; so has humanism. For the modern individual, directly helping the needy is a messy business because you are forced to get involved. Presenting money or goods to a place of worship or to a godman/woman solves the issue neatly. Hinduism has a special place for the parityagi – he who renounces all. The way things turned out, it is the so-called parityagi who ends up making all the money! ... Usual places of worship do not do so well in money-catching because they have no special charisma; or they must build up the god as a miracle-maker through

> competitive marketing. Big money flows only towards the talented individual who can create popular spiritual appeal and surround him/herself with a group of committed disciples. Disciples are the key. By him/herself the godman/woman is like a nuclear reactor waiting to go critical. It is the disciples who trigger the money-machine and the supporting media blast. They have more at stake than the guru. Almost none of them is guru-material. They control immense wealth and power because of the guru's talent.

Among important Indian cults are of Amritanandamayi, Anandamarga, Bangaru Adigal, Brahma Kumaris, Jaggi Vasudev, Kalki, Baba Ramdev, Ravishankar and Sai Baba among Hindus, and of Dinakaran among Christians. The Hindu cults centre on beliefs and rituals or yoga and meditation. Of the several cult figures three among the Hindus and one among the Christians are discussed here.

The Amma Phenomenon

"Negative aspects of Western culture more disastrous than nuclear deal, says Mata", was the headline of a news report in *The Hindu* of September 28, 2007, on the benedictory address delivered by Mata Amritanandamayi (hereafter MA) at her 54th birthday celebrations at Amritapuri near Kollam, Kerala, on September 27. If the MA website (http://amritapuri.org) is any indication, MA's birthday every year is an extravaganza of Brahminic Hinduism of which 'homa' is a hallmark, performed by high-ranking Brahmin priests; with Sri Guru Pada Puja (worship of the 'holy feet'), deification of MA as "mother of the universe", and as goddess; well-organized devotional programmes, launching of charity; and so on.

MA, meaning mother of absolute bliss, is popularly known as Amma (mother). The organizations that promote her include MA Math, MA Centre and MA Mission Trust. *The Week*, published from a place not far from MA ashram, had her for its cover feature of September 21, 2003. The feature, with its main title 'Embracing the world' and sub-title 'Devotees worship her as god', is an important instance of commercial exploitation of cultic religion by the print and electronic media. As *The Week* reported, "MA has grown from an illiterate child with strange spiritual experiences to a global guru who presides over an empire of charity; she is

Kerala's 'hugging saint' who straddles the material and the spiritual worlds; her ashram figures at the top of the list of charities receiving donations from abroad."[18]

Paul Zacharia placed the Amma phenomenon in the context of the regressive ambience of Kerala, which he saw as peculiar for a number of reasons (*Tehelka*, 30 June 2007):

1. Society as a whole in Kerala was more secular, progressive, even rationalist, in the 1950s, 60s and 70s than it is today; those were the heady days of the Left when a democratic revolution seemed about to bloom; Sai Baba was the only godman who made some inroads once in a while.
2. The 1990s saw Kerala's most startling somersault into a black hole of crude bhakti, superstition and blind ritual, cutting across all religions, when religion suddenly emerged as a money machine.
3. Amritanandamayi was the right person at the right time. Owners of unknown backyard deities were hiring MBAs in marketing, and shooting up into the multi-million categories. One could say that three things forced Kerala into being the regressive religious madhouse it is today: (a) the collapse of civil society and of the economic and social dream of the common man under the UDF and LDF coalitions; (b) active promotion of religiosity and caste by politicians for their own ends; and (c) ruthless day-to-day promotion of superstition and religiosity by the media for its own ends.

Zacharia's assessment of MA's religious wheeling and dealing broadly conforms to my own, though he does not look at the cult aspect as academics are, wont to do. More from Zacharia's observations:

> Mata Amritanandamayi is reckoned to be one of the country's richest gurus. She is a handmaiden of the Sangh Parivar, especially the VHP, with its global fund-flows. The hug is her USP. Her media managers and fund-managers are the real miracle-workers, considering what they have made out of a simple woman with a knack for popular religious enactment and the energy to hug all and sundry. In Kerala, where there is much jealous scrutiny on money with foreign strings, Amritanandamayi goes scot-free. Foolish Malayalis just marvel at and admire her wealth as they do that of corrupt politicians. They

> feel she has done them proud by being in the newspapers wherever she goes. The media reports her in terms more cringing and crawling than those of the devotees. A.K. Antony, former CM and now Union Defence Minister, is a devout follower and has pronounced that he saw stars when she hugged him .... She has all the permits from the government of India to receive foreign funds with no questions asked. Amritanandamayi has invested well too. She has an expensive TV channel which is a great conduit. All the millions invested into medical/engineering and other professional institutions go under the head of charity. But the same charity also demands capitation fees of about Rs 30 to 40 lakh for a seat in the professional institutions. Some millions were spent on building homes for the tsunami-hit. That was a God-sent credibility exercise because it looked almost like charity. It was the best mask Amritanandamayi's millions have yet worn. It increased her money-gathering power a hundred times. As we know, what all godmen/women don't like is auditing and accountability. But then, can you audit God?

One cannot infer any malevolence from these accounts. If this is true of regular activities of the organization, the MA cult may seem benevolent. But critics have different views. Among other sources is a website,[19] which claims to act as a saviour of parents who feel they are losing their children to the cult, and provide recovery and healing resources and support options for cult victims and their families. Apart from the fact that the website is US-based, cult-healing is unheard of in India and is typically US in its nexus with psychiatric and psychopathic treatment.

While in the religious practices of the organization what one sees is established Hinduism, in her hug MA does not discriminate between persons on the basis of caste or creed. So, if the organization has to be faulted for any misdeed, it is the *dramatis personae* other than MA. In this context, it is worth considering, in keeping with the theme of some of the Malayalam short stories, whether an illiterate Amritanandamayi who in the traditional caste hierarchy of Kerala belonged to a low untouchable caste has been really a wonder woman or victim of a religious mafia – the unscrupulous commercial ascetics from whose religious trap she has no way of escape.[20]

While Amma's ashram may be building houses for the poor, hospitals and educational institutions, and many other ashrams may be swindling the huge funds which they have been receiving from abroad, the very idea of social service through the conduit of religion, that too primarily the majoritarian Hindu religion, in a secular and pluralist society, where religion is not expected to play any role in the public sphere, raises at least two issues. One, the failure of a democratic state to perform and deliver thereby enabling various self-styled 'divinities' and 'god incarnates' to use it to perform and deliver through make-believe spiritualism through the state though the state is expected to be secular and pluralist in letter and spirit. Two, the effect of this 'divine delivery' on the functioning of a secular pluralist democracy and the role of globalization in creating spurious godheads who would not have had the kind of weird spin doctors, networks and media savvy images but for the technocracy of globalization itself turning into spiritualism.

Whether such a democracy should draw legitimacy from self-made – and those forced into the spiritual trap – dubious godheads, or from people's will is a challenge to the very notion of democracy.

The close nexus of dubious godheads, especially of the internationally sought-after types, with politicians, their hangers-on, criminals, middlemen and fixers is well known. That is an important reason for cults to thrive with state and political patronage, and get away with misdeeds. For, any criminal case against a cult has to be initiated by the police on a complaint or at the instance of the government. When both are devotees of the cult figure they would not act against the cult, and there is every possibility of them making the complainant an accused.[21]

Bangaru Adigal

Bangaru Adigal, now aged 65 years, is at the centre of the Adi Parashakthi movement. Its headquarters, Adi Parashakthi Peetham, is in Bangaru's home town of Melamaruvathur, about 23 miles south of Chennai. Bangaru is made out to be an avatar of Adi Parashakthi. He is revered as Amma (mother in Tamil). His USP is allowing women to perform puja to the Shakti image and use of Tamil for invocations. In fact, the ashram is mostly populated by women of all ages. Any woman who is wearing 'Adhiparasakthi dictated' colour of literally blood red can perform the puja. They are all dressed in crimson red saris. Bangaru himself wears a red dhoti when in 'trance'. It is a kind of uniform symbolizing that the blood of humanity is one colour. He is believed to experience oracles and make miracles which are claimed to attract devotees from across the world, have built careers, cured baffling diseases, and made 'barren' women conceive. The movement's philosophy is non-sectarian. Over the years the movement has expanded and established centres at several places. It has also invested hugely in education, health care, etc., and blended spiritualism and social service. His VIP visitors included Rajiv Gandhi.

Bangaru was a school teacher and is married with children. He is not affiliated to any teaching order. The following anecdote may help in understanding his rise as a cultic phenomenon:

> Three hundred yards from the ... ashram is where it all began. Here was Bangaru's childhood home. Right across from it was a popular Mariammen temple.[22] As is the custom in non-Agamic temples, non-Brahmin families performed the rites. Bangaru's father, Gopala Nayagar, held this responsibility annually during a certain festival period. One year Mariammen appeared to Gopala Nayagar, stating in a few years she would begin communicating through Bangaru. Meanwhile Bangaru himself was worshipping the goddess daily under a neem tree, which ... according to folk tradition was surrounded by 27 siddhas in the form of snakes. In 1970 the tree blew over in a storm, revealing a swayambu (naturally occurring) form of Amman. It became the focus of worship and a rough-hewn temple was built. Bangaru began speaking prophecy. In 1974 the Adi Parashakti image was installed behind the swayambu Amman as were stone images of the snakes.[23]

Such stories are the stuff of many other cults as well. The sophisticated organizational set-up and esoteric and secretive features of some other cults are not visible in this cult. Yet it is a big money-making religious enterprise. Critics charge the activities as benign mass exploitation. However, reports of malevolence of the cult are not heard. In a sociological sense, the cult may be characterized as modern expression of folk religion or popular non-Brahminic Hinduism.

Sai Baba

Sai Baba, who died recently, appeared as a miracle man some fifty years ago in Puttaparthi in Andhra Pradesh and Whitefield in Karnataka. The strange stories about his healing power, producing objects such as ash, pendants and rings from air, burping out pearls, diamonds and such other precious things and their offer to devotees, avatar as Krishna – soon made him a crowd-puller. The hearsays about him were spread far and wide with even more incredible stories. He thrived on people's gullibility, faith in god, belief in his avatar, and in superstitions in the efficacy of his magic powers in gratifying their needs and desires. Some rationalists tried to call his bluff. But their attempts had hardly any effect on him or his devotees as he enjoys the support of many high and mighty in Indian society. The Sai Baba phenomenon has been well established for several decades now. His cult centres are located in different parts of the world. Like MA and Bangaru, he has also invested hugely in social service.

On November 24, 2006, President A.P.J. Abdul Kalam, called on Sai Baba at Puttaparthi, penned a poem in Tamil on him and read out in the presence of thousands of Sai devotees who gathered on the occasion of his birthday. Immediately after Kalam completed his poem, delighted Sai Baba shook hands with him. Last year, websites of a number of Indian newspapers were full of advertisements on Sai Baba. When these advertisements appear even on the website of a supposedly credible newspaper like *The Hindu* people are swayed more by impressions, images and visuals than by reason.

When Sai Baba called on the self-styled atheist DMK President and Tamil Nadu Chief Minister, M. Karunanidhi at his Gopalpuram residence in Chennai, on January 21, 2007, it was a 'godly' welcome, and was characterized by a section of the media as "momentous meeting between an atheist and one worshipped as a living god". Among those who sought Sai Baba's blessings on the occasion were Lalu Prasad Yadav and Karnataka Chief Minister, H.D. Kumaraswamy.

When late Dr H. Narasimhaiah, Vice-Chancellor of Bangalore University constituted a committee on rationalism and took on Sai

Baba about three decades ago, *The Indian Express* proprietor, Ramnath Goenka was the first to defend Sai Baba, glorify him as an avatar of Krishna, and ridicule Narasimhaiah's rationalism using the front page of the newspaper.

If Babas thrive in India and abroad and people throng them it is important to go into the reasons. With the advent of ICT and the related cyber-spirituality, it has become even more difficult to do away with bliss-peddlers.

The literature on cult figures as available on websites, published works, or peddled by their followers is hagiography. Because of this much of the past of the cult figures remains unexplored and unexplained. As a result, their growth and dynamics, to the extent they are accessible to discerning critics, is limited to the period they are in the limelight of god business, that too as they appear outwardly.

MA and Sai Baba were school drop outs from traditional low caste families. Both are believed to have had strange childhood spiritual experiences. MA is believed to have gone into trances as Krishna [Krishna bhava (when she is believed to have suckled Krishna)].[24] She came on the scene in the 1990s as the hugging saint. She continues to thrive with this USP. Sai Baba appeared long before her with his miracles and avatar claims. Compared to both, Bangaru, also from a traditional low caste, came on the scene as an adult responding to an oracle from Adi Parashakti.

There are, however, certain striking features in the god business of all the three. The website of MA Math has the following as her desire: "Everyone in the world should be able to sleep without fear, at least for one night. Everyone should be able to eat to his fill, at least for one day. There should be at least one day when hospitals see no one admitted due to violence. By doing selfless service for at least one day, everyone should help the poor and needy." The message attributed to Sai Baba and highlighted below his image on the website of his organization (http://www.srisathyasai.org.in) is "there is only one religion, the religion of Love; there is only one caste, the caste of Humanity; there is only one language, the language of the Heart; there is only one God, He is omnipresent." The philosophy of Adi Parashakti movement is non-sectarian and anyone, irrespective of caste and creed, can worship at the shrine. All the three are known for their huge investment in social cause and success in a country which is not known for its social commitment or humanism. By this they have redefined traditional spiritualism through a newfound humanism.

While cults of MA, Bangaru and Sai Baba centre on beliefs and rituals, those of Ravi Shankar, Ramdev and their ilk centre on yoga and meditation. In some sense what they do is the Indian version of tele-evangelism. While they exploit the believers and followers financially and otherwise, the crowds they attract from abroad may be seen as part of 'spiritual tourism'.

Dinakaran

Among Christians in India, Chennai-based D.G.S. Dinakaran was the most popular cult figure, though he may not be anywhere near the controversial Benny Hinn, who reportedly performed his "Festival of Blessings" from January 21 to 23, 2005 before an attentive assembly of seven million people at the Jakkur airstrip in Bangalore, leaving the airfield completely devastated. Dinakaran's death on February 20, 2008 attracted a lot of media attention in India and abroad. Of the obituaries probably the most matter-of-fact and at the same time satirical was an editorial in *The New Indian Express*. To retain its flavour the editorial is reproduced here:

The Papa of Pop Christianity in India

> Evangelist DGS Dhinakaran, who passed away in Chennai on Wednesday, leaving millions of faithful followers and admirers in mourning and a multi-million dollar organization as a legacy for his son and family to inherit, was perhaps a pioneer in the popularisation of pop Christianity in India.
>
> His was the brand of modern-day evangelisation that lays stress on prayer – for anything and everything one aspires for in life – and not necessarily on living an old world 'Christian life' devoid of overindulgences and unethical practices.
>
> Through his captivating sermons and lilting songs, Dhinakaran held a sway over his listeners, but it was his passionate prayers that endeared him to his followers. By creating an impression that he was equipped with a hot line to Jesus Christ – what with

the lives of people ever overflowing with woes – he served as an interlocutor, who sought divine solutions to human problems.

His Prayer Tower at Greenways Road, which has been functioning as a round-the-clock call centre diverting earthly pleas to heaven for the past few decades, has helped countless people get solace and unburden themselves of their agonies. Prayer requests through post, too, have been pouring in there ever since the facility was opened. The belief was that the brother would read every letter and then make a prayer to God.

Besides the prayer facility, Dhinakaran, during his evangelical career spanning over five decades, had offered the faithful a variety of schemes – all well packaged with definite price tags. Those who went in for the schemes were assured of an uninterrupted flow of God's blessings.

In his bid to reach out to the masses with God's message, he had exploited every type of mass media, starting with the radio in his initial years. It was in those years, he was a popular preacher in Tamil Nadu who used to be invited to 'conventions' organized by Christian groups or churches in small towns and even villages. He was then just a bank employee, who preached in his spare time wearing a necktie.

More than his soothing words, it was the prayer-heeling sessions at the 'convention' venues that earned him more followers and led to the setting up of his own establishment – Jesus Calls. Subsequently he diversified and started his own publication, which was supported by the faithful through their offerings. Slowly his popularity crossed the state borders and his organization gained more financial strength. People who got God's blessings through Dhinakaran's prayers were liberal in their offerings, besides sending in prayer requests explaining their problems.

It was then he began calling out names in conventions. People waited at his meetings to be called out – on to the stage and prayed especially for their problems that the brother knew through divine revelation. The money flow into his organization's coffer increased and he, too, became dapper. He started wearing suits – only suits – and lived a life marked by conspicuous consumption.

Subsequently he chucked his job with the bank and became a full-time servant of God, thus channeling his energies in devising schemes that were advertised through his publications, whose number had gone up by then. His wife Stella was by his side in his mission, mostly editing the magazines that came out from the Jesus Calls stable. People even started writing to her. Subsequently, his son Paul Dhinakaran, too, joined in the mission to share his burden of praying for the people. Later his grandchildren were featured in the song and dance sequences in the video albums of devotional songs produced and sold by Jesus Calls, which itself is a family trust.

Of his schemes, of course all of them inspired by God, one was the 'Young Partner's Scheme', under which by paying an amount a child can be registered with Jesus Calls. Brother would regularly pray and ensure that God's gaze was upon the child as it grew up. Later on schemes came up for adults, too, but for a fee, even running to lakhs of rupees.

Through his opulence, Dhinakaran's subtle message to his followers was 'prosper with God's blessings'. In his sermons he spoke passionately of God's love and how God waits to shower blessings on those who seek them and of course opened their purse strings – in the modern world manna does not come down from heaven free of cost or even for a cheap price.

His blessed life should be an inspiration for younger generation of wannabe evangelists. For now, one can aspire to serve the Lord without losing on material comforts. Or for that matter, even leave huge fortunes for one's own progeny after a life in the service of God.

Conclusion

The cults of Amritanandamayi, Bangaru Adigal and Sai Baba preach humanism and love. As a result, these cults merge well with the cultural values of the larger society. Whether the three cults engage in mind control is difficult to say. For, only devotees are within and followers are outside their ashrams leading normal life. They have at best an occasional visit to the ashrams, a Bangaru Adigal, Sai Baba or an MA ring or pendant, or photo in their homes along with the images of deities like Krishna. This may be because their message and teachings are part of larger Hinduism. Dinakaran was an Indian avatar of Benny Hinn, making money using Jesus Christ, and the gullible congregation getting addicted to his antics.

India is a secular pluralist democracy. In the normal course the state does not regulate or interfere with religious beliefs and practices of its citizens. As the Constitution of India guarantees freedom to Indian citizens to pursue and propagate the religion of their choice anything can pass for religious pursuit and propagation.

India is still a land of believers. Because of this the much needed scientific temper for the effective functioning of a full-blown secular pluralist democracy is still wanting in it. As the state and its functionaries are drawn from this society, India has a long way to go for using law, as envisaged by the Constitution, to reshape recalcitrant social patterns. As a result, it is rarely that any cult or cult leader has been hauled up by the state and the judiciary for charges of malevolence or for unaccounted sources of income.

Many of the cults are also registered as charitable trusts. As these are private organizations their incomes other than from foreign sources are not subject to government scrutiny. As charitable organizations, they are also exempted from income tax.

Considering that India has been not only a breeding ground but also a haven for various cults, and many of the cults in developed countries are anchored in India, the state's role in formulating public policies about cults, and the yawning gap between governance and public policy, or use of governance and policy space vis-à-vis cults are major issues for cultic studies in Indian context.

The traditional Hindu culture has been a deepening paradox, with the Sangh Parivar trying to drag the country back to the illusory Vedic age, and the younger generation dragging it in different directions, many succumbing to the temptation of consumerism – a fallout of the economic dimension of globalization, the aberrations and absurdities of the tinsel world, and the temptation of migration to the US for making quick bucks. Conventional religion has become computerized religion, as for instance, many in far-flung Chennai or Delhi can have rituals through the Internet in the far-flung US or UK temples and vice versa.

Globalization has given a new lease of life to various religion-related phenomena through the Internet. Cults have been major manipulators of the Internet, and through it, among other things, people's minds, and major beneficiaries of cyber chicanery.

Almost all websites which have some bearing on India have astrology, numerology, palmistry, vaasthu, Vedic predictions, and so on to cater to the needs of the gullible millions; and spiritualism through the TV channels or what has been aptly termed 'TV spirituality'.[25] All these have made god a money-spinner through cyber chicanery. Since gods either do not exist or have failed to deliver, godmen and godwomen, particularly those with cults, are the next best choice of the masses and the main beneficiaries of their need, greed and gullibility. As a result, while traditional worship centres continue to exist, with the advent of globalization cultic religion exists as its parallel with some of the cult figures having immense worldly riches, following, popularity and political clout. If beliefs have to be judged by their usefulness, cultic religion has already overtaken conventional religion at least in some areas.

Notes

1. Population by religion, 2001.

Religion	*In million*	*In per cent*
Hindu	827.579	81
Muslim	138.188	13
Christian	24.080	2
Sikh	19.216	2
Buddhist	7.955	1
Jain	4.225	0.4
Others	6.640	1
Total	1027.883	100.0

"Others" includes the Parsi community. Its population according to the Census of 2001 is only 0.01 per cent, or just about 69,601 in absolute numbers, and the community is well on the way of extinction (Source: Census of India, 2001).

2. B.R. Ambedkar (1979), "Annihilation of Caste", in his *Writings and Speeches*, Vol. 1, Education Department, Government of Maharashtra, Bombay, p. 80.
3. C.J. Fuller (1992), *The Camphor Flame: Popular Hinduism and Society in India*, Princeton University Press, Princeton, New Jersey, p. 29.
4. Shudras are the lowest of the four-fold varna classification of Hindu society, the other three being Brahmanas, Kshatriyas and

Vaisyas, in a descending order. Each varna consists of several castes, most of them hierarchically arranged, of which only those belonging to the first three has the right to wear the "sacred thread", and hence are known as the twice-born.

5. A case in point is the classification of kites as Pariah kite (Chakki Parunthu) and Vishnu kite (Krishna Parunthu), which I noticed in the Trivandrum zoo. Pariah is one of the traditional Untouchable castes of Kerala and Tamil Nadu. Chakki is the name traditionally used for Pariah women. Vishnu is the supreme Hindu god.
6. M.N. Srinivas (1992), *On Living in a Revolution and Other Essays*, Oxford University Press, New Delhi, p. 3.
7. See Rajni Kothari (1994), "Rise of the Dalits and the Renewed Debate on Caste", *Economic and Political Weekly*, Vol. 29, No. 26, pp. 1589–94.
8. Government of India (2006), Social, Economic and Educational Status of the Muslim Community of India: A Report, Prime Minister's High Level Committee, Cabinet Secretariat, Delhi, p. 11.
9. P. Radhakrishnan (2008), "Muslim Backwardness and Sachar Report", *South Asian Journal*, No. 19, January-March.
10. P. Radhakrishnan (2007), "Crossing the Sethu Rubicon", *The New Indian Express* (leader page), September 26.
11. James Kurth (1999), "The Templeton Lecture on Religion and World Affairs", FPRI (Foreign Policy Research Institute) Wire, Religion and Globalization, Vol. 7, No. 7, May.
12. James Petras and Henry Veltmeyer (2001), *Globalisation Unmasked: Imperialism in the 21st Century*, Zed Books, London, p. 11.
13. Clifford Geertz (1965), "Religion: Anthropological Study", in David L. Sills (ed.), *International Encyclopedia of the Social Sciences*, Collier-Macmillan Publishers, London, p. 402.
14. I have dealt with these issues at length in an earlier write-up. See, P. Radhakrishnan (2004), "Religion under Globalisation", *Economic and Political Weekly*, Vol. 39, No. 13, March 27.
15. The reference is to W.H. Wiser (1936) 1969, *The Hindu Jajmani System: A Socio-Economic System Interrelating Members of a Hindu Village Community in Services*, Lucknow Publishing House, Lucknow.
16. See P. Radhakrishnan (2006), "Faith in a Time of Rationality", in *Religion, Caste and State*, Rawat Publications, Jaipur.
17. See for instance, K.A. Shaji (2008), "Human, all too Human", *Tehelka*, Vol. 5, No. 24, June 21; "Snuffing out the Flame of Faith" (edit), *The New Indian Express*, May 29.

18. I have dealt with the MA phenomenon in my article "Religion under Globalisation", *Economic and Political Weekly*, Vol. 39, No. 13, March 27–April 02, 2004.
19. "Cult of The Hugging Saint: Alternative Views on Mata Amritanandamayi: To Balance the Largely Unbalanced and Uncritical Resources published by the Amma Movement and its Followers" (http: //cultofthehuggingsaint.com).
20. A case in point is the Malayalam film *Yuvaturky* about a godman, with Gunasekaran becoming godman Somendraji. The film brings out luridly the politics of communalism, and the politics-godmen nexus.
21. There are, however, exceptions. A case in point is the arrest in May 2008 of Kerala godman Santosh Madhavan for molesting a minor and on charges of fraud, Devaswom Minister, G. Sudhakaran's labeling of all godmen as fraud; his statement that: "We should make these swamis wear clothes; they should start wearing clothes and we should teach them some decency .... I am still saying that 90 per cent of them are all thieves and they are all fit to go to jails;" much to the chagrin of self-proclaimed spiritual groups in Kerala and elsewhere. Timesofindia.com, "All godmen are fake, says Kerala Minister", May 17, 2008. Closely related to this is the announcement on May 24 of crackdown on spiritual fraudsters by Kerala Home Minister Kodiyeri Balarishnan and that an economic offences wing would be formed in the state police to probe sources of income of bogus godmen cheating people in the name of spirituality. See, "Crackdown on Spiritual Fraudsters: Kerala Home Minister", Newindpress.com, May 24, 2008. Also, "Scandal in God's Own Country", *The New Indian Express* (edit), May 21, 2008; "Divine Comedy", *The Week*, June 15, 2008.
22. Mariammen is a goddess of Hindu folk-religion commonly worshipped for protection against disease, particularly the traditionally dreaded Small Pox; and sometimes worshipped as the universal Shakti.
23. "South India's Bangaru Adigal", *Hinduism Today*, November 1985.
24. Implied in this is the claim that she is Yashoda, Krishna's mother.
25. In this context, an article in the *Outlook* dated October 20, 2003, "Bhakti Button" by Harsh Kabra, makes fascinating reading. Its opening paragraph runs thus: "Preaching was never so lucrative. With salvation outsourced, the boob tube now wants to be your drawing-room deliverer, promising armchair enlightenment and remote-controlled emancipation."

8

Usurping Differences, Reproducing Homogeneity

Cultural Changes in the Midst of Global Markets

ROHINI SAHNI AND V. KALYAN SHANKAR

"If I belonged to a bigger town, I would have definitely got more SMS votes", was the remark of a contestant (Amit Sana in an interview on www.rediff.com) voted out in the finals of 'Indian Idol', a popular entertainment contest on television . Beyond the phenomenon of 'a small town guy being undone in the big world', what larger cultural significance does this statement hold? There is a multilayered fine print to it that deserves further attention. As a preliminary speculation, from where are more votes going to come? In the hierarchies of urbanity, how would one's position make a difference?

In the public voting format, merely *viewing* the programme is not sufficient anymore. There is an active soliciting of votes, which has to be translated into tangible SMSs. How would this happen? More SMS would be a function of more mobiles and what if the penetration of mobiles is not prolific enough? Even if one owns a handset and intends to send an SMS, he/she still needs the network range. Plausibly, these hurdles could get more pronounced as you move down the geographic hierarchies, creating systemic limitations for an individual to succeed.

Framing this issue at a broader level, there is an increasing demand for an active viewer rather than a passive one; 'Indian Idol' is only an illustrative example of this. As an integral component of 'popular culture' (Strinati, 1995: xvii), the programme is widely consumed and has reached a high level of penetration in terms of viewership. The next rung of coordinated consumption seeks the transition into an 'active' viewer, and this would not be possible without the means to exercise it. The programme in a way seeks to assimilate two waves of 'material culture' (Miller, 1987): the first of the television that originated earlier and the second of the mobile phones. There could be a certain disparity in the spread of the second when juxtaposed with the first. The culture of 'sending SMS' as a form of consuming the programme may not exhibit the same number of takers as those who consume the programme only as spectators.

The way we engage with popular culture is increasingly getting defined through the *conduits* of material culture. This change has an international dimension to it, wherein both the forms of culture are drawing their influences from global trends. For a programme titled 'Indian Idol', what is so *Indian* about it? The participants are Indian, the songs they sing could be termed Indian by and large (though it cannot be vouched that they may not have been plagiarized from elsewhere); the indigenousness ends here. Otherwise, the show has a 'Made in America' tag in the fine print (being a conceptual rip-off from Fox TV's 'American Idol'); the channel Sony Television that has garnered the eyeballs is a Japanese multinational broadcaster; the televisions for viewing could be LG and Samsung in all probability [considering that the Korean multinationals have a large share of the Indian market (Chandra Mohan, 2005)]; and the mobile handsets could be Nokia or Sony again. Thus, we are affronted with a situation wherein the cultural basket of what we consume knowingly or unknowingly has an international connection at multiple levels, both in popular as well as material forms. Within the aegis of cultures going global, this paper explores two interrelated questions: How does economics matter to the global spread of culture? How does the culture of a particular commodity shape the economics of it?

When we say that consumption cultures go global, more often the ambit of studies revolves around *what* happens on account of it rather than *how* it happens. It is a study of the ends rather than the means. But how do cultures travel after all, particularly when they have acquired material forms? This paper probes through the channels for the global spread of material culture, and argues of how the underlying forces are as much economic as they are cultural. It is about the role that economists have in cultural studies, considering that economic frameworks can either bar or facilitate the movement of consumption cultures. This paper derives its examples from the Indian context but they could be equally applicable across other parts of the developing world.

I
How Does Economics Matter to the Global Spread of Culture?

Cultures Going Global, But How

When we talk of cultures going global, what do we essentially mean? The underlying reference is to the mobility of cultures. Locally confined to begin with, it indicates that cultures are now moving over or transcending into newer geographies and among unfamiliar people. In a default manner, cultures then get ascribed with characteristics that are associated with *mobility per se*. How much of cultures move and how fast, or, in other words, the pace and quantum of cultural movements would define their spread across space and time.

When cultures go global, what does this abstract term 'cultures' stand for? *What* is going global after all and imparting mobility to cultures? The answers to this could be traced to one of the ways in which culture has been defined. In a broader sense, cultures are "sets of beliefs or values that give meanings to ways of life and produce (are reproduced through) material and symbolic forms" (Crang, 1998: 2). Thus, looking at culture as a sum of parts of 'ways of life' and 'material and symbolic forms', it is these integral 'parts' that are gaining mobility.

Do these 'parts' exhibit evenness in the pace of their movements? This is where the enquiry would naturally lead. Of these, 'ways of life' as vectors of culture has a history to it. When Appadurai speaks of how "between travelers and merchants, pilgrims and conquerors, the world has seen much long distance (and long term) cultural traffic" (Appadurai, 2000: 27–28), the attempt is at identifying the role of individuals as *agents* of cross-cultural exchanges and familiarization. When people would move, not only would their 'ways of life' get transported but also the 'material and symbolic forms' building them. While these historic movements may not be the fastest or the most voluminous, they formed the initial waves of cultural influences spilling into unfamiliar territories.

The important point to be noted here is that with individuals at the helm, the pace of mobility associated with 'ways of life' and 'material forms' was consistent. Resulting from their interdependence, neither could ways of life move over and get entrenched without the ancillary existence of the material forms that would be needed to support them, nor could material forms outpace and arrive into new territories independent of the ways of life that would require them. The constraints to movements of individuals were in fact the limiting factors to cultural movements. Cultures could travel only as further as individuals would carry them. This no longer remains the case.

In cross-cultural travels, a substantial disjuncture can be witnessed at two levels. Firstly, individuals still act as agents of culture, and there continue to be more of them travelling across the world and faster than ever before. But, as active perpetrators, their importance has waned since individual movements are no longer a prerequisite for cultural movements. We argue that they have been superseded by 'ways of life' and 'material forms' acquiring a mobility of their own. These latter agents have been accosted with a certain fluidity of moving spatially at a faster pace and in larger numbers, something which is a typical limitation in physical, individual movements. Probing further, a deepening split can be observed in the relation between 'ways of life' and 'material/symbolic forms' as well. From moving simultaneously, there is now a disjuncture in the pace of their travel.

Earlier, there was a simultaneous flow of individuals carrying their lifestyles and merchandise and entrenching them elsewhere. Increasingly, this has been replaced by a haphazard sequence of cross-cultural travels, in terms of what moves first and what follows. Taking the case of Chinese and Indian diasporas and their little cultural hamlets or corners, one can discern the 'package deal' that would get transported as a collective. 'China towns' are miniature representations of what Chinese ethnic immigrants have on offer. Over time, a certain disjuncture can be observed in these collective transfers.

A Chinese or Indian meal is not confined to their respective hamlets anymore. They were exclusive reserves of these collectives once but now have an independent existence of their own.

They have travelled wider and faster, and have ceased to be esoteric offerings of a Chinese or Indian corner. Going further, the *ingredients* could be spread even wider, across general supermarkets and retail outlets, and not in conjunction with where the cuisine is on offer.

Thus, from the earlier definition of culture as the one giving meaning to ways of life and creating material forms, the order appears reversed when cultures go global. It is the material forms that arrive first with their newfound acceleration. As they get entrenched as independent variables, they are pliable to new meanings that may not be what they signified earlier. This is simply because the original symbolism has not moved fast enough. The material forms go on to give meanings to ways of life (same as original or otherwise), and in the process give a new dimension to cultures. From culture/ways of life/material/symbolic forms, as a set of cultural perpetuation, we now have material/symbolic forms/ ways of life/culture).

As we discuss the material forms of culture and explore the drivers behind their accelerated global movements, as economists, the enquiry becomes simpler by replacing 'material and symbolic forms' with the more familiar, economic terms of 'goods and services'. Discussing the diffusion of goods and services through 'trade and capital movements' (things that economists are obsessed with), an economic perspective to cultural movements can be put forth. While treading on the often unexplored, common grounds that exist between cultural studies and economics, the text that follows looks at how economists can *add value* to the discourse on cultural spread. This would be possible if only they were to understand the material and symbolic values that 'goods and services' embody in themselves.

No Culture Please, We are Economists

The indifference of economics to the cultural ramifications of its actions is not uncommon. The vast body of economic literature engaged in explaining the finer details of 'cross-border movements' (read trade and investments) hardly considers the associated 'cross-cultural movements'. Nothing can exemplify this better than the works of economists and theorists dealing with international trade movements, both in terms of theory as well as methodology of trade analysis.

Discussions on international trade theory, about what drives trade and between which countries, begin with the classical expositions of Adam Smith and David Ricardo. Any regular textbook on international economics commences with these foundations (Södersten and Reed, 2006). For establishing the absolute advantages arising from trade, Smith constructs his argument using the variables X and Y, which could simply be any of the commodities that a nation may produce. The Ricardian refinement to this, viz., the theory of comparative advantage further entrenches the gains from trade. Where Ricardo goes a step further than Smith, he also gives an identity to Smith's generic, nameless goods of X and Y by replacing them with wine and cloth. This could be termed a quantum leap in the economic perception of goods.

For Smith, trade arose from price differentiations, no matter what the goods were. By virtue of being nameless, the goods are in fact, *acultural.* Their social and cultural meanings do not have any bearing on the way trade evolves (at least the theory has been constructed that way). Arising from this inconsideration, there is a strong underestimation of what those goods may actually *signify*. Ricardo, on the other hand, does specify the items and gives them certain identities. But, for this improvement, the same inconsideration takes over again. His theory still does not recognize that wine and cloth are not simply items of trade, but are *culturally loaded* signifiers of consumption. What if the wine is champagne and the cloth is a Levi's jeans? Wouldn't they alter the way in which the goods move, and from where? Having been introduced in a particular country, wouldn't they influence the cultural patterns of consumption?

The other problem with trade theories is the implicit assumption that the trading nations are *culturally uniform*, and the same products could be freely extended across international markets. Taking Ricardo's example, even before England and Portugal start trading, they are producing and consuming the same items, namely, wine and cloth. After trade, these countries increase their consumption of both the goods but this in no way alters the consumption basket. The classical and even the modern trade theorists have not seriously considered the cultural outcome of the introduction of a totally new, non-indigenous product as part of trade. If what we consume is closely connected to our culture, then how does the introduction of an altogether new product impact us?

Without undermining the importance of trade theory, there is a need to look at the continued lack of coherence between economists, trade theorists and the cultural significance of goods. It has been little recognized that the traded items signify more than their monetary worth, and culturally their value could be higher/lower. Economics, with its overwhelming obsession with empirics, continues to construct its edifice with an air of indifference to the cultural dynamics ingrained in trade. Looking beyond the theory, even the actual methodology of trade data compilation bears the same imprint. Commodity trade classification systems would be a good example for illustration here.

The Harmonic System (HS) is the universally accepted classification for traded goods with the objective of maintaining uniformity in the definitions of goods. Within this, consider Code 22 that has been assigned to beverages, spirit and vinegar (UN COMTRADE, 2008). The code is a broad-based nomenclature that includes a host of sub-sections including unsweetened beverage waters (Code 2201), non-alcoholic sweetened and flavoured beverages (2202), beer made from malt (2203), grape wines (2204), fermented beverages not elsewhere specified including cider, perry etc. (2205), liqueur, spirits and un-denatured ethyl alcohol < 80 per cent (2208) among other items.

These numeric designations could just as well pass for rather innocuous trading items, until we start the naming procedures. What do these sub-codes stand for? What are the possible brand names that get concealed by them? Unsweetened beverage waters could simply be Kinley and Aquafina – two brands owned by rivals Coke and Pepsi respectively. Non-alcoholic sweetened and flavoured beverages could be Coke and Pepsi, and localized versions like Zam Zam (in the Middle East) and Inca Cola (in Peru). Beer is synonymous with Heineken, Cobra, Budweiser and Fosters, just as ethyl alcohol is the lesser-known identity for Bacardi, Chivas, Johnny Walker and Smirnoff. Without sounding like a paper on alcoholic spirits, this listing of names is simply to bring into focus how brands move trade. If you thought what's in a name after all, then it would be eroding all the strength that moves these brands, all the imagery created around them for bolstering their consumption.

Associated with the brands are also their countries of origin. "While Coca-Cola is promoted as a universal or trans-cultural product, it is at the same time identified with the culture and ideals of the United States. Coke is intimately bound up with the so-called American Dream" (Howes, 1996: 3). The same can be said of blue jeans (Levi's), or burgers (McDonalds) or pizzas (Pizza Hut). From these brand names, the direction of cultural perpetuation also becomes quite apparent in terms of where the goods originate and where they land up. Emerging in the First World, these products have penetrated extensively into the developing markets over the years.

> The Third World has changed dramatically since the concept of a 'developing world' gained popularity after World War II. This is clear from the type of products people consume. Cigarettes and mass-produced textiles have been a worldwide phenomenon for a long time; carbonated soft drinks, though more recent, are today nearly as widespread; cassette players and radios can be found in many villages in countries as diverse as Brazil, India and Nigeria; and the TV and VCR are become necessary status symbols of many peoples of the urban Third World. (Dannhaeuser, 1989)

To this list, we can have further additions in the form of mobiles and CDs, computers and Ipods. The term 'westernization' would refer to this very process of goods from the West proliferating in non-Western markets creating a standardized basket of consumption across geographies. In exchange, the developing world has its own set of items to offer (like Indian films or Thai cuisine) that have gained popularity beyond their domestic markets. But it does not amount to 'easternization' of the West. They remain niche chunks and do not get conferred with the status of mass consumed items; their quantum of movements is rather miniscule. The bulk of items that even the East exports are those that initially originated in the West. The South East Asians are integrated into global production chains of a number of consumer items (Hoekman and Kostecki, 2001: 14–15), and the same can be said of the East Europeans (Hoekman and Djankov, 1997: 471–487). Thus, the homogenizing influences are so pervasive that the same goods (often originating in the West) are being produced, traded and consumed across a larger set of nations.

While consumption has evolved a culture of its own over time, building lifestyles centred on material objects (Miller, 1987), it has also simultaneously created a trade of its own. Trade then becomes not just an 'engine of growth' but also a very discrete, subliminal perpetuator of consumer cultures. The trade-culture correlation is a historical one (Stearns, 2006), but the scale and conspicuousness, as observed today, warrants a new perspective.

Post-World War II, world exports have risen from 50 billion US dollars in 1948 to 12,065 billion US dollars in 2007 (UNCTAD, 2008). What are the implications of these enormous cross-border movements from a cultural point of view? Obviously, there are far more culturally loaded goods being traded than at any earlier point of time in history, but the story does not end at that. The rapidity by which the exchange has got scaled upwards deserves further attention. There is a distinct condensation of the time gap between consequent waves of cross-cultural goods arriving in the markets. Emerging from this, a larger number of people across widespread geographies are getting familiarized and influenced by a common set of beliefs or values that those goods impersonate. Trade, in a way, is a channel for the vast industry creating material objects to extend their markets. The resulting growth in global markets is prodigious, and the omnipresence of material goods would bear sufficient evidence to this global standardization of consumption patterns.

Now, what if these goods that may carry cultures get prevented from entry into particular markets? What if they get barred at national boundaries? Goods and services undoubtedly have greater mobility as cultural carriers, but they would not be necessarily given the freedom to exercise it. So, their potency of transmitting cultures, via the pace and volumes of their movements, gets blunted by preventing their entry. Countries have periodically resorted to putting up external barriers against goods and services. Here again, there are a host of *economic* forces that act as impediments; for example, custom duties and other trade regulations that insulate the country from external goods and, in the process, prevent their cultural connotations from seeping through. The edifice of protectionism that works for goods and services is equally potent in preventing cultural influences from entry. Cultural standardization or homogenization is possible only in those countries where there are lower economic barriers to facilitate better market access.

A 2005 UNESCO report identifies a framework for global cultural trade by categorizing goods into 'core cultural goods' and 'related cultural goods' (UNESCO, 2005: 15). The breadth of core cultural goods covers heritage items, books, newspapers, other printed matter, recorded media, audio-visual media, related cultural goods include equipment and support material, advertising and architectural services. But is the transmission of cultures restricted only to these so-called 'cultural' goods? Where do strong representations of consumption cultures like Coke or McDonalds fit into this scheme of things? The *real* scope of what can be termed as cultural has expanded to encompass far too many items.

To understand the scope of cultural goods, we need a more expansive classification in terms of (a) goods having direct cultural implications, and (b) goods that act as potential transmitters. Items like Coke and blue jeans are direct carriers. On the other hand, media-related equipment like TV, radio, mobiles and computers would all form examples of transmitters. By themselves, they do form a part of the larger framework of material culture, but the services being offered via them are the ones that do the job. For example, in India, being in possession of a television or radio would not have amounted to external cultural influences creeping in if they were to be providing access only to Doordarshan or Vividh Bharati – the official government channels with a distinct national identity. The real cultural explosion (entry of MTV, and the Star network, and the Sony bunch) resulted only after liberalization with the permission to foreign channels to operate in India.

The transmitters could be only the '*physical infrastructure under private ownership*' that could be used for facilitating the spread of cultural material. But they do create a common awareness of ways of life that people are hitherto unaware and expand the scope for mass standardization. For giving those ways of life a material form, the required goods and services might not have still arrived, but they do make their presence felt already via these transmitters. The pace and quantum of cultural spread via media services is even greater than commodities, in fact, it is instant.

Trade volumes have risen exponentially in the post-War time frame, but they have been surpassed by another channel of movements, that of international capital flows.

> The internationalization of production and consumption has been the defining feature of the world economy since the mid-1980s. Foreign Direct Investments (FDI) broadly defined as the creation of enterprises abroad or the acquisition of substantial stakes in existing enterprises now represents a major form of cross-border capital flows. More firms than ever in more industries and in more countries are expanding abroad through direct investment. It has been estimated today that worldwide some 65,000 trans-national corporations, 90 per cent of which are headquartered in OECD countries, have established more than 850,000 foreign affiliates, more than half of which operate in non-OECD countries. Their combined sales of almost $ 19 trillion is more than twice as high as total world exports in 2001. (Ferrarini, 2003: 7)

Thus, the sale of a large number of international goods and services no longer gets registered as part of international trade. The goods themselves do not move, but the money required for their production flows swiftly to establish local production. With investments in place, international goods then qualify as any other local item. The cultural connotations of these goods remain intact though, irrespective of their place of production. As traded items, they would face barriers. Once they acquire local status of production, these barriers get circumvented. Just like trade barriers, there exist hurdles for every penny that comes into the country as investments: monitors, screenings and regulations. As a country liberalizes, it is these barriers that get dismantled progressively both in terms of trade and investments. In the process, they leave the doors open for external cultures to strike root.

The multifarious cross-border movements of goods, capital, individuals and ideas, they all have an intrinsic cultural baggage travelling across. Which of these movements gets regulated at national boundaries and to what extent? Depending upon this, the levels of cultural exposure would vary and international influences on domestic consumption patterns would keep altering. These, in turn, would have their own bearing on the extent of cultural standardization they can bring about.

As seen in the course of this section, there are deep-rooted economic processes that give direction to cultural journeys. The term 'cultural movement' is a sweeping generalization of multiple channels through which the movements occur. Cultural movements via trade, via investments and, as seen later, via seepages are all direct repercussions of background economic forces, and economists are the ones more equipped to throw light on them. Putting it succinctly, economists do have a stake in cultural studies after all.

II

How the Culture of Products Shape the Economics of It?

What product is prone to enter through which channel? What will travel as exports, what will transcend across national barriers via foreign direct investment, and what will go international via value-chains (as seen later)? We argue that this decision is intrinsic to the product, and the *nature of consumption* it seeks. When items of trade get substituted by generic variables like X, Y and Z, or even by somewhat more suggestive indicators like wine and cloth, they offer a relative ease for constructing trade models. But they do not give an indication of the channels through which those items could enter different markets depending upon their cultural dynamics. The discretion exercised by the product to *choose* its modes of entry is not taken into consideration.

Entry of a product into an international market would be determined by (a) how many channels exist at a particular point of time, and (b) which of those get regulated at national boundaries. In closed markets, the channels for entry would be totally restricted. Consequently, the range of offerings in such markets is local in origin. As economies get deregulated, international products can establish their presence in local markets but they still do not have a free hand in choosing the channel of entry. It would depend upon the sequencing of what channel gets liberalized first. As economies increasingly become more open, a product or service may have several modes of entry that can be availed. It still does not imply that the product would resort to using all the channels at its disposal, for it would exhibit its own preferences or predilections to maximize its consumption.

With different channels in place for a product to get routed into new, open markets, the very idea of 'international' goods or services has got blurred over time. For a product to qualify as international, the litmus is no longer limited to the physical good and its entry from elsewhere. It now owns multiple passport identities depending on (a) where it gets produced and where it gets consumed, and (b) who owns the production, whether this ownership is domestic or international. Thus, we have two binaries to contend with: the first dealing with geographic movements, and the second dealing with capital movements. Different products employ different combinations to cross borders and become international. As stated earlier, this is influenced by the nature of consumption it seeks. The following grid constructs the four possibilities for producing and accessing a product:

Table 1

The Location-based Grid for Production and Consumption

		Consumption	
		Local	*International*
Production	Local	Local production and local consumption (1)	Local production and international consumption (2)
	International	International production and local consumption (3)	International production and international consumption (4)

Except for local production and local consumption, all the other combinations in the grid emerge with an international connection to them. They also form the routes for cultural initiations internationally. If searched a bit deeper, even the sole alternative of local production and consumption (Mode 1) is not so local after all, but about that later.

Mode 1
Local Production and Local Consumption

For what evokes an impression of being indigenous, 'local production and local consumption' needs to be probed in terms of the products that qualify under this category. What is so local about them? Or do they also have an international connection after all?

In 1968, when the Indian markets were relatively closed to external influences, Hazelhurst offers the following description of the markets in middle-rung cities of India:

> Behind the hawkers are the shops of resident businessmen. Here one finds, for example, bicycle sales shops and bicycle mechanics, small-scale metal workers who manufacture trunks and agricultural implements, the shops of medical practitioners and dispensers of medicine, cloth shops and brass shops, tailors and dry cleaners, radio repair shops and shops labeled simply 'general merchandise', gold merchants and grain merchants. (Hazelhurst, 1968: 540)

A host of these items have been traditionally part of local markets (gold, grain, cloth) and have their own symbolisms in local culture. What of bicycle and radio (or their repair) shops that have also found a place in the local markets? The markets are thus a composite blend of items that are (a) locally produced and consumed, and (b) locally produced and consumed but introduced from elsewhere. Over time, the assimilation of such introduced products has been extensive in the local markets.

Strictly speaking, the term 'local production and local consumption' would hold valid only in those countries where the products have originated. A large number of items of industrial production, which also qualify as items of material culture, began their journey through tapping the markets where they were first introduced. The automobile is a Daimler invention (read German), and the assembly line a Ford (read American) contribution. Just like this, we can ascribe nationalities to an array of inventions like the radio and television, computers and mobiles that are the beacons of material culture. These items would find a place in Mode 1 wherein they were locally produced and locally consumed *originally*.

Gradually, the firms mass producing these items began their journey across the different alternatives of the grid. For tapping new markets, firms progress through the different alternatives mentioned in the grid. Starting with local production and local consumption, then, came a phase of their exports to other markets, followed by the alternative of producing them locally in those markets through FDI, and finally cutting costs by resorting to value chains.

Across the vast gamut of products symbolizing material culture, the term 'local production and local consumption' holds different meanings for different markets. In the originating markets or countries, it has an added meaning being emerged from a local idea or invention. All other markets would have to acquire the product either through trade or capital investments. But an alternative phenomenon can be observed here. Moving across the grid creates a time lag resulting from a phase-by-phase lifting of barriers across nations, as also the technical gap possibilities. During *this* time lag, the commodities may not be moving as yet, but their underlying ideas or concepts can, and often do. Before the actual 'original' products arrive at the borders, and jump across barriers, the ideas have already permeated and taken root. There is a local production and local consumption (the replicated or reverse engineered Mode 1) of the products emerging from international *ideas*.

When the original international product enters the local market employing any of the other modes, it has to contend with local versions that have already emerged. At the time of Coke's re-entry into post-liberalization India, there were already local substitutes in the form of Thums Up and Campa Cola. When Levi Strauss, the original blue jeans manufacturer, started its Indian operations in 1995, there were a host of Indian blue jeans brands (Cambridge, Buffalo, Flying Machine) that had already got established. Adding further depth to the local jeans sales were 'ready to stitch' jeans that fitted with the Indian idea of custom tailored clothes. Ruf & Tuf jeans were "sold as a kit: two legs, buttons, rivets, zipper, leather label and an instruction booklet for the neighborhood tailor" (Jordan, 1997). Thus, there were local entrenchment of international ideas that had cultural content ingrained in them but had altogether bypassed the regular channels or modes of access. We thus have mirrored forms of 'local production and local consumption' wherein they are not local in the strict sense of the word but more attuned to local culture.

Mode 2
Local Production and International Consumption

Considering the alternative of local production and international consumption (Mode 2), the rationale could simply be explained by international trade in the Hecksher–Ohlin world. When production is confined locally and foreign markets have to be tapped, it assumes the form of trade. If we take the case of "Ricardo's wine", it would be interesting to look at the trade volumes for this category and the nations generating those numbers (see Table 2). The bulk of exports are accounted by a selective club of nations including France, Italy and a few others from Western Europe (COMTRADE, 2008). France derives a large part of its code 22 exports from grape wines, of which there is a substantial proportion of sparkling wines (which would include champagne). Similarly, the United Kingdom trades extensively under the whisky sub-code (220830) and presumably a sizeable chunk of it would be brand sales of scotch and likes. The geographic confinement of these items' production has ensured that they would necessarily have to be procured via trade. In fact, the producing nations have been vehement in safeguarding their exclusivity of production.

Geographical indicators as a form of intellectual property rights are precisely for this purpose. For example, champagne cannot be equated with any other sparkling wine. The "French law has created the 'Maisons de Champagne' to determine exactly the methods and conditions of Champagne production in France and has empowered them to sue in protection and on behalf of the name 'Champagne'" (Knoll, 1970: 310). This legislation now has an international validation to it, with additional protection for geographic indications for wines and spirits under the aegis of intellectual property rights at WTO (World Trade Organization, 2008). The term 'champagne' is no longer associated just with French culture but is linked with the larger domain of the culture of consumption. Thus, nations have resorted to a safeguarding mechanism to protect what would seem as cultural connections of items; but the motive is just as well to prevent their economic spillovers being accrued to other nations.

Table 2

Exports from Selective Countries for Code 22 and Sub-categories in 2006

Country	*Product (HS Code 2002)*	*Export value (billion$)*
France	Beverages, spirit and vinegar (22)	13.299
	(of which) grape wines (2204)	7.830
	(of which) sparkling wines (220410)	2.844
United Kingdom	Beverages, spirit and vinegar (22)	6.998
	(of which) liqueur, spirits and un-denatured ethyl alcohol (2208)	5.352
	(of which) whisky (220830)	4.642

Source: UN Comtrade database.

In case of champagne, annual "sales by all producers total more than 300 million yearly bottles, roughly Euro 4.3 billion. Roughly two-thirds of these sales are made by the large champagne houses with their *grandes marques* (major brands). Fifty-eight per cent (58%) of total production is sold in France, and the remaining 42 per cent exported worldwide" [http://en.wikipedia.org/wiki/Champagne(wine)]. Even as the champagne brand remains imbued in French culture, France as a nation remains the sole authorized beneficiary of this cultural symbol.

Within the spheres of consumption and material culture, a similar status could be denoted to the French or Italian couture or luxury goods industry. "The worldwide luxury goods market now represents a total of 35 billion US dollars. On that market, the French companies have contributed a little less than 50 per cent of total turnover in the mid-1990s" (Djelic and Ainamo, 1999: 625). Comité Colbert, an elite 70-member association governed by

French law includes an enviable list of firms from the world of luxury goods: haute couture (Chanel, Dior, Givenchy, Lacoste, Yves Saint Laurent), leather goods (Hermes, Louis Vuitton) and perfumes (Caron, Guerlain, Dior, Chanel) among others. With a 'Made in France' tag, "the Comité Colbert members generate 82 per cent of their sales on international markets" (Comité Colbert, 2006) with their international presence not through production sites but through retail avenues. "Scattered all over the world are about 3,300 exclusive points of sale representing French luxury" (ibid).

Table 3

Exports of Select Categories of Luxury Goods from Select Countries in 2006

Product (Code)	*Country*	*Export value (in dollars)*	*Trade quantity*	*Per unit valuations ($)*
Leather goods				
Articles of apparel and clothing accessories of leather (4203)	China	2,892,898,808	108,709,894	26.61
	Italy	931,015,176	8,217,050	113.30
Other articles of leather or composition leather (4205)	China	597,042,385	68,032,029	8.77
	France	291,099,662	1,438,224	202.40

Source: UN Comtrade database.

Table 3 gives the trade figures for certain categories of leather goods, where China is consistently the top exporter, followed by Italy (4203) and France (4205). But what does it suggest about the 'Made in China' versus 'Made in France' or 'Made in Italy' labels that those goods represent? Beyond the trade figures that standardize the items, what would the comparison amount to? Can such a comparison be made after all?

Firstly, the Chinese exports are simply bulk in nature and cannot be equated with the niche French exports of leather goods, which must be originating from the Comité Colbert members or similar firms aspiring to emulate them in the world of luxury goods. It would be equating a branded, named identity with a nameless one that sells in volumes. Secondly, the high culture that the French goods intend to construct does not come cheap, as can be seen from the high per unit valuations fetched by them. So effectively, France is deriving its valuations through much less quantities traded, considering that its exports have an added 'brand' value. Thirdly and more importantly, what can be understood about the positioning in the international market for a 'Made in France' versus 'Made in China'? The Chinese exports, being mass-based and derived from price competitiveness, would face competition from other developing countries which can replicate the same characteristics. There is a certain threat of substitution for the 'Made in China', which could easily become a 'Made in Vietnam' or 'Made in India'. As a result the Chinese goods persistently have to be low-priced and mass-based. The French or Italian goods do not face such a danger of being overrun, considering that their items of exports have acquired the status of luxury goods. They cater to a niche market that is keen to demonstrate the ownership of a Yves Saint Laurent or Gucci (for a price, of course). These exports would be stickier and would continue to be based out of France or Italy, even if the production costs are higher. The same branded identities could also be behind the high French exports of perfumes (see Table 4). Comparisons are odious, and this would be just another case of how trade data comparisons completely mask the underlying cultural dynamics that move trade.

Table 4

Export of Perfumes (Code 33) and Sub-categories from France

Country	*Product*	*Export value (in dollars)*	*Trade quantity*
France	Essential oils and resinoids; perfumery, cosmetic or toilet preparations (33)	12,446,238,233	—
	(of which) perfumes and toilet waters (3303)	4,088,282,601	120,801,932
	(of which) beauty or make-up preparations (3304)	4,769,564,699	179,614,107

Source: UN Comtrade database.

Niche luxury brands that are symbols of the culture of elite consumption show a high degree of reluctance in extending their production through capital movements internationally. They are at the roots of differentiating between elite and mass consumption.

These are not supposed to be mass consumer goods, and as such, have pricing barriers to their access. It is a natural choice, considering that their brand equity revolves around regulating the possession and consumption of the product. Under these circumstances, their production would tend to be concentrated in the parent country, from where they would be exported.

While it is easy to state that 'exclusive' products are conspicuous examples that choose the trade route, the categorization of an item as 'exclusive' is a difficult proposition. What may have been exclusive once may not remain exclusive over time. Ample examples could be stated here; in fact, most of the consumer durables that have been stated as cultural transmitters were once niche items. Naturally, they found a mention in the trading lists of nations. Progressively, they have become mass consumption items. At this juncture, they move beyond trade channels and into the domain of capital movements. Thus, the grid constructed above is not two-dimensional (those of production and consumption) but has a third dimension of time in which the production and consumption take place.

Mode 3
International Production and Local Consumption

International production and local consumption could be interpreted as 'normal' trade again, this time via import channels. But, the objective here is to bring out the vast global expansion of production facilities brought about by the global movement of capital, commonly referred as Foreign Direct Investment (FDI) or its emerging forms of private equity ownerships. In such cases, the validity of the term 'international production' is based on the fact that the money, technical know-how is international, even though the production is local.

Existing economic literature enumerates the motives behind FDI movements from the perspective of *why* it takes place and *when*. In answer to the why, the reasons include circumvention of trade barriers or 'tariff jumping' (Blonigen and Feenstra, 1996; Blonigen et al, 2002); reducing transport costs (Horstmann and Markusen,1987); relocation of production that is either resource seeking (skilled labour, raw materials) or efficiency seeking (low labour costs) (UNCTAD, 2007: 3). In answer to *when* FDI would move in, the focus has been on understanding the early or delayed effects of entry (Ellis and Fausten, 2002).

But this still does not answer the question of what drives capital movements in *some* products as against others? The reasons could be as much cultural as economic. We argue that depending upon their specific culture of consumption, products may or may not go the FDI way. If we take the case of exclusive wines discussed in the previous section, they would continue to remain in the trade channels irrespective of trade barriers and the possibility of low production costs elsewhere. It is intrinsic to the culture of consumption they seek, distinctly elite in this case. In contrast, there are goods that seek a mass base and their production and consumption is built on stupendous volumes. The channel of trade becomes an incompetent carrier for such items because of (a) the large volumes that have to be handled, and (b) the added costs of transport would bring down the affordability and therefore reduce the mass appeal of the product.

In terms of production, they would not remain restricted to selective countries (as in case of wine). Their ownership though remains dominated by multinationals from few countries. These products thrive not through centralized production in selective countries and their eventual exports, but through a more decentralized network of production. To achieve this goal, they diversify their production and distribution facilities as seen from the extensive global operations for some of the major culturally symbolic brands.

The category of 'sweetened beverages' would form a good example to be cited here. "I would like the world to buy a Coke", goes the title of the biography of a Coca Cola CEO (Greising, 1998). In tune with this, the Coca Cola 2007 annual report boasts of being "the largest manufacturer, distributor and marketer of non-alcoholic beverage concentrates and syrups in the world", that are now "sold in more than 200 countries" (The Coca Cola Company, 2007). There is a fascinating account that traces the dynamics of Coke's existence and enormous expansion over the century (Pendergrast, 2000). Table 5 shows the stupendous rise in Coke servings over the century.

Table 5
Rise in Coke Servings over the Century

Year	*Coca Cola bottles sold*
1886	9 glasses per day
1903	Over 300 million
1915	Over 5 billion
1936	Over 100 billion
1952	Over 200 billion
1965	Over 500 billion
1973	Over 1 trillion
1982	Over 2 trillion
1993	Over 4 trillion
2003	Over 6 trillion

Source: http://www.rzuser.uni-heidelberg.de/~el6/presentations/pres_c2_hoa/CCSalesfigures.htm

If the entry of international goods and services forms the quasi-front for spread of cultures, capital movements are the massive force driving their pace and quantum. Through their orientation towards generating a mass consumer base, they are instrumental in defining or projecting what eventually become mass cultures. In a rather suggestively titled chapter named 'Exporting Americana', John Love writes of how McDonalds, a quintessential American food service chain, now derives a substantial chunk of its revenues from *outside* the United States.

> What is more surprising than the scope of its success abroad is that McDonalds cracked the international market with more or less the same formula it had perfected in the United States. Given the enormous lifestyle differences between domestic and foreign markets, a unique approach to international expansion might have been expected. McDonalds might have greatly modified its system to adapt to foreign cultures. Instead, it stuck to the basics of its system and *changed the cultures to fit it.* (Love, 1995: 416) (italics ours)

This cultural moulding is not just through some millions of servings of a Coke or a Big Mac that are standardizing what we drink and eat. These are flagrant examples that only form the upper crust of a phenomenon that runs deep. There are blue jeans forming a part of what we dress. There are cosmetics that decide on how we should look and for what occasion. Across all of these categories, there are multinational firms trying to sell their products *en masse* and they have all penetrated across nations through the FDI route. Looking through the FDI figures for India, we can segregate them into two broad categories of items: (a) direct cultural signifiers that would include a host of consumer durables and fast moving consumer goods, and (b) support structures required for servicing these direct signifiers.

Table 6

Industry Classification for Cultural Transfers Through FDI in India

	Industries	*Examples*
Direct signifiers	Food and beverages	Coca Cola, Pepsico, Kellogg
	Clothing	L'evis, Lee Cooper, Benetton, L'acoste
	Personal care	Revlon, Avon, L'oreal
	Consumer durables	LG, Samsung, Nokia
	Computers	Compaq, Microsoft
	Automobiles	Hyundai, Daimler Chrysler, Ford
Support structures	Power and electric equipment	Alstom, ABB
	Banking and finance	HSBC, Citicorp, ABN Amro
	Telecommunication services	Vodafone

For people to indulge in this plethora of goods, their capacity to consume needs to be expanded. People have to be familiarized with what they have to consume for what occasion, and how. They have to be convinced of how an occasion is incomplete without having consumed a certain set of items manufactured for the purpose. This platform gets created through the media instruments. The 2001 Census of India reports of over 60 million households having television sets and over 67 million in possession of radios (Census of India, 2001). If we take the case of televisions, a large part of this growth can be traced to the post-liberalization period when a host of MNCs like LG, Samsung etc., entered the Indian markets and consolidated the base of their production. The televisions become the instruments for broadcasting of a host of MNC channels including the basket of Star TV and Sony that too entered simultaneously.

So long as India restricted market access to external products and services, it remained a static destination that was able to regulate external influences from creeping in. Gradually, with the easing of FDI norms, it has opened the scope for such a possibility. The range of foreign influences on the Indian television spans from (a) direct transmissions of international sitcoms (e.g., Friends, The Bold and the Beautiful) to (b) localized versions of international shows (e.g., *Kaun Banega Crorepati* that derives its name and content from 'Who Wants to be a Millionaire', 'Indian Idol' that traces itself to American Idol, or the more recent *Kya Aap Panchvi Pass Se Tez Hain* based on the American show 'Are You Smarter than a Fifth Grader'). In the absence of a widespread network of television sets, the viewership for these programmes would have been limited. In some cases, the mere consumption or viewership would not suffice. Those consuming the programmes have to be led to the next rung of consumption, which is by soliciting their active participation in the decision-making process of selecting winners. Indian Idol for instance, was based on hundreds and thousands of SMS's, which gives an idea of the massive network of mobiles at work. Reverting back to the opening statement, it firstly points out at the further scope for penetration of mobile networks and services in the interiors and at a deeper level, the scope for further standardization of who consumes what. The success of international capital would depend on the achievement of this dynamism.

Mode 4
International Production and International Consumption

This final alternative involves a complex combination of trade, FDI and international labour markets as manifesting in the form of international splitting of supply chains, also referred as 'value addition chains'.

> The Barbie Doll's label says "made in China". This suggests, correctly, that in the production of Barbie, China provides the factory space, labour and electricity, as well as cotton cloth for the dress. It conceals however, the facts that: Japan provides the nylon hair, Saudi Arabia provides oil, Taiwan refines oil into ethylene for plastic pellets for the body, and Japan, the United States and Europe supply almost all the machinery and tools, most of the molds (the most expensive item) come from the United States, Japan, or Hong Kong; the United States supplies

> the cardboard packaging, paint pigments and molds; and Hong Kong supplies the banking and insurance and carries out the delivery of the raw materials to factories in Guangdong Province in South China, together with the collection of the finished products and shipping. (Snyder, 2002: 4)

If "the Barbie doll is quintessentially American in origin, style and culture" (ibid) as Snyder writes further, there are a couple of things evident here: (a) a product symbolic of material culture has many seemingly non-cultural processes backing it, and (b) these processes are geographically dispersed in operations, resulting in a large number of nations backing this cultural end-product.

"The rising integration of world markets has brought with it a disintegration of the production process, in which manufacturing or services activities done abroad are combined with those performed at home" (Feenstra, 1998), giving rise to the phenomenon of value addition chains. As the mass base of consumer products increases, and becomes more global in spread, the need for tapping nation-specific comparative advantages becomes necessary. Production gets fragmented wherein "materials and components produced in one country may pass through a sequence of other countries that each add value through fabrication, assembly, or other processing before a final product is delivered to consumers. Countries, which specialize in different stages of the production process according to factor-cost or other locational advantages, are thus linked in a vertical chain through trade in intermediate inputs" (Borga and Zeile, 2004).

There is extensive economic literature explaining the emergence and rationale of these international production networks (Gereffi et al., 1994; Feenstra, 1998; USITC, 1999), and going further about how there is extensive multinational firms' involvement in these chains (Borga and Zeile, 2004). The crux of the matter is that this mode exhibits a combination of both trade and investment activities. Borga and Zeile (2004) give a detailed account of how affiliates of American MNCs (read firms established via FDI) import a substantial chunk of their inputs from parent firms. Such chains are not just restricted to Barbie dolls or Pokemon games but are highly penetrated in case of electronic and transportation equipment.

The cost reductions resulting from global sourcing and economies of scale are enabling a further expansion of the material culture represented by the products coming out of these networks. The items that get produced through such assemblages are then offered across varied markets, validating the terminology of international production and international consumption. This possibility would be somewhat nipped if there were to be barriers to trade or to capital movements.

Where do Local Markets End and Global Markets Begin?

As nations liberalize, there is an increasing interaction of local and international markets resulting from the lifting of economic barriers. In the process, the identity of local markets would be shaped from its response to the presence of international markets (as represented by international products or brands). There are different levels of this interaction, and the hierarchy of the changed local markets needs to be deciphered.

At one extremity are those chunks of the local markets that continue to remain stubbornly local, and go on to become representatives of the local or indigenous market cultures. Their binding set of customers is drawn out of this claim to authenticity. The example to this would be old sweet shops, cloth stores, gold and silver ornaments, metalware shops etc., which highlight their long-standing local traditions.

But for these, all other forms of local markets do have a changing face. It would be more visible and swifter in metropolitan markets, though their presence can be noted at different levels of urbanity. There could be alterations in terms of their offerings, their representations and their displays, which may show semblance of international practices. In our urban markets, particularly the metropolises, we are witnessing the direct participation of international products with their exclusive spaces in consumption-oriented constructions (e.g., malls, multiplexes). Such international products as stocked in international stores, and located in local duplications of international construction spaces, have their own set of customers. But their influences are more long-standing in nature, and permeate through the entire breadth of the local markets and have a larger pool of customers. The process of this percolation varies from product to product, but some insights can be drawn from the numerous examples from Indian markets.

Firstly, we have the cascading bandwagon effect (Featherstone, 1992), which comprises of the introduction of a commodity or an idea in a niche section of the society, from where it progresses to mass consumption. Considering the diversity of purchasing powers in our urban markets, the bandwagon effect assumes a different dimension here. A product could gain mass consumption through its affordability. But when the product has a substantial awareness created through media, and its symbolic significance has been accepted by the masses, there is a latent demand for the product. Even if the product or idea *per se* remains unaffordable, this demand is then tapped by cheaper substitutes or variants of the original. In either case, the introduction of the product deepens the markets. For example, expensive fashion statements like Tommy Hilfiger or Gucci are introduced in niche, elite markets. But within a short span of time, the brand moves to the masses, and on to the streets, with every coat or jacket having the name inscribed on it, often with 'wrong spellings'. This phenomenon is largely restricted to low technology intensive commodities, such as apparel, footwear, sun-glasses, among others. They are fashion statements nevertheless, and people take cognizance of the fact that they could construct their lifestyles through indulging in these forms of material culture.

Secondly, we have the creolization effect (Howes, 1996) where a commodity or an idea, when inherited, an indigenous set of meanings are added on the concept. For example, we could consider cross-cultural cuisine like a 'pizza with tandoori topping' or 'Chinese bhel puri', or 'Bhangra pop', or a linguistic concoction like 'Hinglish'. This transformation is catalysed by the media, which makes an impression on mind spaces through repeated reinforcements. Through this indigenization, the product then finds place in the consumption basket of the masses on a regular basis. It does not remain a novelty any more. Acceptance of one wave of cross-cultural commodities or ideas paves the way for a second wave of them. Individuals, who have indulged in the first set, are likely to respond favourably to the subsequent set of new commodities on their introduction. This is another phenomenon that deepens the markets, increasing the mass base of the product. Again, low technology goods are more prone for such assimilation.

Thus, when firms enter new emerging markets either through trade or through investments, they are actually betting on extending their patterns of consumption internationally. But, the complexity of this process emerges not just from the national barriers, but also the local variants that have already made headway in the local markets. The material culture as signified by the original products may not seep through as much. But there already exists a local, developing form of it.

In the context of consumerism, a Third World country like India 'imports' readymade commodities or concepts. The underlying meanings of these objects and concepts are already assigned and established in the developed world, where these concepts have originated. It could be blue jeans or Rolex watches or a celebration package like the Valentine's Day (Sahni and Kalyan Shankar, 2006). In their attempt to expand their markets, the developed world (multinationals) transfers these packages to a Third World consumer. As a 'second hand' user of these readymade concepts, a Third World market or consumer does not really get the opportunity to assign meanings to these objects of consumption. The transfer of meanings and symbols inherited from the West acts as a benchmark of consumption standards, even working as a force of standardization of urban culture. The rapid speed of urbanization and pressures of globalization rarely provide Third World urban societies with the space and time to evolve their own patterns of urban culture and consumption.

References

Appadurai, Arjun. 2000. *Modernity at Large: Cultural Dimensions of Globalization (Public Worlds)*, Vol. 1, Minneapolis: University of Minnesota Press, pp. 27–28.

Blonigen, Bruce A. and Robert C. Feenstra. 1996. Protectionist Threat and Foreign Direct Investment, Working Paper 5475, NBER.

Blonigen, Bruce A., KaSaundra Tomlin and Wesley W. Wilson. 2002. Tariff Jumping FDI and Domestic Firms' Profits, Working Paper 9027, NBER.

Borga, Maria and William Zeile. 2004. "International Fragmentation of Production and the Infra-Firm Trade of US Multinational Companies", Working Paper, Bureau of Economic Analysis.

Chandra, Mohan N. 2005. "Running Away with the Indian Market", *India Now Magazine*, Vol. 2, Issue 3, IBEF, 6 September.

Comité, Colbert. 2006. "The French Lead in Luxury, a Strategic Industry", *Annual Report 2006*, p. 8.

Crang, Mike. 1998. "Cultural Geography", *Routledge Contemporary Human Geography Series*, Routledge, p. 2.

Dannhaeuser, Norbert. 1989. "Marketing in Developing Urban Areas" in Stuart Plattner (ed.) *Economic Anthropology*, Stanford: Stanford University Press.

Djelic, Marie-Laure and Antti Ainamo. 1999. "The Co-Evolution of New Organizational Forms in the Fashion Industry: A Historical and Comparative Study of France, Italy and the United States", *Organization Science*, Vol. 10, No. 5, September–October, p. 625.

Ellis, Christopher J. and Dietrich Fausten. 2002. "Strategic FDI and Industrial Ownership Structure", *Canadian Journal of Economics*, Vol. 35, No. 3, August, pp. 476–94.

Featherstone, Mike. 1992. "Cultural Production, Consumption, and the Development of the Cultural Space", in Richard Munch and Neil Smelser (eds.), *Theory of Culture*, Berkeley: University of California Press, p. 268.

Feenstra, Robert C. 1998. "Integration of Trade and Disintegration of Production in the Global Economy", *The Journal of Economic Perspectives*, Vol. 12, No. 4, Autumn, p. 31.

Ferrarini, Benno. 2003. "A Multilateral Framework for Investment?", in *The Singapore Issues and the World Trading System: The Road to Cancun and Beyond*, State Secretariat for Economic Affairs and Simon J. Evenett (eds.), Bern, Switzerland: Federal Legal Publications, Inc., p. 7.

Gereffi, Gary, Miguel Korzeniewicz and Roberto P. Korzeniewicz. 1994. "Introduction: Global Commodity Chains", in Gary Gereffi and Miguel Korzeniewicz (eds.), *Commodity Chains and Global Capitalism*, Westport, CT: Praeger Publishers, p. 1.

Greising, David. 1998. *I'd Like the World to Buy a Coke: The Life and Leadership of Roberto Goizueta*, New York: John Wiley.

Hazelhurst, Leighton W. 1968. "The Middle Range City in India", *Asian Survey*, Vol. 8, No. 7, July.

——. 1968. "Modernization in South Asian Studies: Essays in a Changing Field", *Asian Survey*, Vol. 8, No. 11, November, p. 540.

Hoekman, Bernard and Simeon Djankov. 1997. "Determinants of Export Structure of Countries in Central and Eastern Europe", *World Bank Economic Review*, Vol. 11, pp. 471–87.

Hoekman, Bernard and M.M. Kostecki. 2001. *The Political Economy of the World Trading System: From GATT to WTO*, Oxford: Oxford University Press, pp. 14–15.

Horstmann, Ignatius J. and James R. Markusen. 1987. "Strategic Investments and the Development of Multinationals", *International Economic Review*, Vol. 28, No. 1, February, pp. 109–21.

Howes, David. 1996. *Cross Cultural Consumption: Global Markets, Local Realities*, New York: Routledge, pp. 1–2 and 5–8.

Jordan, Miriam. 1997. "Arvind Sates Global and Local Hunger for Jeans: An Indian Textile Mill Strikes Gold with Denim", *International Herald Tribune*, Business, November 20.

Knoll, Alfred Phillip. 1970. "Champagne", *The International and Comparative Law Quarterly*, Vol. 19, No. 2, April, p. 310.

Love, John F. 1995. *McDonald's: Behind the Arches*, New York: Bantam Books, p. 416.

Miller, Daniel. 1987. *Material Culture and Mass Consumption*, Oxford: Basil Blackwell, pp. 3–5.

Pendergrast, Mark. 2000. *For God, Country and Coca-Cola: The Definite History of the Great American Soft Drink and the Company that Makes It*, New York: Basic Books.

Sahni, Rohini and Kalyan Shankar V. 2006. "Romancing Material Culture in Urban Public Spaces: The Case of Valentine's Day in Pune", *Economic and Political Weekly*, Vol. XLI, No.7, February 18, pp. 649–54.

Snyder, Francis. 2002. "Governing Economics Globalization: Global Legal Pluralism and EU Law", in Francis Snyder (ed.), *Regional and Global Regulation of International Trade (Studies in European Law and Integration)*, Oxford: Hart Publishing, p. 4.

Södersten, Bo and Geoffrey Reed. 2006. *International Economics*, 3rd Edition, London: Macmillan Press.

Stearns, Peter N. 2006. *Consumerism in World History*, New York: Routledge.

Strinati, Dominic. 1995. *An Introduction to Theories of Popular Culture*, London: Routledge, p. xvii.

UNCTAD 2007. World Investment Prospects Survey 2007–09, United Nations, New York and Geneva, p. 3.

UNESCO 2005. International Flow of Selected Cultural Goods and Services 1994–2003: Defining and Capturing the Flow of Global Cultural Trade, UNESCO Institute for Statistics, UNESCO Sector for Culture.

USITC 1999. Production Sharing: Use of US Components and Materials in Foreign Assembly Operations 1995–1998, USITC Publication 3265, December.

Websites

Census of India 2001. Website: http: //www.censusindia.gov.in/ accessed on 21st April 2008.

The Coca Cola Company 2007. *Annual Report*, Website: http: //www.thecoca-colacompany.com/investors/pdfs/form_10K_2007.pdf accessed on 17th April 2007.

"Amit Sana's doing Fine, Fine, Fine!" Website: http: //in.rediff.com/movies/2005/mar/22amit.htm uploaded on 22nd March, 2005, accessed on 21st April 2008.

http://www.iht.com/articles/1997/11/20/denim.t.php
http://www.rzuser.uni-heidelberg.de/~el6/presentations/pres_c2_hoa/ CCSalesfigures.htm accessed on 14th January 2008.

http: //en.wikipedia.org/wiki/Champagne_(wine), accessed on 14th January 2008.

UN COMTRADE 2008. "United Nations Commodity Trade Statistics Database", http: //comtrade.un.org/accessed on 7th April 2008.

UNCTAD 2007. "UNCTAD Handbook of Statistics 2007 Online", http://www.unctad.org/Templates/Page.asp?intItemID=1890&lang=1, accessed on 7th of April, 2008.

WTO 2008. "Agreement on Trade Related Aspects of Intellectual Property Rights", Article 23, p. 329.
Website: http://www.wto.org/english/docs_e/legal_e/legal_e.htm accessed on 11th April 2008.

Part IV
Discourses in Social Movements

9

Gender Discourse and Its Many Avatars

How Critical? How Mainstream?

MAITRAYEE CHAUDHURI

That women's studies and women's movements have had an inextricably linked history is a core assumption of this paper. A related premise is the belief that the women's movements have succeeded in making gender a major issue in the public sphere. Major actors, such as the state, civil society, market and international institutions, have had to take cognizance of gender inequality. This 'mainstreaming' of gender, whether in developmental programmes or in the corporate sector or in the media, has most certainly made gender issues more visible. However, this has often led to a delinking with broader visions of liberation and justice articulated by women's movements. Significant reconfigurations have therefore occurred with the very ideas of freedom, justice, equity, autonomy, choice, activism and empowerment that women's movements raised. This forms one part of the story of the shifts in gender discourse – a shift which in some ways has redefined public discourse.

There is another part to the manner in which the women's movements and women's studies have redefined dominant and broad understandings of society and history which informs the common sense of state, society and nation. Critical rethinking has taken place around caste, labour, nationalism, colonialism, family, body and violence, which has led to new knowledge formations and most importantly questioned the domain assumptions that go into the making of knowledge in patriarchal societies. This paper seeks to look at both these developments, namely, the intended and unintended consequences of 'mainstreaming' of gender; and the critical interrogation of extant social science knowledge by women's studies.

Some of the changes can be linked directly to the global rise of a neo-liberal vision and India's own tryst with it. But not all trends evident in the growing body of women studies can be attributed to the rise of neo-liberalism. Many fundamental interrogations of both women's movements and women studies are linked to the challenges thrown up by new movements that have focused on the rights of "the discriminated and socially excluded". These interrogations have brought fresh insights to our understanding of central categories, such as nation and caste, class and community and therefore also of possible ways of looking at 'globalization' itself. It is in this context that the first part of the paper revisits histories of the women's question. For the many interrogations of conventional accounts of the history of the women's question have emerged from both women's movements and women studies. They offer new understandings of the past and thereby also of the present.

The first task this paper (part II) therefore sets out to do is a very quick and an essentially schematic history of movements that raised the women's question in India and the corresponding nature of women's studies. It is a quick, sweeping account of the major trends from the colonial period into early years of independence, to the mid-1970s that witnessed a range of movements, including what is often termed as the second wave of women's movements. This broad etching has two purposes. One, it will help us better appreciate the nature and direction of changes in recent years. Two (and this purpose is critical to this paper), it will foreground how new perspectives emerging from new movements narrate histories differently. The second task (part III) involves an overt focus on the contemporary period, focusing primarily on the changes that have come with the New Economic Policies of the Indian state since 1991. The effort will not be towards an exhaustive treatment of either studies or movements but will be more in the nature of an illustrative treatment of what one identifies as distinctive features of the current phase of both social movements and studies on women. Significantly here too new narratives emerge with the increasing presence and role of new actors, especially that of international institutions. The beginning of women studies, indeed the women's question itself, is assumed to have begun with the declaration by the United Nations of the International Women's Year and Decade in 1975. Such narratives focus on how women have emerged as a target group in agency programmes/projects of various UN organizations such as the UNFPA, UNIFEM, UNICEF and UNDP. This is the dominant storyline of development practioners. But there are other narratives too which highlight both the old and new issues that women's movements have raised since the 1970s whether they be poverty or health, violence or education, law or sexualities, diversities or inequalities.

Women studies have had a specific institutional trajectory from the mid-1970s since its establishment within the ICSSR and furthering through the UGC (Mazumdar and Sharma, 1979; Mazumdar, 1994). This paper refers to that, central as it is to the evolution of women studies in India. However, one also includes within its orbit a very large body of writings on gender in India that have emerged in and outside India, and that may have had tenuous links with the institutionalized history of women's studies.[1] And if one were to explore the manner that many women studies scholars entered the field from the mid-1970s, a homogeneous and unilinear narrative is an unlikely outcome. But most likely in some tangential way their entry into women studies would be linked to the emergence of womens' movements and other social movements or even to some intellectual currents. Significant contributions were made by them, located as they were differently in disciplines, such as history, literature and cultural studies, economics, sociology/social anthropology and political science. And, in different locations such as universities and colleges, research institutions and women's organizations. They were from different regions in the country and sometimes from outside the country. I make this point deliberately for regions even in a rapidly globalizing India matter. They matter in the nature and prioritization of issues raised by women's movements and women's studies (human rights in the north-eastern part of India, caste elsewhere, work in yet another). Research from outside the country, whether

North America or elsewhere in the West, also matters. That academic fashions emerging from the West tend to travel fast and strong is a well-known fact. On the other hand, we also have an increasing trend for western universities to develop a global curriculum, where versions of our stories of gender discourse are incorporated. But that is another story.

Within women studies one also includes more recent trends as evident in the new efforts to 'mainstream' and 'gender train' or 'gender sensitize' by a wide set of actors such as the state, NGOs and increasingly by corporations. Much of this is also evident in mainstream media, whose manifold expansion in recent years cannot be overemphasized. My own study of the manner that 'feminism' is portrayed in the media since the 1990s suggests a clear disengagement with earlier notions of women's movements and an affirmation of the individuated, entrepreneurial woman (Chaudhuri, 1998, 2000, 2001). Here I argue are two strands at work: one, a backlash and two an illustration of both an aggressive assertion of class, gender (and nation, albeit a refurbished one) that is very typical of a globalizing corporate India. Corresponding to the ascendancy of the new individuated entrepreneurial middle class women in the public discourse is a major shift in the developmental vision vis-à-vis the poor woman with a rise in the 'empowerment' discourse. Both flow from the neo-liberal vision. This period is also marked by the retreat of traditional left-led mass movements of workers and peasants and by the growth of new social movements. Perhaps the most notable of them has been the Dalit movement that has raised some of the most challenging questions about dominant women's movements. Not yet so visible in public discourse but likely to become so increasingly is the 'adivasi' or 'indigeneous' or 'tribal' movements. Indeed, some very interesting debates emerge from the naming process itself (Xaxa, 2010; Omvedt, 2005). There has been an increasing acknowledgement that women's issues and women's movements are diverse. Voices for recognition appear to have overtaken claims for redistribution, even as we witness violent upsurge of tribal-led Naxal movement. Likewise, class and capital as categories of analysis have surprisingly retreated at a time marked by an almost unchallenged ascendancy of capitalism. Significantly, western scholarship has witnessed a rise in returning to class. In India, we see gender discourse shaped by both this retreat of questions of redistribution and affirmation of recognition – whether it be of the individuated entrepreneurial women, the emblem of the gains of globalization or of the 'empowerment' of the 'poor' woman. Significantly, this 'empowerment' is painless for no one gets 'disempowered'. It obviously goes against the well-known understanding that power is exerted by some against the will of another.

II

Histories of Women's Movements

We have moved a long way from a time when history was simply a narration of what appeared self-evident facts from the past. The arbitrary nature of history writing, the political character of its project, and the affirmation of multiple and plural locations have made the task a daunting one. But one is here not in the guise of a professional historian. My effort is limited to garnering what one would think are largely well-established ideas about the way the women's question emerged in modern India and evolved over time. The story has been written and rewritten, each time as responses to challenges of movements and re-conceptualization. (This has been one of the salient contributions of both women's movements and women's studies.) It runs roughly like this (and I attempt to build in the mainstream account and the challenges): a mandatory mention of the 19th century social reform movements and the articulation of the women's question; the growth of women's writing and voices in the same period; the emergence of women's groups in the early part of the 20th century; the links between the women's movement, the national movement and the early left movements; the caste and gender question within and outside the national movement that history writing had excluded for long; independence and the state domestication of the women's question; the 'second phase' of the women's movements in the 1970s, its character and its interrogation, and new issues and institutionalization of women's studies; and the new economic policies, the new social movements and the gender question from the 1990 onwards.

India's tryst with modernity has been inextricably linked with its entry within British colonialism. The two cannot be disengaged much like the manner the women's question from our complex relationship with colonialism. The complexity is rendered more so not just because of the nature of colonialism but also because of 'our' differential relationship with colonialism. This difference could be on the basis of regions, classes, castes and communities. Not surprisingly, therefore, there has been considerable interrogation from the Dalit viewpoint about the nationalist framework as well as the purported role of colonialism.[2] One also finds that similar interrogations are being made about the present role of globalization. In other words, there are differences not just about its differential impact on a beneficiary middle class and impoverished masses but of the differential impact on sections such as Dalits, tribes, and even fractions of the lower middle class. A significant political current from the past, not talked about much today, is the left's own mixed and uncertain response to independence from colonialism that raised issues of nationalism, capitalism and class. An interesting comparison may be made with some trends within the Dalit movement and Dalit studies, both to the issue of colonialism and capitalism.

British colonialism entered and spread over much of India at different stages, impacting different regions differently both because of the stage of colonialism as well the nature of different regions. Thus, there were periods of reluctance to meddle with India's social customs such as those related to women, particularly abolition of sati in 1829 or raising the age of consent for women in 1863, which brought forth a fury of hostile reaction leading again to a phase where the British preferred to rely more on their conservative allies. What one can however infer is that the colonial rule, the humiliation of the subject population, the impact of western education, the role of Christian missionaries, growth of an English-knowing Indian middle class all led to an intense and contested debate on the women's question in the public sphere. This debate itself has been scrutinized carefully from different perspectives. We thus have a questioning whether the debate on sati was about women or about reconfiguring tradition and culture; we have questions on why Dalit women's public initiatives and interventions went unwritten about; we have arguments that suggest social reforms were more about efforts to introduce new patriarchies rather than about women's rights and gender justice. Much of this questioning is of recent times. And importantly women studies scholars have been at the forefront of this. I think, this needs reiteration to challenge widely held ideas about the ghettoization of women's studies. For long, the nationalist rendering of an account of social evils and unproblematic role of male reformers persisted and perhaps still does, given our very uneven spread and use of new knowledge in the country.

Commenting on the kind of studies done on gender in the pre-independence period, Vina Mazumdar observes:

> The *objective of pre-Independence research* was often to justify social reform or to provide a backbone for India's cultural pride, which had been battered by colonial rule and the onslaught of Western culture. *The focus of such research was on the minority of women in the upper classes.* For a variety of reasons such research declined after Independence. (Mazumdar, 1994: 42; emphasis mine)

However, one did have other accounts and orientations also even if they were not the dominant strands. What readily comes to one's mind is the document "Role of Women in a Planned Economy" (WREP) which revealed a curious mix and contestation of three dominant ideas of liberalism, socialism and notions of cultural revivalism within the same text. It contained substantial data on the conditions of women workers in the unorganized sector, in agriculture and the public and private issues that they faced (Chaudhuri, 1996). It could be argued however like Rege does that even such accounts of labour and other subaltern groups still privileged the role of nationalism. Talking about studies, however, what appears interesting also is that we need to clarify what we mean by studies. For much pulling out the hidden history swept under social reform or nationalism involves new ways and approaches of reading old texts and of course discovering new texts. Thus, while at one time (and this is but one illustration) Tarabai Shinde's *Stree Purush Tulana* (1882), disapproving, women's subordination as well as the Brahmanical patriarchy, would not be thought of either as a crucial text of social history or as a reading on women's studies. It would be considered both today. This rethinking of history and the enormous and rich body of research that has emerged in India is of course not accidental. I have argued earlier and would like to restate why I think so much of feminist work and theorization happened within history:

> If I had been searching for writing on Indian feminism *per se* on the lines of debates in the West between radical and socialist feminism for example, I was obviously on the wrong track. I was also obviously on the wrong track because I felt troubled about my reliance on western theoretical sources while teaching a course on gender. My own hands-on attempt at resolving the dilemma was to emphasis the specific history of the women's question in India (Chaudhuri, 2002). The centrality of history (and colonial history in particular) led me into a second and related mode of rethinking – a kind of post facto realization about why I insisted on teaching *history*, and why so much feminist scholarship in India has been historical. *Indeed historical research has laid the ground for theorizing feminism*. Self-conscious history writing is crucial for any modern society but more so for one with a colonial past, such as ours; in this narrativizing, women have been made key markers of the nation's culture and identity. A great deal of feminist theorizing, therefore, has interrogated the imagining of a nation that conflated itself with a sanitized image of Hindu upper caste women. While writings on modern India has explored the recasting of women in colonial India (Sangari and Vaid, 1989; Chaudhuri, 1993; Tharu and Lalita, 1993) scholars of ancient India have interrogated the Altekarian vision of the high and noble status of women in ancient India (Chakravarti, 1989; Roy, 1996). (Chaudhuri, 2004: xiii)

In other words, I am trying to affirm that women's studies and feminist perspectives involve not just more information but necessarily imply new modes of interrogation and new perspectives to approach the study of society. I mention this for it enables us to look more critically to the charge of ghettoization of women studies.

Early Years of Independence

There is a general sense of dismay that the women's question, so central to colonial India, appeared to retreat from public discourse with independence in 1947, which also marked the unprecedented violence of partition. We are aware that the Hindu Code Bill faced stiff opposition (Chaudhuri, 1993) and that a Committee for Abducted Women was formed. Feminist scholars have etched out from the tragic narratives how the women's voices were violently brushed aside before the decisions of the state and nation (Butalia, 2000; Menon and Bhasin, 1998).

The other paradigm that seemed to dominate notions of gender in this period was the 'modernization' driven vision that was premised on a simple dichotomy between 'traditional' and 'non-traditional' societies. Traditional societies were rural, stratified and 'backward' while non-traditional societies were urban, dynamic and progressive. This privileged a certain 'modern' domesticated women and studies of women largely operating with a role conflict paradigm. The central question of the private-public dichotomy returned to be a naturalized entity as in Talcott Parson's analysis of the family in an industrial society. Indian sociology from the late 1970s had a body of works inspired by this model (Chaudhuri, 1982). The language of the WRPE seemed a distant forgotten legacy. As we know far more conservative programmes of community development came to be implemented in the 1950s and 1960s.

> Instead, the 1950s and 60s saw the reemergence of "women" in the community development programmes (financed by the Ford Foundation) whose projects were geared to enable village women to become, in the words of the director of the Women's Programme in 1959, "a good wife, a wise mother, a competent housewife and a responsible member of the village community". Women's work and labour are not alluded to. (John, 1996: 3073)

A question often raised is how did the left-oriented WRPE completely disappear from public discourse on development and gender? Why did transformation of gender relationships disappear when the other aspects pertaining to social equity and state planning, characteristic of WRPE persist? I offer two sets of explanations. One that is specific to gender. There was a clear retreat from a more radical questionings of sexualities and sexual division of labour of an earlier period to a time when the Hindu Code Bill was being opposed not just by conservatives but also by many within the Indian National Congress. Significantly, one should recall that much of the 19th century middle class social reforms were self-consciously seeking to refashion the family in an ideal typical modern, western bourgeois family with a male breadwinner and a domesticated genteel mother and wife (Chaudhuri, 1993). Feminist scholars have worked on conduct books that were written at that time. The challenge clearly stemmed from a patriarchal notion of social order, identity and tradition, heightened in the aftermath of unprecedented violence of partition. This period also marked the confrontation of the Nehruvian Congress government and the Communists with the Tebhaga and Telengana movements and a little later by the 1962 war with China. Reference to such international developments is critical for a great deal of manoueverings of the state often happened vis-á-vis strategic moves with a global order that had its own strategies[3], may be in the form of Community Development Programmes in the Cold War era. In the contemporary period women studies can provide a vantage point to understand these moves of global politics and dominant global frames of development – be it in the rapid growth of micro-credit and self-finance groups or in shifts in higher education policies or in new discourses of choice and autonomy.

Women's Studies in the Post-1975 Context

Vina Mazumdar reiterates time and again the embryonic relationship between women's movements and gender studies. She writes:

> The *revival of the women's movement in the late 1970s brought new dynamism and directions to women studies*. Issues of *violence* – domestic and social, sexual exploitation in old and new forms, identification of *complex structures of domination* and their reassertion in new forms in the *ideology of revivalist, fundamentalist, communal and ethnic movements* – are some of the most significant of these new dimensions that the movement has brought into women's studies. Similarly, investigations of *peasant women* in the rural economy and of their undiscovered history have prompted new questions and drawn women's studies closer to issues being also raised by *ecological and environmental* movements. Investigations into *women's marginalization and exploitation in the economy, formal and informal, in the educational process, in communication and*

> *media and, also in the political process*, have turned women's studies into one of the *major critics of the pattern of "development"* and the choice of strategies. (Mazumdar, 1994: 44; emphasis mine)

Significantly, this focus on women in the rural economy and the unorganized sector brought forth new conceptualization of 'work' as well the meanings of the public and private domains. The report of the Committee on the Status of Women in India *Towards Equality* presented a grim picture of social reality that sharply contrasted with the goals of equality laid down by the Indian Constitution. The result of the report was to define a new agenda for women's studies in the country – an agenda that stressed the dynamism and pluralism of Indian society in contrast to the often monolithic discourse of the nationalist or development schools. A new programme for women's studies, initiated by the Indian Council of Social Science Research (ICSSR), emerged after the report with three distinct objectives: (1) to identify and work for needed policy change; (2) to persuade the social science community to re-examine the methodology, concepts, theories, and analytical apparatus of social research, which had successfully excluded women's role, status and situation from the entire arena of social investigations; and (3) to revive the social debate on the women's question which had emerged as a major issue during the freedom struggle but had faded in the post-independence period. Further, Mazumdar (1994: 43) argues that the extension of the post-1975 research to peasant women and women in the informal sector generated new sources of information for the fast growing women's movement. Most significantly, as we shall shortly see in the next section, these studies were then used by the developmental agencies and the state in the neo-liberal era to legitimize a form of development that rested on an unregulated informal economy of flexible labour.

For quite some time the central concern appeared to be the greater visibility of women. In a body of research on women's role in various sectors such as *bidi* industry, construction work, domestic work, professional woman has emerged. Very soon, however, more fundamental conceptual and theoretical questions were raised. Soon after the First National Conference on Women's

Studies, in Bombay in 1981, a group of practitioners in India defined women's studies as

> ... the pursuit of a more comprehensive, critical and balanced understanding of social reality. Its essential components include (i) women's contribution to the social process; (ii) women's perception of their own lives; (iii) roots and structures of inequality that led to the marginalization, invisibility and exclusion of women from the scope, approaches and conceptual frameworks of most intellectual enquiry and social action. (cited in Mazumdar, 1994: 45)

III

The Paradigm Shift from the 1990s

The 1990s in a fundamental sense brought in changes that can be clearly seen as a break with the earlier periods. A neo-liberal vision emerged to capture governmental imagination and much of public discourse. Neo-liberalism is not a unified economic theory or political philosophy – it is a label denoting an apparent shift in social, scientific and political sentiments that manifested themselves in theories and political platforms supporting a reform of largely centralized post-war economic institutions in favour of decentralized ones, a shift in control of the economy from the public to the private sector, a push for free trade, removal of tariff barriers, 'undistorted' market prices etc. In India, the media has played a key role in pushing this agenda. However, before delineating the role of media in refashioning both developmental models and recasting women in globalizing India, one needs to look at the shift in developmental vision itself. Therefore, the order in which I seek to map the paradigm shift is as follows: (i) a developmental vision that privileges the role of the 'informal sector' and encourage initiatives such as micro-credit; (ii) new popular discourses in the media on the new ideas about class and gender assertions; (iii) corporate visions on gender justice; and (iv) the appropriation of 'gender concerns' by the entertainment industry, which has been sometimes termed as 'infotainment of gender' and interestingly a 'professionalization' of both 'feminism' and 'activism'. In many ways all these trends flow from the fact that from the early 1990s the Indian state has moved away from a language of growth with equity, standard hallmarks of an earlier

Nehruvian period to a language almost exclusively of growth and growth rate.

In consonance with the neo-liberal paradigm the discourse on alleviating the conditions of the masses of people has shifted from a vision of state support, development and social support to a language of poverty alleviation through micro-credit and self-finance groups. Very interesting discursive shifts have taken place in the developmental discourse generally and the manner that gender has been reconfigured within the discourse. I first seek to address this before looking at some of the different ways that the women's movement and women's studies itself have looked these new developmental initiatives.

Development and Gender

We have already referred to the new energy with which the women's question re-emerged with the women's movement in the mid-1970s. New debates and new issues emerged. And, as noted, a concerted attempt was made to build up a body of research on women studies questioning fundamental categories of social sciences. Categories such as work, family, violence and sexualities were interrogated with fresh data and new perspectives.

A very interesting development that emerged in this period was an appropriation of findings of women studies for purposes that went fundamentally against the models of development and notions of social justice that women's movements were premised upon. This happened as Mary John has argued with a body of literature that women's studies produced from the mid-70s onwards and were used for quite another purpose in the 1990s by developmental agencies and the state. And, as I have argued elsewhere, a similar process happened with ideas of autonomy and freedom raised by the women's movements (Chaudhuri, 2000).

One of the crucial texts to come out of the subsequent decade of the 1980s was the *Shramshakti* – a report on self-employed women and women in the informal sector that was published in 1988.

> Drawing from a now vastly expanded literature and from extensive field surveys in different parts of the country, the authors produced detailed studies of women in the informal

> sectors of urban and rural India. The report was intended to show women's extremely vulnerable working conditions across diverse occupations under high levels of discrimination, as well as the range of health hazards women were exposed to on an everyday basis. The recommendations of the report – addressed to various ministries and departments at the central and state levels, but possibly also international agencies – run to almost a hundred pages. Their demands included enlarging the definition of work to encompass all women engaged in production and reproduction, recognizing women's position as major rather than supplementary wage earners, and finding strategies to enhance women's control over and ownership of resources. Also important was the demand to extend the rights and benefits for the privileged 10 per cent of the general labour force who make up the formal sector (in the case of the female workforce the corresponding figure is barely 7%) to the rest of the working population. (John, 1996: 3074)

Mary John takes off at this point to argue that:

> The special focus of this report on the informal sector, it seems to me, can help serve as a bridge for the 1990s. The *World Bank Gender and Poverty Report*, with which I began, followed only a few years later. The World Bank report draws directly from the efforts of the National Commission on Self-Employed Women and Women in the Informal Sector as well as from most of the literature on women and development produced in India and elsewhere over the last decades. In other words, it is not based on case studies of its own. *By drawing upon the past years of research, activism and government action in India, however, it is able to perform a remarkable feat; lay claim to an overall consensus on the nature of women in poverty, while in fact coming to often diametrically opposite conclusions from prior feminist concerns.* (John, 2004: 247; emphasis mine)

In the neo-liberal framework, the informal sector is at the heart of the market economy and represents its prime model. And, most important of all, since women are seen to predominate in this sector, it is their creativity and potential that needs special attention. The World Bank's report, drawing upon this kind of understanding, focuses on "the incredible range of tasks poor women perform, their often greater contribution to household income despite lower wage earnings, their ability to make scarce resources stretch further under deteriorating conditions, all of which were documented and debated in the past, are now reworked: through a crucial shift in signification, these findings are no longer arguments about *exploitation* so as much as proofs of *efficiency*" (John, 1996: 3074).

Not surprisingly therefore a great deal of development gender discourse is now exclusively addressed within the micro-credit framework, premised upon the idea that women are efficient managers and can be trusted to repay. A recent work is a collection of micro-finance activities and women's empowerment interestingly initiated by UNDP and ICICI Bank.

> Micro-credit as a tool of poverty alleviation and empowerment, particularly of women have gained credence in development dialogue the world over. The provision of micro-credit involves initiatives on the part of the state and non-state organizations in making available very small amounts of credit to poor citizens. There is an acute need among the poor for credit, both for consumption and production, which often forms the deciding line between survival and succumbing to poverty. In other words, credit is sought for basic requirements such as food, as well as for income generation activities. *The rationale of micro-credit is based on the hypothesis that the poor can be relied upon to return on time the money that they borrow. It has been proved that the poor are capable of thrift and savings.* (Deshmukh et al., 2005: 31; emphasis mine)

Other studies have suggested that micro-credit also develops banking habits among poor women and leads to increase in deposit accounts (Varman, 2005). In the discourse on micro-credit and self-help groups the categories of class and production relations disappear. The 'poor' and 'poverty' appear to be self-contained entities with no structural connection with production relations.[4] In a great deal of research a few indicators is all that is required to collect data whether it be 'poverty alleviation' or 'empowerment' to assess the impact of any intervention to alleviate 'poverty' or lead to 'empowerment' of women (Krishnaraj, 2005). Often deep-seated patriarchal assumptions persist even as new ideas of gender budgeting are included; for example, the idea that anything that has to do with children and contraception is for the excusive benefit of women (Das and Mishra, 2006). Research on development interventions suggests that often the programmes fall short of both progress towards gender equality and broader social equity. Nitya Rao writes:

> While several projects have encouraged women to participate in development and decision-making processes by specifically targeting them, it is now recognized that a more gender-focussed approach is necessary .... Women's groups do provide a forum for women to come together, share ideas, exchange information and develop a social network. Yet strategic shifts in access to resources and benefits (linked as they are to responsibilities for maintaining them) can only emerge if men support a shift, and take on a more equal share of both productive and reproductive work. In the context of structural reform, poor men too are facing a crisis in terms of accessing productive assets, markets and income, leading to a crisis of masculinities that is often reflected in growing trends of violence against women. (Rao, 2005: 4707)

Naila Kabeer, who has a more careful take on the role of micro-credit, however, does not dispute the point that it is the "imperatives of cost-recovery and financial sustainability which drive the financial systems approach clearly resonate neo-liberal orientation to market principles" and that "it is not surprising therefore that it has come to assume a hegemonic position in international development thinking about micro-finance as a tool for poverty reduction" (Kabeer, 2005: 4709).

Contending takes on Women and Globalization

Central to the neo-liberal frame is the informal sector as we saw and one needs to foreground the political implications of this. The political implications of making the informal sector, with the greater proportion of women workers, the hub of the new economy are as Breman argues:

> ... the informalisation of gainful employment which has become a major trend especially in developing countries in this late phase of capitalism hampers steady increase in the wretchedly low wages and regular employment with casual, spasmodic work arrangements, paid not in time-based wages but on piece rates. *An economic regime of this kind discourages militancy and obstructs the mobilization of the labouring poor into other unions and other representative organizations.* (Breman, 2004: 3872; emphasis mine)

Not all within the women's movement have a similar take on a neo-liberal-driven globalization. Gail Omvedt contends that "being anti-globalization" has become the correct standard of political correctness. She agrees with Rohini Hensman who argued that in a globalized world, labour needs global regulation, and therefore the left should argue for the extension of these and not of withdrawing from the world system (Hensman, 2004). But if one looks at what Breman and John are arguing the very assumptions of the growth of a global labour movement on which Hensman's take rests needs relooking. Debates on outsourcing in the US in this regard are illuminating. Indeed there have been labour regulations but too often not at the insistence of the labour movements. Omvedt's contention is:

> The only meaningful question is, for a Marxist (or Dalit, or feminist) activist, what advances the revolution, that is, the movement towards a non-caste, non-patriarchal, equalitarian and sustainable socialist society? (Omvedt, 2005: 4881)

She has an interesting take on adivasis, extraction of natural resources and local control before she moves on the possibilities of 'tribes' becoming non-caste nationalities.

> ... the increasing extraction of natural resources and their channeling to the world market via multinationals, the state and local powerholders .... The problem regarding local control (community control) and the extraction of resources is precisely that the two may go together. Anti-globalisation activists often do not see this; but in fact gaining local control will at best – mean that resources will be extracted more sustainably, that local people will get a share of the profits and raise their standard of living. It does not mean that they will resist the world market and extraction or listen to the activists when they try to tell them to do so; self-determination after all does mean just that, that they will do what they want. And *this will primarily mean getting a better deal from world capital.* (Omvedt, 2005: 4883; emphasis mine)

In arguing for the need to revisit narratives of women's movements, I had emphasized both a Dalit take on colonialism, nationalism and now globalization. For indeed there is a strong Dalit pro-globalization view (Omvedt, 2001; Prasad, 2000).

Reconfiguring Feminism: New Popular Assertions of Class and Gender in the Media

In the above discussion on gender and development, we saw that critiques by women studies of the assumption that women were passive victims were turned around to justify state withdrawal of subsidies for poor women. Developmental discourse now valorized the steely determination of 'poor' women. In the media, in what can be seen a similar turn around, notions of women's feminism were being given new meanings. I draw from an earlier writing of mine to illustrate this 'reconfigured' idea of 'feminism'. Readers would note that the discussion revolves around the theme of 'women at work' – key feminist issue in the unlikely high fashion women's *eLan* magazine:

> ... A writing on *'women at work'* initiates the discussion by suggesting that 'dressing for work must rank high in the list of life's arduous-but-inescapable chores ... a dilemma' but suggests that better days are here now for 'Savio Barretto presents workwear that will ease your journey into the boardroom'.
>
> ... women over the ages have learned to use their ingenuity, creativity, even daring to adapt – centuries ago, a cave woman somewhere would have discovered that soft fluffy rabbit fur, while nice for a stroll through the jungle, was no good near the cooking ire. Quite the same way, one imagines that a woman today would discover, that the sari while a sophisticated ensemble, isn't refined after a train journey, or a drive through hot, grimy city roads. *So, is the Indian woman condemned to a lifetime of endless inevitabilities? Must she quietly resign herself to helplessness when choosing to dress to work?* Not really. Especially not if designer Anita Dongre has her way .... And while what you choose to wear is really a very personal choice...it's up to us designers to cater to that...*Today's Indian woman is different from her predecessor. She is more comfortable with herself and her body. She doesn't find a need to shy away from expressing herself. She is not afraid of trying new things, even what the close-minded call 'western'. And what's more, she is doing it all looking good.* (cited in Chaudhuri, 2000)

The phrase which reiterates that "what you choose to wear is a very personal choice" but "it's up to us the designers to cater to it" is illustrative of the thesis that the concept of identity is necessarily defined by two opposites: sameness and difference. To be unique is to be the same in two senses: to be identical to others in your class (and different from those in 'other' classes) as well as to yourself over time. I have argued for long that the media since 1991 has played an incredibly important role in changing the public discourse on development and gender, on the nation and on notions of national pride and shame. I use the vantage point of media to foreground how gender has been used in the overall production of a new discourse and developmental model partly because I have worked on it. More significantly, the media today occupies an overarching space in the public discourse (Chaudhuri, 2010). There is a transformed visibility of the public, new possibilities of the growing middle class and fractions of the lower middle class, new sensibilities and aspirations, new gender identities, and new ideas of leisure, pleasure and consumption. Together they have tangibly worked towards producing new aspirations of success and freedom, a heightened sense of individuated selves so critical for a consumption driven society. Gender identities are recast in the media (Chaudhuri, 1998, 2000, 2001). Further, gender issues resurface also in a new fashion directly in the corporate world which I look at, albeit sketchily, below.

The Corporate Vision: Brand India or India Incorporation

Often today the nation itself is referred to as India Incorporation or Brand India and there has been an incredible move towards corporatizion in all spheres including that of the academia and other centres of knowledge production. The corporate language has acquired a legitimacy that has increasingly been difficult to challenge. Not surprisingly, the gender question and feminism itself has also been subject to reconfigurations. Advertisements and sponsorships have played a huge role in redefining dominant public discourse. We have seen above how the very term 'feminism' has undergone a shift that moves it away from a collective emancipatory project to a lifestyle statement of choices.

There are other moves within the corporate sector to implement what they perceive more gender-friendly work space. One would like to describe it as a kind of corporatization of gender rights. I draw upon just one example from the January 2008 issue of the magazine *India Today Woman* to illustrate this.

A two-full-page advertisement with three shelves of shoes, placed some distance (space) from each other, has a brief write-up. The title is Match Point.

> Four companies redefine gender equality and are recognized by the Nasscom INDIA TODAY *Woman* awards for excellence in gender inclusivity as they strive to create work paces for women that enable them to excel.
>
> The IT industry has been busy wooing women. And why not? A Nasscom study predicts that the percentage of women in the IT industry will grow from 30 to 45 per cent by the year 2010. *Gender inclusivity aims at creating work spaces to entice a college graduate, a career woman and a mother.* Recognizing this change, Nasscom and *India Today Woman* announced winners of the corporate awards for *Excellence in Gender Inclusivity*, recognizing companies that have implemented outstanding practices in promoting gender empowerment. The independent team of judges choosing the winning companies was a veritable who's who: N.R. Narayana Murthy, Chairman, Infosys Technologies Ltd; Aroon Puriee, editor-in-chief, India Today Group; Kiran Karnik, President, Nasscom; Vinita Bali, managing director, Britannia Industries Ltd., Hema Ravichander, strategic HR advisor and Rekha Jain, professor, IIM Ahmedabad. (emphasis mine)

Another small advertisement may help us further appreciate gender in the corporate vision. This is about a Workshop on Work Life Balance for Working Women, Date: 28–29 November, 2007; Venue: India Habitat Centre, New Delhi; Organiser: Associates.

> Across generations, gender, industries, and international borders, work-life balance is surfacing as a common concern. What is the high price of a life that is out of balance? Within the past decade or so, the global workplace has seen increased numbers of working women; dual-career and single parent families, and increased numbers of employees with eldercare responsibilities; a decrease in job security; and a blurring of work-family boundaries due to technological change.
>
> *Life is a balancing act. Striking the right balance is the key to a fulfilling life. Female Executives have multiple responsibilities, diverse needs, and often, conflicting priorities.* Organisations are becoming increasingly conscious of the important role that work

> life balance policies play in attracting and retaining high calibers staff. Striving to achieve a better work-life balance should become a national obsession.
>
> The workshop is targeted at Working Women to raise awareness of the importance of work life balance policies at the level of the enterprise.

What we see at work above are two sets of assertions. One, that of an upwardly mobile middle class, and two, that of women from a certain section within the corporate sector. What is also discernible is a model of 'fulfilling life', a 'balanced life' and of course a more discreet affirmation of the new individuated self. Quite clearly many issues raised by women's movements and women's studies have entered public discourse and new everyday commonsense. Ideas of an earlier unproblematic notion of role conflicts acquire more nuanced shades. But what also happens is that gender issues get redefined as lifestyle statements and personal management questions rather than social questions.

On occasions we have a crasser version of how gender has travelled in public discourse. The examples below are illustrative of this process. Gender issues, such as female foeticide and rape, which are very visible in the public domain, are used in a gender, insensitive manner by many in the corporate sector, notwithstanding the above instances of ongoing exercises for 'gender inclusivity'.

Infotainment of Gender

The declining sex ratio has been a prime concern of both women's movements and women's studies. It was in early 1980s when aminocentis tests arrived on the Indian scene. Primarily devised for detection of genetic diseases in the foetus and to assist in delivery, they soon metamorphosed themselves into determination of sex of the foetus in the craving for a son in the Indian families. Two decades later and with the figures of the 2001 census staring us in our face the corporate world has a long way to go. A recent case was registered against a leading telecom firm under the Pre-Natal Diagnostic Techniques (Prohibition of Sex Selection) Act for displaying an advertisement on its website pertaining to sex determination of the foetus (*Hindustan Times*, February 1, 2005) with a suggestive 'Better Rs 500 now than Rs 5 lakh later' message. The ad series launched by Maruti-Suzuki for their new car model Zen is representative of yet another current trend. The controversial ad showed a young beautiful blonde being stalked by a tiger through the city at night. The girl passes through various parts of the city. Whenever she is on the road, it is the new look car that follows her. The moment she is on stairs or overbridge, the car is transformed into a tiger. The ad ends with the girl finally giving up the chase with a deep male voice-over "Surrender, to the new ...." The advertisement fashioned on the 'predator concept' was chosen to attract young consumers below the age of 35, and it was deliberately selected to "build excitement around the brand in a completely different manner" (30 September, 2004 Countercurrents.org).

One will recall that this paper is premised on the belief that the women's movement has succeeded in making gender a major issue in the public sphere. Major actors, such as state, civil society, market and international institutions, have thus taken cognizance of gender inequality. Yet as would be evident from this paper, this 'mainstreaming' of gender, whether in developmental programmes or in the corporate sector or in the media, has led to significant reconfigurations of the very ideas of freedom and justice raised by women's movements and women's studies. The 'infotainment' usage of gender issues (and this is just one instance) throws up major challenges to the hard-won gains of women's movements. Indeed, as shown so often by women studies, serious women's issues are not just trivialized but turned around to perform a titillating role.

The Transformed Relationship between Women Studies and Women's Movements

In the early part of this paper it may be noted how pioneering scholars time and again reiterated the close links between women's studies and women's movements. I had further stated that the close connection between the two formed a given premise of this paper. I maintain this position but argue that in the changed historical context where neo-liberal visions dominate the relationship itself can undergo fundamental transformations. In the changed circumstances women's studies possibly can be understood as service providers to the state, corporations and NGOs. In an effort to illustrate the manner this process takes place I take recourse to drawing attention to two developments. The first refers to an advertisement for hiring in a feminist activist organization and the second to a comment on the changes in autonomous women's organizations. Both are indicative of a broader trend towards institutionalization.

In an earlier account of my experiences in teaching gender I had mentioned the growing trend among students to choose gender studies as a useful add on to one's CV, a requirement for the job market (Chaudhuri, 2002). Here I quote at length an advertisement for an 'activist' for an *international feminist organization*. The emphasis added is mine and would help indicate what I imply by professionalization of women's organizations and 'globalization' of women's strategies.

> THE ORGANIZATION:
>
> The Association for Women's Rights in Development (AWID) is an international feminist organization working to strengthen the voice, impact and influence of women's rights advocates, organizations and movements *internationally*.
>
> AWID is seeking a Research Associate to work with the Young Feminist Activism Program. For over 7 years, AWID has supported young feminist activists in shaping *the future of women's human rights* and defining women's rights and development from their perspective. The Program focuses on thematic issues including:
>
> - Funding for young women's rights work
> - Young *women's strategies* to challenge and resist religious fundamentalisms
> - Young feminist visions for *movement building*
>
> The Program provides skills-building and information resources for young feminists, and uses information and communications technology to create spaces for discussion, debate, dialogue and networking. In 2008 the Program will also work on young feminist activities at the AWID Forum 2008, and will continue to engage with the youth sector globally.

NECESSARY QUALIFICATIONS AND EXPERIENCE:

- Aged between 18 and 29
- *Two or more years activist/advocacy experience with/for young women, young women's organizations and women's movements globally and/or regionally*
- Knowledgeable about women's human rights and/or gender and development at the regional or international level
- Proven research and writing skills
- One or more years previous work on an action-research research project
- Strong communications skills
- Good organizational skills (including time-management)
- Highly motivated to work independently and to work as part of a dynamic virtual team
- University degree preferably with a focus on gender and development, women's human rights, international development studies, community development, women's leadership training, women's studies or a related social science field
- *Written and spoken fluency in English*
- *Language skills in French and/or Spanish highly desirable*
- *Some experience living and/or working in the Global South preferred*

The Research Associate should be able to start with AWID by or before the beginning of March 2008. The successful candidate must be based in either Cape Town, Toronto or Mexico City or willing to relocate at their own expense. The candidate's preference for location will be taken into account, but the final decision on where the position will be located will be made by AWID.

The successful candidate must be willing to work after hours twice a week in order to communicate with team members located in other *time zones.*

Advertisements of such kind are so common today in India that it is not easy to dislodge the 'natural' 'given' assumptions that it communicates about women's movement and its necessary linkages with gender and development, women's human rights, international development studies, community development, women's leadership training and women's studies. The globalized nature of such operations is obvious, captured very well in the advertisement – the requisite need for the successful candidate must be willing to work after hours twice a week in order to communicate with team members located in other *time zones* apart from knowledge of French, Spanish, English being *highly desirable*. And most revealingly some experience living and/or working with the Global South is a *preferred requirement*. Significantly *two or more years activist/advocacy experience with/for young women, young women's organizations and women's movements globally and/or regionally* form integral part of the eligibility criteria for the job. What is clearly at work is yet another instance and site of reconfigured notions of women's studies/women's movements.

The other instance I draw as illustrative of what I had termed (with reservations) the NGOization of women's movements. This pertains to the reflections of a women's movement activist after the 2006 Kolkata conference of the autonomous women's movement.

> ... Whatever might be the case, it needs to be understood that this gap between self-perception and self-actualisation of the autonomous politics is having a very negative fallout? It has created a situation where 'institutionalised' or 'state sponsored feminism' – which has the potential of deradicalizing feminism – has been accorded new legitimacy as being part of the 'autonomous women's movement'. *It has created a situation where the division between NGOs – running projects centred around women – and mass organisations of women who have been valiantly raising issues since decades has been deliberately blurred. And a key difference between the sustenance of a project – which is external – and a movement – which is driven mainly by its internal momentum and legitimacy among the masses, is being largely forgotten*. It has led us to a situation where the failures of the autonomous women's politics – even its failure to define itself or suggest any alternative organisational structure – have not even come on the agenda. (Sinha, 2007; emphasis mine)

IV

Conclusion

This paper has sought to map the two very broad directions that gender discourse in India has moved towards: one, towards greater mainstreaming and institutionalization; and the other towards great critical interrogation and new imaginings. How does one look at these processes? One strand within western scholarship has sought to describe this anxiety about institutionalization as an unfortunate expression of melancholic mourning, of a sense of loss for an once 'pure' normative feminist past that paves way for contemporary conservative politics. While this may be an intellectually seductive narrative, it offers little in a way of understanding the dynamics of the present juncture. One agrees wholly with the idea that there is never a 'pure' originary past of feminism or of nationalism or of socialism. And hard-won gains brought from past struggles do become part of our institutionalized present. Just as equal wages for men and women may not appear frightfully feminist today (Chaudhuri, 2004: xvi). Or for that matter socialist or even liberal, even though unequal wages remains a major issue today. But acknowledgement of this inevitable and not quite unwelcome logic of mainstreaming should not blind us to what could be possibilities of productive theoretical analysis of the nature of mainstreaming and its linkages with other 'mainstream' or dominant developments in society. The urgent question today is the manner of feminism's evolution in the dramatically charged social context of rising neo-liberalism (Fraser, 2009). In Nancy Fraser's provocative framing, how do we understand "the movement's extraordinary successes" but also "the disturbing convergence of some of its ideals with the demands of an emerging new form of capitalism – post-Fordist, 'disorganized', transnational" (Fraser, 2009: 97–98).

What I am arguing here is for using theoretical tools for analysing the manner that gender and other social formations are linked and reproduced. To again use an easy catchword I am arguing for an intersectional analysis that has defined feminist analysis in India prior to the production and circulation of the term 'intersectional' itself. That critical intersection between gender and capital, state and family, labour and sexuality may offer us ways to understand that the structural critique of mainstreaming is critique of institutionalization of a certain kind, of a socio-political order where it is entirely acceptable to use rape as good copy for advertisements or where invoking women's agency is to legitimize withdrawal of state subsidy for the poor.

Notes

1. It is quite outside the scope of this paper to focus on a detailed listing out of scholars and their writings. The point being made is that there were different entry points and trajectories.
2. Sharmila Rege writes: History of late colonial India has always prioritized Indian nationalism, such that it came to be assumed that the world of political action and discourse can be comprehended only through the categories of nationalism, imperialism and communalism. The radical historiographies of colonial India, though they emphasized the autonomous role of peasants, labour and other subaltern groups, equated the historiography of colonial India with that of Indian nationalism. .... The non-brahmanical re-constructions of historiography of modern India ... have underlined the histories of anti-hierarchical, pro-democratising collective aspirations of the lower caste masses which are not easily encapsulated within the histories of anti-colonial nationalism. In fact these histories have often faced the penalty of being labelled as collaborative and have therefore being ignored in a historiography which is dominated by narratives of nationalism (Rege, 1998).
3. Interventions in Afghanistan have often sought to be legitimized by all the "good things" that it has brought to Afghan women. The global attention on trafficking of women itself has been debated intensely, with some arguing that strict controls over western borders is an issue that has driven some of the western policy makers to focus on it. Debates on reproductive health have been yet another issue.
4. An interview of Radha Kumar: "I would say that the women's movement in India has grown so hugely that it is difficult to categorise it as one movement; rather there is a focus on women at different levels by almost every social and economic group. *Perhaps the one defining distinction of the past decade has been a thrust towards encouraging women's self-help and entrepreneurship skills – this is a trend that is reflected in the corporate world, government planning, NGOs and women's groups*" (Radha Kumar, 2008; emphasis mine).

References

Butalia, Urvashi. 2000. *The Other Side of Silence: Voices from the Partition of India*, Durham, NC: Duke University Press.

Chakravarti, Uma. 1989. "Whatever happened to the Vedic Dasi? Orientalism, Nationalism and a Script for the Past", in Kumkum Sangari and Sudesh Vaid (eds.), *Recasting Women: Essays in Colonial India*, New Delhi: Kali for Women, pp. 27–87.

Chaudhuri, Maitrayee. 1982. "Sociology and Women's Studies", *Social Scientist*, October, pp. 21–29.

——. 1993. *The Indian Women's Movement: Reform and Revival*, Delhi: Radiant

——. 1996. "Citizens, Workers and Cultural Emblems: An Analysis of the First Planned Document in India", in Patricia Uberoi (ed.), *State, Social Reform and Sexuality*, New Delhi: Sage, pp. 211–35.

——. 1998. "Advertisements, Print Media and the New Indian Woman", *Social Action*, Vol. 48, No. 3, July, pp. 239–52.

——. 2000. "Feminism in Print Media", *Indian Journal of Gender Studies*, Vol. 7 No. 2, pp. 263–88.

——. 2001. "Gender and Advertisements: The Rhetoric of Globalisation", *Women's Studies International Forum*, Vol. 24, No. 3/4, pp. 373–85.

——. 2002. "Learning through Teaching the 'Sociology of Gender'", *Indian Journal of Gender Studies*, Vol. 9, No. 2, pp. 245–61.

——. (ed.). 2004. *Feminism in India*, New Delhi: Women Unlimited.

——. 2010. "Indian Media and its Transformed Public", *Contributions to Indian Sociology*, Vol. 44, Nos. 1 & 2, pp. 57–78.

Deshmukh, Ranadive et al. 2003. "Placing Gender Equity in the Family Centre Stage", *Economic and Political Weekly*, Vol. 38, No. 17.

Fraser, Nancy. 2009. "Feminism, Capitalism and the Cunning of History", *New Left Review, 56*, March-April, pp. 97–117.

Hensman, Rohini. 2004. "Globalisation, Women and Work: What Are We Talking About?", *Economic and Political Weekly*, Vol. XXXIX, No. 10, March 6-12, pp. 1030–84.

John, Mary E. 1996. "Gender and Development in India, 1970s–1990s: Some Reflections on the Constitutive Role of Contexts", *Economic and Political Weekly*, Vol. 31, No. 47, pp. 3071–77.

Kumar, Radha. 2008. "Infochange Defining Development", infochangeindia.org, October 15.

Mazumdar, Vina. 1994. "Women's Studies and the Women's Movement in India: An Overview", *Women's Studies Quarterly*, Vol. XXII, Nos. 3 and 4, pp. 42–53.

Mazumdar, Vina and Kumud Sharma. 1979. "Women's Studies: New Perspectives and Challenges", *Economic and Political Weekly*, Vol. 14, No. 3, pp. 113–20.

Menon, Ritu and Kamla Bhasin. 1998. *Borders and Boundaries*, New Jersey: Rutgers University Press.

Misra, Yamini and Subrat Das. 2006. "Gender Budgeting Statement", *Economic and Political Weekly*, Vol. 41, No. 30, 29 July–4 August, pp. 3285–90.

Omvedt, Gail. 2001. "Marx and Globalisation" (Parts I & II), *The Hindu*, March 1 & 2.

——. 2005. "Capitalism and Globalisation, Dalits and Adivasis", *Economic and Political Weekly*, Vol. 40, No. 47, November 19, p. 4881.

Prasad, Chandra Bhan. 2000. "New Life Movement versus Narmada Bachao Andolan", *The Pioneer*, October 22.

Rao, Nitya. 2005. "Women's Rights to Land and Assets: Experience of Mainstreaming Gender in Development Projects", *Economic and Political Weekly*, Vol. XL, Nos. 44 & 45, pp. 4701–08.

Rege, Sharmila. 1998. "Dalit Women Talk Differently: A Critique of 'Difference' and Towards a Dalit Feminist Standpoint Position", *Economic and Political Weekly*, Vol. 33, No. 44, October 31, WS39–WS46.

Roy, Kumkum. 1996. "Where Women are Worshipped, there the Gods Rejoice: The Mirage of Ancestress of the Hindu Woman", in Tanika Sarkar and Urvashi Butalia (eds.), *Women and the Hindu Right: A Collection of Essays*, New Delhi: Kali for Women, pp. 181–215.

Sangari, Kumkum and Sudesh Vaid. 1989. *Recasting Women: Essays in Colonial India*, New Delhi: Kali for Women.

Sharma, Kumud. 2003. "Institutionalising Feminist Agenda(s)", *Economic and Political Weekly*, Vol. 38, No. 43, October 25–31, pp. 4564–66.

Shinde, Tarabai. 1882. *Stree Purush Tulana*, extracted in Maitrayee Chaudhuri (ed.), 2004. Op. cit., pp. 82–93.

Sinha, Anjali. 2007. "Autonomous Women's Movement?" countercurrents.org, April 13.

Tharu, Susie and K. Lalitha. 1993. *Women Writing in India: 600 B.C. to the Present*, Vols. 1 & 2, Delhi: Oxford University Press.

Xaxa, Virginius. 2010. "The Concept of Gender: Its Travels and Travails", in Maitrayee Chaudhuri (ed.), *Sociology in India: Intellectual and Institutional Practices*, Jaipur: Rawat Publications, pp. 340–59.

Websites, Magazines and Newspapers

countercurrents.org September 30, 2004.

infochangeindia.org October 15, 2008.

Hindustan Times, February 1, 2005.

India Today Woman, January 2008.

10

When Neo-liberal Agenda Negotiates Dalit Agenda

The Case of BSP in Uttar Pradesh

PRASHANT KUMAR TRIVEDI

Last two decades in India have seen gaining prominence of two phenomena: one, unabated advance of neo-liberal agenda, and two, identity-based social movements getting stronger and becoming assertive. The former advocates shunning of old-styled welfare state model and takes market as panacea of all developmental problems while social movements of marginalized groups are expected to be concerned about equality and social justice. If one has to go by the stand of Rodrigues (2008) on the issue that globalization welcomes only those who have something to start with and Dalits lacking this see these neo-liberal changes as another conspiracy against them, these two coinciding phenomena seem to be contradictory objectives. But still they are co-existing with each other for such a long time. This observation raises certain questions relating to negotiation of these seemingly conflicting agendas – the neo-liberal agenda and the agenda of movements of marginalized groups. If co-existence is just coincidence? And, if co-existence remains peaceful or there exists tension between the two.

To further explore these questions we propose to look into the political mobilization of Dalits in Uttar Pradesh in its latest manifestation as BSP. We are particularly concerned about the economic policy adopted by BSP governments in the state. For this we will focus on policy moves taken by the present BSP government that has been in the office for last three years since we believe that earlier governments, though led by the BSP, were coalition governments and that definitely would have had a bearing on government's policies. On this count, the present government is different being a majority government with full control on its functioning. Besides, the period of 2–3 years is really very short period for any government to come out with its desired comprehensive plans and also to mature initiatives taken by it. One more thing before we move ahead, BSP as a political party and the BSP government are not two identical things. And we do not wish to shy away from the fact that the BSP is also working within same set-up that defines limits of any government especially state governments. In this case, we are interested to see how BSP as a political party negotiates these limitations.

The BSP in Uttar Pradesh

BSP is one of the national parties with influence spread even outside Uttar Pradesh (UP) while UP remaining its main base. BSP's official website (bspindia.org) introduces the party as the party of 'Bahujan Samaj' which comprises of the Scheduled Castes (SCs), the Scheduled Tribes (STs), the Other Backward Classes (OBCs) and religious minorities such as Sikhs, Muslims, Christians, Parsis and Buddhists which accounts for over 85 per cent of the country's total population. The party, it is stated, works for the social transformation and economic emancipation of these classes that have been the victims of the 'Manuwadi' system in the country for thousands of years, under which they have been vanquished, trampled upon and forced to languish in all spheres of life. The party affirms its full faith in the Constitution of India about which it states that because of pivotal role played by Dr Ambedkar, oppressed classes were given a number of rights but these rights will not be fully realized until governments are dominated by Manuwadi persons and parties. Keeping in mind political power as the master key to all kinds of progress, BSP owns the responsibility to form governments at the centre and states to enforce all the constitutional and legal rights of the Bahujan Samaj and provide opportunities to its people to move forward in all spheres of life besides enabling them to lead a life of self-respect.

The website further states that to achieve these goals Kanshi Ram founded the party on 14 April 1984 and lead it for almost two decades till 2003. This was most vibrant period in BSP's history during which it not only established itself as a champion of Dalit cause but, with rapid expansion in its mass base, also made impressive electoral victories. Before founding the BSP, Kanshi Ram had founded two other organizations, viz., All India Backward and Minorities Communities Employees Federation (BAMCEF) and Dalit Shoshit Samaj Sangharsh Samiti, popularly known as DS–4. Out of these two, the former was mainly an organization of educated government employees belonging to marginalized communities, although, its founders, Kanshi Ram and D.K. Khaparde, did not conceptualize it as an employees union. They formed it as a resource centre – both intellectual and financial – for broader Dalit agitations. Being primarily a middle class organization, limitations of BAMCEF were clearly evident to Kanshi Ram, who would have wanted to take things to broader masses. For the purpose, an activist organization Dalit Soshit Samaj Sangharsh Samithi (DS-4) was founded in 1981. In 1984, Kanshi Ram dissolved the DS-4 to give way to a completely political wing Bahujan Samaj Party (BSP). This caused major strains in BAMCEF ranks. In early 1986 a major split took place. Kanshi Ram announced at that time that he was no longer willing to work for any organization other than BSP.

The initial formative years of the party saw most aggressive attack on the so-called upper castes. Its most popular slogan "tilak, taraazu aur talwar, inko maro joote chaar" received sharp reactions from the upper caste people who perhaps for the first time heard this kind of a derogatory language for themselves and that too from the people abusing whom was part of their daily life. As much as frustration of the upper castes against BSP kept on mounting, proud filled Dalits got consolidated with the party. Now, for the first time in the history, they were able to pay back their erstwhile masters in their own coins. Not only this, in the early days of BSP, Kanshi Ram used to publicly ask the upper castes in the audience to leave the meeting place. This offensive strategy cultivated identity and created self-confidence among the Dalits (Teltumbde, 2007). It is true that Dalits did not create a separate identity for themselves; instead they were assigned a separate place by caste Hindus (Padavala, 2007). Kanshi Ram only attempted to organize them politically on the basis of this identity. The significance of this phase of Dalit movement precisely lies here: an oppressed identity got converted into an assertive identity and Dalits demonstrated that instruments of oppression can also be used as instruments of struggle. This is the period when Dalits were subjected to very high level of violence by a section of so-called upper castes and OBCs. What was reported in media as 'Jat-Jatav clash' in several places of western UP during the late eighties and early nineties was mostly an attack on Dalit–Jatavs by dominant Jats to suppress their growing assertion.

Although, BSP leaders later made a U-turn and lowered their tone against non-Dalits when they started forging alliances with parties like BJP and Congress and adopted a strategy of reaching out to the upper castes but all through this symbolism has remained most important resource for the party. The first of its kind was a programme that continued all along was the installation of Ambedkar statutes in villages and towns. This received both support and opposition, in their extreme forms. On the one hand Dalits favoured this move, even at the risk of their life and livelihood, non-Dalits opposed it with all their might. Perhaps there are only a few villages in the state, which would have not witnessed sharp polarization between Dalits and non-Dalits on the question of installation of Ambedkar statutes. In some cases, this kind of a confrontation took shape of physical violence against Dalits and in some other cases economic boycott, banning Dalits from using village roads passing through upper caste localities, taking back land leased out to Dalits etc., took place. Many Dalits lost their lives in these clashes across the state. My own recent fieldwork in the central Uttar Pradesh suggests that Dalits in a number of villages are still struggling to instal statues of Dr Ambedkar. In two villages studied in Barabanki district, Ambedkar statues are kept in safe places for several years but their installation in public places are getting postponed due to conspiracies hatched by non-Dalits. One reason for which the efforts to instal statues of Dr Ambedkar would have continued in spite of the changing tone of BSP was that Dalit movement in the state is much broader than the party and it involves numerous local initiatives. In addition to installing statues, Ambedkar's birth anniversary on 14 April continues to be most popular programme for Dalit activists, while in the government, BSP organized these programmes with much fanfare in every corner of the state. Besides Dr Ambedkar, Shahu Ji Maharaj, Jyotiba Phule and Buddha were other anti-caste social reformers in whose names big *melas* were organized and newly constituted districts were named after them.

Beyond this symbolism that had its own role in bringing a sense of confidence and dignity among its following, BSP never appeared to be serious about the socio-economic development of Dalit masses. Perhaps, it was the only party that has not declared its plan to deal with problems like landlessness, inadequate wages, loss of livelihood, inaccessible education and health causing great deal of deprivation among Dalits. Take one example of the issue of land distribution. Eva-Maria Hardtmann (2009) narrates her experience in following words:

> During 1990s there was a tendency among many Dalit groups across the state to occupy government land under the BSP slogan "jo zamin sarkari hai, who zamin hamari hai" (government land is our land). Dalit activists put up Ambedkar statues on government land and claimed ownership of it. What did Kanshi Ram have to say about these activities?
>
> Yes, I want to distribute land. There should not be any big land-owners and also no landless people. Everybody should have what he can cultivate, no more no less. We have our own plan of how things should be done. When my ideas are carried out it should be done across the whole India simultaneously, not just in one or a few states. (interview with Kanshi Ram, New Delhi, 9 April, 1994)

Kanshi Ram was never very specific about his plans during interviews; he simply made it clear that he did not find it meaningful to work for minor changes in one or a few states. The way he spoke about ordinary local politics stands in sharp contrast to the detailed knowledge he seems to have had of distribution of caste and religious groups in different districts and urban areas (Hardtmann, 2009).

One can draw a few conclusions from this account. One, land hungry masses were ready to fight for land but the party leadership kept it limited to the government land only. It never took active interest in dismantling unequal land ownership structure that has got close interface with social structure too. Two, in his statement, BSP leader appears suggesting that landless Dalits would have to wait for land distribution until the party forms governments at the centre and in most of the states.

At the economic level, one may accuse BSP of adopting a callous attitude but at ideological-cultural level, this phase of Dalit movement asserted itself with much vigour, especially during the first decade of the formation of BSP. Studies done during the eighties and nineties confirm this trend. Melucci (1985: 797) says that simply by talking about themselves as Dalits and not as untouchables, Harijans or SCs, they make power relations visible and challenge dominant symbols and meaning systems in everyday life (ibid: 1988: 250; quoted in Hardtmann, 2009). Although the term 'Dalit' was already in the use in Dalit literature for long but the BSP invested all its energies in popularizing it among the masses. Anti-Gandhism was another significant tenet of this political mobilization. The party might have ignored many other advices of Dr Ambedkar but it took aggressive stand against Gandhi. Following serious objections raised by Dalit activists on the use of term 'Harijan', it was declared unconstitutional later.

One more thing that distinguishes BSP from several other social movements of marginalized groups and Dalit movement in other parts of the country is its attitude vis-à-vis the state. Unlike those movements that oppose the state, BSP wants to get closer to the state and follows a line of using state power to curb caste oppression. Sudha Pai (2002: 14) defines it as a "statist party, i.e., it hopes to break the hold of the select Brahmanical elite on the state and use its power for Dalit upliftment". For BSP, political programme meant nothing more than voting for its candidates in Vidhan Sabha and the Lok Sabha elections. Its firm belief seems to take control from above, by jumping into electoral fray which alone is a key to power in an electoral democracy (Kumar, 1999).

In 2003, due to illness of Kanshi Ram, Mayawati, till vice president of the party, became president. During this entire period Mayawati became the chief minister of the state for four times – three times heading coalition governments supported by extreme right Hindu fundamentalist Bhartiya Janata Party (BJP) and finally in 2007, leading BSP's single party government. BSP leaders always believed that political stability was not in favour of Bahujan politics but it is only after formation of this majority government lead by BSP, a long era of coalition governments in the state has ended.

The extraordinary performance shown by BSP could be possible with further consolidation of Dalit votes, especially near 100 per cent mobilization of Jatav–Dalits, the largest Dalit community constituting around 56 per cent of total Dalit population in the state. This was complemented by selective move of certain sections of OBCs, Muslims and so-called upper castes, especially Brahmins, in favour of the party at local levels. This is seen as culmination of a long campaign launched by the party to woo non-Dalit voters. This campaign not only included Brahmin Sammelan but also dismissal of "the party's 'pro-Dalit' image as a canard spread by the opposition" (Sharma, 2005). BSP's success in combining all three sections has surprised many. Some of them call it 'congressization' of BSP but they fail to note that successfully forging the electoral alliance of Brahmins, Dalits and Muslims that remained the rock bed for Congress rule for four decades, there is a marked change: earlier leadership was in the hands of Brahmins that slipped into the hands of Dalits in contemporary political scene. Dipankar Gupta and Yogesh Kumar (2007) put it in more interesting words:

> The resemblance with Congress, that appeared so compelling at first sight, is actually spurious. Under Congress' giant umbrella the list of invitees was sent out by upper caste/class Congress members. In the BSP alignment the leading partners are the SCs and other poor communities. As their interests are now paramount it is highly unlikely that everybody would be invited unlike Congress' large garden parties.

Kanchan Chandra (2007) identifies another very significant difference between both the situations:

> The Congress party usually played a coded ethnic card, invoking ethnic identities – identities based on caste, religion, region, language or tribe – quietly in its selection of candidates but not openly in its identification of issues, and targeting these groups through the distribution of patronage but rarely through the rhetoric of identity .... The BSP, by contrast, has always made open appeals to ethnic identity central to its election platform. And the slogan based on which it began appealing to upper-caste voters – "jiski jitni sankhya bhari, uski utni bhagedari" (each group should obtain a share of political power proportional to its share in the population) – keeps these open appeals to ethnic

identity intact. The only difference between this and earlier slogans is that upper castes are now included in the open ethnic appeals while they were earlier excluded.

Some other commentators say that it appears that the BSP and the Congress have swapped their caste cards. Congress general secretary Rahul Gandhi tries to woo Dalit votes by way of visiting their families and eating with them and at the same time BSP is all out to reach Brahmin voters.

Whatever one says about BSP's electoral tactics, it is the first party of Dalits in the country that has formed a government on its own. Besides one cannot afford to ignore the fact that BSP's coming to power gives extreme confidence and sense of dignity to Dalits, who have been kept deprived of these for thousands years. Similarly, as Subhashini Ali (2008) notes, "another distinction of the party is that it is headed by a Dalit woman, Kumari Mayawati, who rules her organization with iron hand. There is no doubt that she inspires tremendous admiration among the masses of Dalit women who see in her and her incredible successes and authority hope for themselves in the midst of hopelessness and despair". On the same line, while placing Mayawati's emergence as a militant Dalit leader in the socio-historical context of Uttar Pradesh, Vivek Kumar (2009) underlines that she has deconstructed the established image of Dalit women which was earlier portrayed as 'devadasi' or 'dayan'.

BSP Government's Initiatives

The initiatives taken by the BSP government reflect a quest to retain its traditional mass base and simultaneously reach out to other social groups, especially Brahmins and Muslims. At the same time, it has to do another balancing act of implementing neo-liberal macro-economic policies and again see that its mass base is not isolated from it even though they bear the brunt of these policies. A revealing example of this kind of a dilemma is Chief Minister's announcement regarding making reservation mandatory for private organizations to which the government outsources its work.

Besides, while studying the BSP government's policy initiatives, one can also make a distinction between pre-general election and post-general election periods. Political observers feel that before parliamentary elections BSP was vigorously pursuing inclusive politics of 'sarvajan hitaya' (everybody's interest). This political line was very much successful during assembly elections in 2007. These elections would be remembered for Mayawati's brilliant performance in social engineering which, combined with anti-Samajwadi Party mood of the voters, resulted in landslide victory of BSP. Before these elections, in her attempt to woo upper caste votes, Mayawati went on to the extent of dismissing the party's 'pro-Dalit' image as a canard spread by the opposition, and extended an open offer of tickets to the upper castes in the assembly and parliamentary elections (Sharma, 2005). And after not so impressive performance in these elections, all eyes were focused on strengthening its roots among Bahujans. In the Lok Sabha elections, the BSP had won 21 seats, ending up behind the Congress and the Samajwadi Party (SP) in the seat tally – both of which had won 22 seats each. The number was far below the party's expectations. The party had won only two of the 17 reserved seats, while the SP won 10 reserved seats – that set the alarm bells ringing.

Reservation in Private Sector

An *Indian Express* report says that all private establishments, interested in doing business with government, public sector undertakings, boards and government-aided bodies, will have to implement reservation. This includes contracts given to construction agencies by various departments like Public Works, Irrigation and others. Before this, the Mayawati government had enforced a 30 per cent reservation – 10 per cent each for SCs, OBCs and the poor from upper castes – in new industrial units. The government had also implemented reservation for SCs and OBCs in units coming up under the public–private partnership (PPP) policy. While announcing the decision taken by state cabinet, the Chief Minister says that with the shrinking of the government's role as an employer, in this era of economic reforms and liberalization, job opportunities for SCs and OBCs were on the wane and owing to the scarcity in government jobs, steps are being taken so the deprived sections of society also get their due share in the growing economy (Express News Service, 2008). The underlying argument here is that implementing globalization-liberalization policies is inevitable and government will have to continue outsourcing its works in order to downsize itself as per the neo-liberal policy direction. The Chief Minister also seems admitting the adverse impact of these policies on marginalized communities and offers some remedial measures to salvage them. This is another issue that even the government reports and studies admit that bulk of the employees in private sector work without any formal contract leaving aside livable wages and humane working conditions. How will these employees avail benefits of reservation is to be seen in the future. At the level of manual labourers, however, these private organizations would quickly follow government instructions as already this class of labourers is largely composed of marginalized communities.

Reservation in Government Contracts

Another major decision taken by the Mayawati government in favour of SCs and STs was the implementation of reservation in government contracts for both these communities. The government order of June 30, 2009 had made 21 per cent reservation for SCs and 2 per cent for STs in contracts up to Rs 5 lakh. The order applied to all boards, corporations and local bodies. It was later on challenged in Allahabad High Court but the court upheld constitutional validity saying that the order was not violative of Article 19(1) (g) of the Constitution. The scheme was an instant hit, as in the first two months after became operational the number of contracts awarded to SC/ST contractors was almost the same as were awarded in the previous four months. In the first three months, as many as 5,344 contracts had been awarded of which 2,392 went to SC and ST contractors. After four months of introduction of the scheme, the state government had initiated an exercise to extend the reservation to contracts of higher value as several departments had found that there were not many 'E' category contracts. They tried to create some new 'E' category contracts by splitting work, but this created a synchronization problem and parts of the same project had differences in quality. A proposal was moved to enhance the limit upto Rs 40 lakh but the government turned it down on the ground that most SC and ST contractors might not be able to mobilize the required resources.

Although this scheme was welcomed by many but not all agree with these kinds of strategies which they call strategy of 'individual salvation'. An article posted on radical Dalit website dalitvoice.org comments that "when somebody tries to set up some kind of "Dalit Capitalism" like Nixon's "Black Capitalism", which created only traitors like Jesse Jackson, Dalit Bahujans must become extremely vigilant and doubly careful. They must become alert, because otherwise the Brahminical order will successfully manufacture similar traitors from Dalit Bahujans". Commenting on similar steps taken by the Digvijay Singh government as part of implementation of Bhopal Declaration, this article further suggests that "the original Brahminical party of Congress is out to increase the number of such traitors using economic tools – by creating a sort of permanently handicapped 'Dalit Capitalism' integrated into the supply chain of the overall Brahminical economic structure" (Ayyankali, undated).

The PPP Model

The perceived inevitability of neo-liberal policies for the state government is also reflected in its economic policies premised on public–private partnership (PPP) model. Although the idea of PPP was not a discovery of the state government and was conceived during the Eleventh Five-Year Plan at the national level but the BSP government has been vigorously pursuing it in all sectors including education, health, infrastructure, power, agriculture etc. The state cabinet, while approving the New Economic Policy at its meeting held on December 24, 2007, had taken a decision to make PPP an important component of the policy. After this we witness a series of decisions by the government opening up sector by sector for PPP. Besides setting up polytechnics and ITIs, six new medical colleges and two para-medical colleges coming up in the state would be run under a PPP arrangement. Most of these colleges were in an advanced stage of construction at the time of this decision. Although the modalities of the PPP model and the award of necessary contracts were to be worked out later but it seems that these colleges were constructed by the government at the expense of state exchequer and private sector would participate only in running of these institutions and take away its share of profit generated. If it is so then these colleges would have to be necessarily profit-making enterprises and they would charge hefty amounts somewhat similar to the private sector.

Not just education but it was for the first time that the state has formulated a policy for handing over core activities in the health sector to the private sector on PPP model. According to a newspaper report, as part of the strategy for involving the private sector through the PPP model, the state government has already engaged consultants such as Pricewaterhouse Coopers, Grand Thornton and EPOS to explore the possibility and finalize the bid papers for handing over as many as six projects to private companies. They are: setting up and operating mobile medical units in 20 districts of the state, operating ambulance services in another 20 districts situated close to the highways, handing over 18 regional diagnostic centres to the private sector, handing over the management of urban health centres in six cities to private parties, inviting PPP for managing and running 50 community health centres (CHCs) in the rural areas and for setting up super specialty centres in six cities of the states (Jainani, 2008).

On the same lines, the Uttar Pradesh Power Corporation Limited (UPPCL) has initiated the process for privatization of power transmission in the state. In this connection, it has invited bids from consultant companies which will formulate the financial and technical models for the project. Seven companies – Pricewaterhouse Coopers, Ernst and Young, CRISIL (Credit Rating Information Services of India Limited), SBI Capital, Feedback Ventures, ICRA and Srei Infrastructure Finance Limited – have shown their willingness to assist the state government in its project through the PPP model. Similar arrangements are in the pipeline for water supply in urban areas in selected zones. If PPP model succeeds in these zones, then the government might think of extending it to other areas as well. Alongside the Uttar Pradesh government has proposed to adopt the PPP model for proper procurement and marketing of agricultural produce. Another newspaper report says that aiming to expedite the disinvestment of public sector undertakings under its policy of infrastructure development and divestment through public–private partnership, the Uttar Pradesh government has decided to invoke the Swiss Challenge Method for bidding. The disinvestment process is on in Uttar Pradesh in key sectors like tourism and sugar mills.

Investment-friendly Environment

Two seemingly separate incidences in NOIDA–Greater NOIDA area shot to headlines of national dailies in 2008. On August 14 that year during a protest by farmers on the issue of the land acquisition the police had to open fire in which five persons were killed and many others injured. This was followed by another incidence in which hundreds of sacked agitated workers gheraoed the Graziano Transmissioni's CEO on September 22. On the day of the incident, workers accused that the Graziano authorities, which planned to get the leading elements of the agitation beaten up using goons, after getting them inside the factory premises on the pretext of talks. They say that while the workers' delegation was inside and being assaulted, one worker ran out to the gates (which had been shut) and told those assembled outside that their delegation members were being beaten. Then, workers stormed in and the confrontation took place, which resulted in the CEO being killed.

Both these incidences were taken very seriously by the state government, which was worried about an 'anti-industry image' of these twin cities. To restore 'investor-friendly environment', apart from taking stern police action against Graziano's workers, a number of measures were initiated by the state government. These include giving of the additional charge of Labour Commissioners to the CEOs of the twin towns. Besides, to regain the trust of industries, the government has constituted an Industrial Relations Unit comprising two deputy superintendents of police to sort out the industry-related issues. One need not to be judgmental about it but this is anybody's guess what an Industrial Relations Unit comprising of only police officers is supposed to do. Similarly, it seems that decision of giving additional charge of Labour Commissioners to CEOs of these towns is meant to give a message to industrial houses that they do not need to bother about labour laws.

Land Acquisition

The BSP government took a welcome decision that no agricultural land would be forcibly acquired for industries and SEZs without consulting owner farmers. The decision actually came in the backdrop of protest movements in several parts of the state, including one in Dadri, against the decision of Mulayam Singh government to acquire land for a proposed power plant to be constructed by Reliance Power Company. But, at the same time, the government is willing to go ahead with its much ambitious project 'Ganga Expressway', an eight-lane 1,047 km long expressway from Greater Noida to Ballia. It is said that it will reduce travel time between western and eastern ends of the state from 24 to 8 hours. But it will also involve acquisition of over 62,000 hectares of fertile land. Although the project is not moving fast in the wake of farmers' protests against land acquisition and BSP also seems to be cautious after its defeat in general elections held in May 2009 in most of the constituencies through which this proposed road has to pass. But, the government is firm to pursue this project and necessary formalities including setting up of UP Expressway Industrial Development Authority and selection of developer have been completed. As it involves an investment of Rs 30,000 crore, it will be built and operated by private sector and the government would only play the role of a facilitator.

The government may have put the Ganga Expressway project on the back burner but it is vigorously pursuing Yamuna Expressway project. Yamuna Expressway, the 6 lane expandable to 8 lanes, 165 kms under construction road would connect Greater Noida with Agra. At a cost of around Rs 9,500 crore, the expressway will need 4,300 hectares of land, for which more than 1,400 villages were notified. The construction of the expressway, which is almost half way through, has progressed without much resistance from the farmers. Trouble began when farmers came to know that the government planned to acquire more land for proposed hi-tech cities around the expressway. As 'sweetener' in the deal developer, the JP Industries was given 25 million square meters of land along the expressway for commercial, industrial, institutional and residential development. This land shall be provided at five or more locations of which one location shall be in Noida or Greater Noida with an area of 5 million sq. mtrs. Land acquisition for this project met with stiff resistance from the farmers. At several places, the police retaliated with firing on agitating farmers. Several people have died in these clashes.

In response to this explosive situation, the Uttar Pradesh government has come out with a new rehabilitation policy. The new rehabilitation policy provides for Rs 20,000 per acre per year for 33 years with annual increase of Rs 600 and 7 per cent developed land returned to the farmer if land is acquired for residential purpose. Later on, the government decided not to acquire land for private players and also enhanced 7 per cent developed land component to 16 per cent.

Social Welfare Initiatives

At the time of completion of one year in the office, the Mayawati government, like all its preceding governments, released a document providing details of its achievements. This document focuses on political stability, improvement in law and order situation, curbing corruption, NOIDA–Ballia expressway, filling up vacancies of reserved categories backlog, lifting up ban on recruitment of general category seats, and large-scale recruitment of teachers in primary schools and *safai karamcharis* (scavengers) in municipalities. In addition, as the government claims, the expansion of educational and medical facilities, its decision to avoid acquisition of farmers' lands for industrial purpose and banning sale of mortgaged land belonging to small farmers by banks would make Uttar Pradesh a 'prosperous and better state'. The document further states that the government's missionary project is aimed to make an egalitarian society based on mutual respect and brotherhood. It appears that the government is more concerned about state as a whole and does not wish to present itself as a pro-Dalit government. The government released another report a year later but with a very different tone. It says that to initiate a process of social change in Uttar Pradesh was the most important task before this government. It further states that the Chief Minister Mayawati has always tried to uplift Dalit, exploited and oppressed and standing on the last ladder and these are the people who remain in the centre of all initiatives taken by this government too.

What would have led to change of heart is only a matter of speculation but the biggest event that happened in between these two reports was 2009 Lok Sabha elections in which BSP performed far below its own expectations. In the elections, the BSP lost votes from almost all sections in the state, including from Mayawati's own community of Dalit–Jatavs. An educated, socially-conscious community – the Dalit–Jatavs – later on realized that Mayawati had allocated them only as many seats as there are reserved constituencies in the state. The BSP chief owed her success to them; they transferred their votes almost wholly to whoever she named. In return, they did not get even one seat more than their constitutionally sanctioned share (Subrahmaniam, 2009). From the above one can infer that the BSP's efforts to expand its base among non-Dalits went to an extent where they started posing danger of weakening of core base among Dalit–Jatavs. It is from here BSP takes a lesson not to overlook its own constituency while reaching out to others.

Concluding Observations

The above discussion indicates that while the BSP's electoral tactics keep changing with changing political environment but economic policies pursued by the BSP government remain consistently not so different from that of Indian state, which has coined the term 'inclusive growth' to market its neo-liberal policies. In this schema, the overall economic strategy remains based on the same exclusionary neo-liberal ideas but few social development initiatives are also attached to it as add-on. In other words, few inclusive initiatives are placed in an overall exclusionary context for tension management and no wonder in the age of several emerging rights – right to employment and right to food – unemployment and starvation deaths are on its peak.

In the same way, the BSP government pursues the economic policies which exclude Dalits on a large scale but simultaneously take few relief measures as well. The most revealing example of such an approach is the provision of reservation for marginalized communities in the companies to which the government outsources its work. Outsourcing government work is not a new thing nor is the BSP government the first government to outsource increasing quantum of its work. The case for outsourcing flows from the neo-liberal line of argument that keeping government employees is a wasteful expense. Instead, governments should rely on and strengthen market by outsourcing most of its work to minimize public expenditure and keep budget deficit under control, a legal prerequisite to get aid from central government or from international funding agencies. As a result, large-scale secured employment opportunities are lost in public sector and people are forced to opt for unsecured and underpaid jobs in the private sector that are available to fewer people. Needless to say that Dalits are worst sufferer of all this, not only because they lost their hard-earned employment rights in the public sector but also because studies (e.g., Jodhka and Newman, 2007) have shown that private sector applies more exclusionary practices in the name of 'merit'. Besides, we all know that the Dalit middle class, which initiated current phase of Dalit movement in the state, is the product of public sector education and employment. The state government, led by the BSP, has shown keenness similar to BJP, Congress or Samajwadi Party to please capitalists at the expense of rights of labourers, majority of whom belong to marginalized communities. The development of NOIDA indicates all this.

Having a look at the developments that took place in the state in last couple of years, one gets an impression that BSP has not shown any distinct attitude towards neo-liberal policies. Few relief measures initiated by it are not so different from the 'inclusive growth' slogan coined by the Congress-led United Progressive Alliance (UPP) government at the Centre. In fact, one feels that implementation of the neo-liberal policies by a party that appeals to marginalized communities also nullifies to an extent the possibility of opposition from the sufferers of the said policies. In this way parties based on identities actually facilitate capital and market to hold sway over things.

While discussing the dynamics of identity politics and neo-liberalism, critiques feel that both these phenomena getting prominence simultaneously since 1980s should not be seen just as coincidence. They further argue that global finance capital finds it convenient to deal with people fragmented on the basis of multiple identities as their fragmentation prevents their coming together to challenge the exploitation of capital. While not undermining the role played by identity-based movements in bringing up several hitherto hidden issues, one can add that the capitalist state in the phase of imperialist globalization also finds it easier to deal with competing groups claiming for access to resources.

It is true that different social groups such as Dalits, adivasis and women suffer from different types of social oppression but at the same time they are also exploited by the capital. In this situation, non-recognition of this commonness prevents these exploited groups coming together to pose a challenge to the rule of capital. Identity politics theorists take state as autonomous and neutral. This understanding misses an important point that even if oppression based on caste, race or gender is taken care of, the exploitation of same groups would continue as long as capitalist order remains untouched.

Logic of the identity politics rests upon the premise that experience of a particular oppression by the people of that identity is the only genuine reality. This focus on 'experiences' and 'difference' has led to an endless process of sub-divisions. In place of Dalit or OBC parties and organizations, emergence of organizations based on individual caste is a logical development of this process. Demands for quota within quota, for MBCs and for 'Mahadalits', are gaining ground and Mala–Madiga question remains unresolved. BSP itself is largely seen as a party of Jatav–Dalits instead of all Dalits. Conceptually too, emphasis on 'difference' brings forth horizontal differences and overlooks vertical hierarchy and inequality.

How this kind of a politics translates at the local level is another important question to be asked. Commenting on the dynamics of electoral politics in the state, Gupta and Kumar (2007) rightly argue that "the leaders of most parties come from elite backgrounds and have similar mindsets. They too believe that caste is the most dependable variable. Those that might have some qualms about this, nevertheless, feel that there is nothing other than caste membership that they can display in their favour as they have failed to deliver on other fronts. This converts a bulk of our politicians, and their advisors, into becoming professional casteists or communalists. That is there is such a plethora of professional Yadavs, Jats, Brahmans, and so on, by the same token, professional Hindus or Muslims".

Although the BSP also seems follow the same ideology of identity politics but one cannot fit to it into any of the two categories – struggle for redistribution and struggle for recognition – conceptualized by Nancy Fraser (Alcoff, 2007). Even though constructed around Dalit identity, it demands redistribution of resources but one can of course raise the question, what kind of resources and for whom? Experiences reveal that BSP is more concerned about the redistribution of government jobs and now government contracts through reservation. No doubt, this is important and necessary. But if we look at the composition of state's labour force, we find that still a vast majority of them depend on agriculture for their livelihood – directly or indirectly. Same is the case with Dalits too. That is why land continues to be the most important resource around which privileges and marginalization revolve. But we do not see BSP making any attempt to rupture land relations in the countryside. It continues with the existing schemes of distributing government land among landless and regularizing possession of Dalits on government land. It has also reinstated number one priority to landless Dalits in land distribution scheme. This scheme was started in 1970s but looking at quality and quantum of land distributed under this, it is clear beyond any doubt that it has done little in bringing down land inequality in rural Uttar Pradesh. Being primarily a Dalit party, one would obviously expect BSP coming out with a programme of more radical distribution of land but unfortunately in 25 years of its existence, it has never taken these issues seriously.

The BSP government can rightly claim to have upwardly revised the minimum wages for unskilled manual labour – another crucial mode of redistribution in favour of labourers, of which larger chunk is constituted by Dalits – three times in two years, time. But, again, there is a catch. Critiques say that these wage hikes were largely due to NREGA for which the central government had already made an arrangement. Besides, the minimum wages declared by the government are yet to be implemented at the ground outside NREGA. Field studies (e.g., Trivedi, 2010) show that daily wages for agricultural labour remain far below than minimum wages even in the comparatively better off cash crop growing areas almost throughout the year. This is not a new situation but if Samajawadi Party overlooks the wage issue, it is understandable considering its base among middle and rich farmers. But if BSP adopts the same callous attitude towards enforcing a statutory requirement, millions of Dalit agricultural labourers who vote en mass to BSP, have every right to question party's stand on issues concerning this class.

This scenario gives an impression that BSP is primarily concerned with redistribution of resources that are important to a tiny well-off section among Dalits, that emerged mainly through state's policy of positive discrimination, especially reservation in government jobs. It is not being argued here that BSP would have not liked to redistribute the resources in favour of labouring classes but only thing is that few steps here and there can be taken to cater to the needs of an extremely small section without disturbing existing structures. But when you want to redistribute resources in favour of a large mass of exploited class, this cannot be done without giving a serious blow to the interests of propertied class. BSP has surely not shown any inclination in this direction.

Thus, while discussing 'redistribution' 'recognition' dilemma of identity politics, one should always question 'coverage of redistribution programme' as well as 'coverage of identity'. It may happen, as appears in the case of BSP, that identity covers the whole community but benefits of redistribution reaches only to a small well-off section of the community.

References

Alcoff, Linda Martin. 2007. "Fraser on Redistribution, Recognition, and Identity", *European Journal of Political Theory*, Vol. 6, No. 3, p. 255.

Ali, Subhashini. 2008. Status of Dalit Women in Uttar Pradesh, paper presented at XII National Conference of Indian Association for Women Studies, held at Lucknow, February 7–10.

Ayyankali. Undated. Converting Dalits into Exploiters: Latest Congress Party Plan, www.dalitvoice.org downloaded on 5 December 2009.

Chandra, Kanchan. 2007. A Benign Rupture in Uttar Pradesh, http: //www.indianexpress.com/ (Posted online: 12 May 2007 at 1541 hrs) downloaded on 10 December 2009.

Express News Service. Reservation, a Must in Private Firms Working for UP Govt, http: //www.indianexpress.com (Posted online: 19 January 2008 at 2222 hrs) downloaded on 5 December 2009.

Gupta, Dipankar and Yogesh Kumar. 2007. "When the Caste Calculus Fails: Analysing BSP's Victory in UP", *Economic and Political Weekly*, August 18.

Hardtmann, Eva-Maria. 2009. *The Dalit Movement in India: Local Practices, Global Connections*, New Delhi: Oxford University Press.

Jainani, Deepa. 2008. UP Mulls PPP for Better Healthcare, http: //www.indianexpress.com (Posted online: 18 September 2008 at 2315 hrs) downloaded on 6 December 2009.

Jodhka, Surinder and Katherine Newman. 2007. "In the Name of Globalisation: Meritocracy, Productivity and the Hidden Language of Caste", *Economic and Political Weekly*, Vol. 42, No. 41, pp. 4125–32.

Kumar, Pradeep. 1999. "Dalits and the BSP in Uttar Pradesh: Issues and Challenges", *Economic and Political Weekly*, April 3.

Kumar, Vivek. 2009. "Locating Dalit Women in the Indian Caste System, Media and Women's Movement", *Social Change*, Vol. 39, No. 1, pp. 64–84.

Melucci, Alberto. 1985. "The Symbolic Challenge of Contemporary Social Movements", *Social Research*, Vol. 52, No. 4, Winter.

——. 1988. "Social Movements and Democratisation of Everyday Life", in John Keane (ed.), *Civil Society and the State*, London: Verso.

Padavala, Chittibabau. 2007. "On Judging Mayawati", *Economic and Political Weekly*, August 18.

Pai, Sudha. 2002. *Dalit Assertion and the Unfinished Democratic Revolution: The Bahujan Samaj Party in Uttar Pradesh*, New Delhi: Sage Publications.

Rodrigues, Edward. 2008. The Changing Content of Dalit Discourse in Post-Liberalisation India, paper presented at the National Seminar on Structural Transformation and Developmental Politics in Post-Liberalisation India, organized by Council for Social Development and India International Centre on 24–25 January 2008 at New Delhi.

Sharma, Amit. 2005. Not Pro-Dalit, BSP Open to Upper Castes: Maya, http: //www.indianexpress.com/ (Posted online: 10 June 2005 at 0143 hrs) downloaded on 10 December 2009.

Subrahmaniam, Vidya. 2010. A Quarter Century of Kanshi Ram and Mayawati, http://www.thehindu.com/2010/03/22/stories/ 20100322 50571000.htm (posted online on 22 March 2010) downloaded on 22 March 2010.

Teltumbde, Anand. 2007. "A 'Mayawati' Revolution", *Economic and Political Weekly*, June 9.

Trivedi, Prashant Kumar. "Changing Agrarian Scene: Sociology of Land, Wages and Indebtness", in Manoranjan Mohanty (ed.), *Social Development Report 2010*, New Delhi: Oxford University Press.

Index